Linux for Small Business Owners

Using Free and Open Source Software to Power Your Dreams

David Both
Cyndi Bulka

Apress®

Linux for Small Business Owners: Using Free and Open Source Software to Power Your Dreams

David Both
Raleigh, NC, USA

Cyndi Bulka
Raleigh, NC, USA

ISBN-13 (pbk): 978-1-4842-8263-2
https://doi.org/10.1007/978-1-4842-8264-9

ISBN-13 (electronic): 978-1-4842-8264-9

Managing Director, Apress Media LLC: Welmoed Spahr
Acquisitions Editor: James Robinson-Prior
Development Editor: James Markham
Coordinating Editor: Jill Balzano

Cover image photo by nibras al-riyami on Unsplash

Distributed to the book trade worldwide by Springer Science+Business Media LLC, 1 New York Plaza, Suite 4600, New York, NY 10004. Phone 1-800-SPRINGER, fax (201) 348-4505, e-mail orders-ny@springer-sbm. com, or visit www.springeronline.com. Apress Media, LLC is a California LLC and the sole member (owner) is Springer Science + Business Media Finance Inc (SSBM Finance Inc). SSBM Finance Inc is a **Delaware** corporation.

For information on translations, please e-mail booktranslations@springernature.com; for reprint, paperback, or audio rights, please e-mail bookpermissions@springernature.com.

Apress titles may be purchased in bulk for academic, corporate, or promotional use. eBook versions and licenses are also available for most titles. For more information, reference our Print and eBook Bulk Sales web page at http://www.apress.com/bulk-sales.

Any source code or other supplementary material referenced by the author in this book is available to readers on GitHub.

Printed on acid-free paper

*We dedicate this book to all small business owners – dreamers
with the power to change the world.*

Table of Contents

About the Authors

 **David Both** is an open source software and GNU/Linux advocate, trainer, writer, and speaker. He has been working with Linux and open source software for more than 25 years and has been working with computers for over 50 years. Yes, he's *that* old! He is a strong proponent of and evangelist for the "Linux Philosophy for System Administrators."

David likes to purchase the components and build his own computers to ensure that each new computer meets his exacting specifications.

He has written articles for magazines including *Linux Magazine*, *Linux Journal*, and *OS/2 Magazine* back when there was such a thing. He currently writes for OpenSource.com which is supported by Red Hat. He especially enjoys learning new things while researching his articles.

David has published four previous books with Apress, *The Linux Philosophy for SysAdmins*, released in August 2018, and a three-volume self-study training course, "Using and Administering Linux: Zero to SysAdmin," released in December 2019.

David currently lives in Raleigh, NC, with his very supportive wife. David also likes reading, travel, the beach, and spending time with his two children, their spouses, and four grandchildren.

David can be reached at LinuxGeek46@both.org or on Twitter @LinuxGeek46. His personal website is www.both.org, where you can find information about his current projects and errata for his books.

Cyndi Bulka has been a yoga teacher for more than 25 years, a Thai yoga bodyworker, owned a yoga studio, is an Integrative Health Coach, a writer, and now provides a fresh perspective and blueprint to living a healthy, happy life of abundance without stressing over the scale or what you can or can't eat.

Her yoga classes, workshops, and retreats have touched thousands of lives all around the world.

She's a mom to two wonderful adults, nana to four beautiful grandkids, and partner to a wonderful man who is her best support. Two fur babies, an 1100 pound horse named Dak, and an 11 pound dog named Lucie are her regular companions. When she's not at the barn or on the end of Lucie's leash, you can find her hiking the local greenways and trails, piddling in her organic garden, or cooking up something fresh and healthy in the kitchen.

Cyndi can be reached at Cyndi Powers Coaching at cyndi@cyndipowers.com. or via her website: https://www.cyndipowers.com/.

About the Technical Reviewer

Seth Kenlon is a UNIX geek, free culture advocate, hacker, independent multimedia artist, and D&D nerd. He has worked in the film and computing industry, often at the same time. He is one of the maintainers of the Slackware-based multimedia production project Slackermedia.

Acknowledgments

David

Writing a book is not a solitary activity, and this one is no exception.

My amazing wife, Alice, has been my head cheerleader and best friend throughout yet another book. I could not have done this without her support and love.

Collaborating with Cyndi to create this volume has made this an exceptionally rewarding experience. As my yoga teacher, she has guided me through improving my physical and mental selves. As co-author for this book, she has guided my writing to ensure that small business owners like herself would be able to understand what I have written. Her own contributions to this book have made it much more accessible to nontechnical people such as most small business owners than I ever could have. In fact, our editors have told me that they like her writing better than mine.

Cyndi

Writing my first book has been a great experience that required much guidance and support. I'm eternally grateful to David for the invitation to collaborate and his patience and humor along the way.

I want to thank my partner Dean for his support and understanding even when my writing took me away on weekends and evenings. His faith in me means a lot.

Finally, I want to thank my mother who from the time I was 9 years old and ever since has encouraged me to write.

Both of Us

We are grateful for the support and guidance of Jill Balzano, coordinating editor for open source at Apress, who believed in us and our vision for this book. This book would not have been possible without her.

Seth Kenlon, our technical reviewer, has done a fantastic job of ensuring the technical accuracy of this book. He has also helped to make it more appropriate to our intended audience of small business owners. His suggestions for rewriting, reorganizing, or deleting certain sections altogether were perfect and have made this a much better book that it otherwise would have been.

ACKNOWLEDGMENTS

We also want to thank James Markham, our development editor, for helping to ensure that this book is clear and on point.

Of course, any remaining errors and omissions are our responsibility alone.

Introduction

Small business owners are an amazing group of people. We dream bold dreams and then overcome all manner of obstacles as we turn those dreams into a reality that enables us to serve our customers, provide jobs for employees, support ourselves, and provide us with a level of enjoyment and fulfillment that we could never attain while working for someone else. And we like to be in charge.

We just want to do our thing, whether it is teaching yoga, consulting, public relations, creating our works of art, writing, playing or writing music, fixing things, or... you get the idea, all those things we started our business to do because we like to do them.

But one of the obstacles that many small business owners crash into is that of technology. This is especially true of computers and all the stuff that surrounds them. Who even knows what a Gigahertz is, or RAM, GUI, CPU, or any of the other multitude of terms and acronyms surrounding computers? How many Giga- or Mega-somethings do we need?

As Cyndi says, "Technology has always intimidated me, and in the early years when I used Microsoft as an OS, I was continually challenged with regular malware, viruses, and system snafus that held up my business, leaving me frustrated and hamstringing my ability to earn a living. Finding reliable and affordable help to remedy the ongoing challenges was a continuous problem."

If this sounds like you and your small business, you have chosen the right book. In this book, we try to answer the critical questions and provide you with enough knowledge to enable you to purchase and use a computer while eliminating many of the challenges and dangers of using Windows.

You will learn how you can take complete control and run your small business with powerful, free open source software (FOSS). This book introduces small business owners to the power and security of Linux and other FOSS tools to manage any small business as well as the many advantages it has over expensive, proprietary software. While exploring the reasons for using free open source software, this book investigates the assertion that "The value of any software lies in its usefulness not in its price," set forth by Linus Torvalds, the creator of Linux.

This book helps small business owners like you learn about and evaluate the usefulness of Linux and other open source software for your own businesses. We start by looking at why the two of us have chosen to use Linux for both personal and business reasons and explore a bit of history that can provide some insight into why Linux is the best choice for an operating system and application software.

We then discuss how to choose hardware and explain those pesky terms in a way that can help you understand what you are getting with a new (or new to you) computer. We also explain how to install our favorite Linux distribution, Fedora, onto a USB thumb drive so that you can test drive Linux on your existing computers or even in the computer store – without touching any of the existing data on those computers.

We provide a detailed, step-by-step guide to backing up your data, removing Windows from your computers, and installing Linux and some commonly used open source software like the LibreOffice suite of office programs, accounting, and other software useful to many small business owners. We also provide information and tools necessary to manage and maintain Linux and applications up to date and secure.

After a little orientation, we guide you through the process of restoring your backup data to your home directory on the storage drive of your computer.

We discuss the use of Linux and also the other free open source software you need to meet your business challenges including the usual accounting, email, web browsing, word-processing tasks, and much more. We show you how to find and install new software you need to run your business and keep it up to date using the tools already provided by Linux and the secure, trusted repositories (repos) available online. We've got you covered when it comes to learning the basics of file management and migrating your data from Windows to Linux – it's really not hard. We also provide you with tools and instructions for installing updates when *you* want to, upgrading to a new release of Fedora, installing and deleting software, performing regular backups, and even how to keep your Linux computer safe and secure.

Without getting bogged down in deep technical discussions, our book provides some logic, reasoning, and explanation for each of the steps that are needed and the tools used to implement Linux in your small business, although you can find some of that deep technical stuff in the appendixes.

This book is ideal for small business owners and owner-operated small businesses looking to streamline operations and save money, time, energy, and the frustration of managing the common problems associated with using more popular operating systems.

## CHAPTER 1

Using Linux – The Personal Case

Objectives

After reading this chapter, you will be able to

- State the reasons that each of the authors has chosen to use Linux in their significantly different businesses and careers

- State the difference between "Free as in Beer" and "Free as in Speech" with respect to software

- List some of the technology challenges facing small businesses

- List at least five reasons the authors use Linux

- List at least five business application programs that are available for Linux

Introduction

Computers are much like our bodies. Wait – what?!

That does seem a bit – well more than a bit – unlikely at first. Let's look at what we mean by that. Human bodies and computers both require power, programming, and regular maintenance. Both process data and produce various types of output, whether speech, information on a display, or printed on paper. Bodies and computers are both complex although we can all agree that our human bodies are far more complex.

1

© David Both, Cyndi Bulka 2022
D. Both and C. Bulka, *Linux for Small Business Owners*, https://doi.org/10.1007/978-1-4842-8264-9_1

Most of us understand that our bodies require our regular attention to stay healthy so we can operate in all the facets of our lives with ease and efficiency. In order to make the best decisions about what we put into our bodies and what we ask our body to do, we have to dedicate time and attention to gather information and then discern what works best for our body's needs at the given moment. It's a constant and fluid process. Along the way, we learn what works and doesn't work for our unique constitution. Often, it's a trial-and-error process to discover the right balance of nutrition, exercise, rest, and emotional and mental well-being. As we age and as life hands us the inevitable challenges, we learn to adapt to maintain that balance.

Computers are complex but in a much different way. Computers ingest power in the form of electricity, and their programs are created by humans and intended to perform specific tasks. Computers don't think and are – so far – incapable of being truly intelligent or self-aware.

Computer maintenance consists of performing regular updates, removing old files and directories that are no longer needed, and performing backups in case files get damaged or deleted. Other maintenance includes the probability of having to replace defective parts such as failing hard drives, memory, or peripheral devices such as mice, displays, and printers.

The brain and personality of the computer is its operating system and the software that we use to perform our daily tasks. It makes sense that if we take care of our bodies and our computers, we want the best for both. For our computers, Linux and free open source software (FOSS) is truly the best as we shall show you throughout the rest of this book.

Both of us have chosen Linux and FOSS as the software for our computers. We did it for different reasons and for similar reasons. We both made this choice because it makes sense for us and the computers we use.

In the rest of this book, we will show you how Linux and free open source software can be the best choice for you, too.

Who We Are

Most small business owners use computers in this age of automation, and we are no exceptions. We have both found that Linux is the right operating system for us and that the free open source software (FOSS) that is available for Linux is all we need to run our business and personal affairs.

Cyndi

I come from a wildly different background having worked most of my career as an independent small business owner in the health and wellness industry. Having had a brief stint in my 20s and early 30s in corporate America, mostly as an office manager and some in sales, I learned fairly quickly that I needed to make my living working for myself doing something that felt congruent with my passions and interests. Hence, I opened my first yoga studio with a partner in October 1999. Less than two years later, I parted ways with that partner because we did not share common ideas about the spirit and direction of the business.

I happily owned and operated my own studio called Moving Mantra Yoga for the next 15 years wearing all the hats, teaching, managing a staff, creative director, operations manager, marketing manager, and community liaison. It was a big job and I loved it.

When my youngest graduated university and set out on his own leaving me an empty nester, I wanted to expand my horizons, so I closed the studio and created Zakti Health, giving me the opportunity to be a one-woman operation doing the things I loved most – teaching yoga, doing therapeutic bodywork, leading wellness retreats, and offering wellness coaching to individuals and groups.

For the next few years, I built Zakti and then the Coronavirus pandemic hit, essentially annihilating my hands-on and in-person business. The pandemic forced my hand to once again reinvent and refine my work. I set about building digital learning programs and found more than ever how important, reliable, secure, and dependable my OS, an open source software, needed to be.

When it comes to business, I'm smart enough to know my shortcomings, so I relied upon the expertise of contractors to help me in the areas I did not have the skill set or interest in, namely, technology and accounting. That was a wise move that helped my businesses grow and thrive over their tenure.

Technology has always intimidated me, and in the early years when I used Microsoft as an OS, I was continually challenged with regular malware, viruses, and system snafus that held up my business, leaving me frustrated and hamstringing my ability to earn a living. Finding reliable and affordable help to remedy the ongoing challenges was a continuous problem.

David, a.k.a. LinuxGeek46, was a regular student of the yoga studio, and we became very friendly over the years. I knew he was a techie, so when I got in a real pickle with a crashing system, he came to my rescue, restored my OS, and recovered important lost data. I thought I was staring down the barrel of replacing my computer, but that wasn't

3

the case. David was able to rebuild and restore my existing computer like new, only faster and much safer. He was instantly my hero!

Prior to knowing David, I'd never really heard of Linux. David was kind and patient enough to support my failing OS for a good stretch, until we'd both had enough of the headaches that came with all those recurring problems. When he first suggested switching to Linux, I admit I was intimidated. Although Microsoft had its headaches, it was familiar and I knew how to use it. I didn't have a lot of confidence when it came to learning new technology, so I was a bit reluctant. David assured me it was easy enough even for tech-phobes like me, so I bought in. He was a patient angel getting me built and up to speed. Turns out he was right… learning Linux was easy. Plus, it eliminated the virus and malware problem completely. I quickly saw how much money and time it saved me since I rarely had to give any time or attention to fixing problems. I was able to use that freed time and energy to do what I was best at – building my business on the human side. Other than system updates and the occasional upgrade, my experience as a Linux user has been pretty seamless.

I've not looked back even once. Not to say I haven't had questions for David from time to time, but the answers were most often simple and straightforward, and I can't recall a time when I was out of pocket because of a system shutdown. Since developing online learning programs most recently, David has also introduced me to invaluable open source software to help me create signature podcasts and videos that sound great. I wish I could own being proficient and confident when it comes to technology these days, but I won't. I'm still a tech-phobe – although it has become infinitely easier and I feel really good about the products I'm putting out in the world.

People like me need for technology to be reliable and simple so we can do the other kind of creative stuff we are best suited to do. I thrive when I am able to dedicate my energy to building programming and community. OS problems stress me out and suck my energy. The peace of mind, the time and money savings, and the freedom from frustration I've garnered as a Linux user is why I'm a dedicated user to this day.

David

I am a free open source software and Linux advocate, trainer, writer, and speaker. I have been working with Linux and open source software for more than 25 years and with computers for over 50 years. I do like to purchase the components and build my own computers from scratch to ensure that each new system meets my exacting specifications.

I have worked for several large organizations and a couple small ones over the course of my career and have used a lot of different operating systems and software. I like Linux and free open source software best. I have never used Windows as the primary operating system on any of my own computers – ever – but I have used a couple versions of Windows in virtual machines[1] (VMs) on my Linux workstation for testing.

I have published four previous books with Apress, *The Linux Philosophy for SysAdmins*, August 2018, and a three-volume self-study training course, *Using and Administering Linux: From Zero to SysAdmin*, released in December, 2019.

I have always been a geeky sort of person. I am the guy in high school who carried around my physics and chemistry books – along with my slide rule which I still have.

I got started in computers in about 1969 and have been playing – er, working – with them ever since. Computers are truly my hobby, and I have been fortunate enough to be able to find work that has been an extension of that hobby.

In 1981, I was working for IBM as a course development representative in their Boca Raton, Florida, facility when I was assigned the task of writing the training course for the very first IBM PC.[2] I had a great deal of fun doing that and decided I just had to have one for myself. I bought one using the employee purchase plan and have always had at least one computer ever since. I currently have 11 working computers in my home office space. Some people do boats, others golf, I do computers.

I have never liked Windows. I used PC-DOS and then IBM's OS/2 which has always been more stable than Windows was.

After leaving IBM in 1995, I started a small business consulting and teaching IBM's OS/2 operating system. Because I could see that IBM would soon drop support for OS/2, I looked around for something else to use for my own operating systems and software as well as something around which I could build my career. I had not heard yet about Linux, but I knew about and was interested in learning Unix which, as it turns out, is the model for Linux.

I found a job at a company that wanted me to support their aging fleet of OS/2 servers and, as part of my employment, would provide me with the opportunity to learn Unix. This arrangement allowed me to learn Solaris, a Unix variant which was created and supported by what was then Sun Microsystems.

---

[1] VMWare, "Virtual Machine," www.vmware.com/topics/glossary/content/virtual-machine
[2] Wikipedia, "IBM Personal Computer," https://en.wikipedia.org/wiki/IBM_Personal_Computer

One day, while I was still working at that company, I was discussing Solaris and Unix with one of the other system administrators (Sysadmin) and mentioned that I wanted to spend time learning Unix at home but could not afford a computer that would run it, nor could I afford the cost of the software itself.

Then my friend told me about Linux.

Linux, she said, was very much a Unix-like operating system; it was free of charge; all the common and much uncommon software that runs on Linux was free of charge. It was also free to copy and share with friends. And here is the best part – it would run on all of my IBM PC-compatible computers.

I figured, "Why not?" and installed Linux on a couple of my (many) computers. I quickly changed all of my computers over to Linux and have never looked back.

After almost 25 years of using Linux as my only operating system, I have a lot of reasons for using Linux as opposed to Windows. Installing Linux on the computers I build is an easy decision.

Fedora is my favorite Linux distribution.[3] There are several reasons for this, but that does not mean that I have anything against other distros or that the others are bad. Fedora is on the leading edge of much Linux and open source software. I kind of like being out there because Fedora gets a lot of the really good and fun stuff first while being stable enough to use in a small business.

I have tried other distributions for various reasons, but I always keep coming back to Fedora.

Why I Use Linux

Linux Is Free (as in Beer)

I place this first because it is a great reason for most people to switch to Linux. This meaning of "free" includes all of the software I have used to run my businesses and all my personal computing needs. I have not paid for software of any kind for almost 25 years except for one testing tool that I no longer use because free (as in beer) software is now available to replace it.

---

[3] A Linux distribution consists of the Linux kernel, standard GNU utilities, and a selected set of tools and application programs that are packaged into a downloadable image file. This image file can be stored on a USB thumb drive and booted on a computer, and the user can try Linux or install it directly. Some common distributions are Fedora, Mint, Debian, Red Hat Enterprise Linux (RHEL), and Ubuntu.

I have not always had enough money to purchase all of the software I wanted or needed. Software that costs nothing in monetary terms enabled me to obtain all that I needed and to keep it up to date.

That said, now that I can, I donate to many of the projects that create and maintain the software I use. Sometimes, I donate money; other times, I donate time to test new releases or simply report bugs I have found using the provided mechanisms. Bug reports are important and appreciated. There is never any obligation.

Linux Is Free (as in Speech)

I can get the source code for all our applications. If I want to know how a certain part of the Linux operating system or an application works, I can download the code and find out. Most people never need or care to look at the source code – except for geeks like me.

The fact that Linux and so much FOSS application software is free as in speech does mean something to everyone like you. It means that you can share the software you download with as many people as you like. You can install it on one or ten thousand computers all for the amazing low price of ZERO. No license police will come looking for you and force you to pay for those licenses copied by employees that you were unaware of. Not to mention the monetary penalties.

Linux Is Safe

This is a big issue for many small business owners, and it always has been for both of us.

The open availability of the source code means, in practical terms, that many people have examined it for bugs and for security vulnerabilities. Those bugs and vulnerabilities are fixed quickly and are well tested before they are released.

Security fixes are released as they become ready and not on a monthly schedule. You only need to perform updates regularly, follow some standard security procedures, and your data and personal information are as safe as possible.

If you are extra paranoid, which is not a bad thing, your data can also be encrypted. This would make it very difficult for the data to be accessed were the computer or storage device[4] to be stolen.

---

[4] In this book, a storage device refers to either a hard disk drive (HDD) or a solid state drive (SSD). Both perform the same task of storing programs and data even when the computer is turned off.

Linux Is Reliable

I have found that Linux and the FOSS application software I use is the most reliable I have ever encountered. I have never had an instance where Linux itself has crashed. There is no blue screen of death (BSOD) in Linux.

I currently have 12 computers in my home and several others for which I have system administrator responsibility. Linux just keeps running 24 hours a day. For various reasons, I never turn them off. I may reboot them if an update to the kernel is installed, but I never turn them off. They just keep running and never crash.

That said, I have encountered hardware problems that can crash the entire system. And I have had some applications crash which happens very infrequently, and recovery is usually quite easy because Linux itself keeps running. And any software can crash, even Linux, but I have personally never had the Linux operating system itself crash.

Linux Is Powerful

Linux is much more powerful and capable than anything else available today. For example, as of this writing, all 500 of the world's largest supercomputers run Linux as their operating system. NASA's Mars helicopter, the first vehicle from Earth to fly on another planet, runs a version of Linux. The computers on the International Space Station all run Linux.

Linux also runs Android phones and watches, cable and satellite set-top boxes, your smart TV, the entertainment systems in many cars, and much more.

It also runs on the amazing Raspberry Pi[5] which costs as little as $35US and can be used by children to learn programming. Because of its low cost, it can be used to provide access to a computer for many low-income children. I have given three of my grandchildren a Raspberry Pi.

Linux Gives You Complete Control

I am a control freak. I like to be in control. I got my pilot's license so I could fly an airplane for fun, but it also helped me understand what is happening when I fly commercial. So now, I find myself explaining to other travelers that, while not a normal occurrence, landing with the malfunctioning flaps in the up position is something that all pilots train for extensively.

---

[5] `www.raspberrypi.org/`

I am like that about my computers, too. I like to be able to control everything. Most small business owners like to be in control, too.

Have you ever tried stopping a process in Windows and it wouldn't let you? Ever tried deleting a file – and you couldn't?

Linux lets you do anything. You can terminate any process you own or delete any file you own. If you log in as root – also called the administrator or superuser – Linux assumes you know what you're doing. Once you become root, everything is allowed; you can even delete files and terminate processes that belong to other users.

Another aspect of complete control is that you decide for yourself when updates are performed. I cannot tell you how many times I have seen Windows running displays in commercial establishments like my gym or when a presenter was onstage stuck in the blue screen of updates (BSOU) because Windows decided that *right now* during your presentation was the right time to force your computer to do updates, during which you can do nothing else.

Linux even allows you to perform updates while doing other things. If a reboot is required, you can choose when you want to do it. Of course, I strongly suggest you never begin an upgrade during a presentation.

Linux Extends the Life of Your Hardware

How long should a normal computer live? *Business News Daily* suggests that desktop computers should last from five to eight years, while laptops three to five years.[6] Like many articles and so-called experts, they suggest that one sign that a computer needs to be replaced is when it slows down. This is just not true.

I currently have multiple computers that are over ten years old and still running fine. I have had to replace storage drives in a few computers over the years and power supplies in several of those computers. I also replace internal cooling fans quite frequently; those are the three most common points of failure in computers. Most computers don't need replaced when they break. They just need fixed.

The oldest computer I currently have is a Dell OptiPlex 755 from 2008 with a Core 2 Duo CPU and 8 GB of RAM that runs at 2.333 GHz. This computer is running Fedora 34 which is the most recent version of Fedora as of this writing. So the newest version of Fedora is keeping this 13-year old computer that has been running the

---

[6] Walter, Derek, *Business News Daily*, www.businessnewsdaily.com/65-when-to-replace-the-company-computers.html, 2020

World Community Grid[7] software full blast, 24x7x365, for 3 years searching for cancer markers, information about the COVID-19 virus and potential drugs to combat it, rainfall forecasting in Africa, a project to help determine cures and treatments for childhood cancer, and more. This old computer passed through multiple other owners before being "gifted" to me by someone who thought they needed a new computer. Well, it is pretty slow compared to today's computer, but it is certainly not ready for the recycling center near my home. All of my computers run this software.

In the past, I managed to keep one old IBM ThinkPad (before Lenovo) laptop running for almost 12 years using successive releases of Fedora.

As long as the hardware continues to work – and many times the hardware itself can be repaired or parts replaced far less expensively than purchasing a new computer – Linux will keep running on your computer, and it will never slow down.

Linux Is Easy

Linux is easy to install, use, and maintain. It is also easy to try out as we will show you in an upcoming chapter. It is not necessary to install Linux on your computer to try it out. You can boot from a "live" USB thumb drive with Linux installed on it and try it without changing or modifying your computer or data in any way – unless you want to intentionally try using LibreOffice to work with an existing Word Document or Excel Spreadsheet – which it will do just fine.

Lots of Software

Another thing I like about Linux is that all kinds of software are available for it and most are high quality and also open source and free of charge. In fact, most current Linux distributions, Fedora included, come with almost all of the software anyone could ever use, or it is quite easily available.

When you install Fedora – or most any of the modern, user-oriented Linux distributions – you also get access to a huge, secure repository of digitally signed software that can perform almost any task needed in a small business. And one of the amazing facts about Linux and FOSS is that you will almost always have multiple options from which to choose the software you need.

Here are a few examples from my own experience:

---

[7] World Community Grid, `www.worldcommunitygrid.org/`

- **Office suite**: I use LibreOffice software which is a complete, compatible replacement for Microsoft Office. LibreOffice Writer is what I am using to write this book – and my four previous books. LibreOffice Calc is a powerful spreadsheet program, and Draw allows you to create vector graphic illustrations. LibreOffice Impress creates and displays presentations. All of your existing MS Office files will work in LibreOffice.

- **Email client**: Thunderbird is quite popular for email, but others are Claws, Geary, Sylpheed, and KMail. If you like the command-line text mode interface, you could also use Mutt or Alpine. Alpine is my current favorite for email.

- **Web browser**: I prefer Mozilla Firefox for my web browser. Other choices are Midori, Chrome, Brave, and Konqueror. The browsers Links and Lynx are also available if you prefer a text mode user interface. Yes, that is a thing.

- **File manager**: This is a tool like Windows Explorer. According to one search result, there are 47 open source file managers. My current favorite is Thunar, the default file manager for the Xfce desktop. Others include Krusader, Gnome Files which is the default for the Gnome desktop, and Xfe. My favorite for the text mode interface is Midnight Commander.

- **Screen capture**: I use Spectacle. It is easy to use and most of the screen images in this book were captured using Spectacle.

- **Image manipulation**: GIMP is a great replacement for Photoshop. I use it occasionally to add text to images or to manipulate color and brightness or to overlay multiple images.

- **Audio editing**: I use Audacity to edit and splice together multiple audio files into a single file while adjusting the volume and sound quality for different segments. Audacity has many filters which can be used for fade in/out, noise reduction, pop removal, and more.

- **Audio playback**: Audacious is an easy-to-use yet powerful media playback tool. Juk is also an excellent choice.

- **Video**: OBS studio is my choice for video recording and streaming. Having made some videos while I was at IBM, I can say that this software looks and feels very much like a TV studio.

- **Video editing**: I have tried OpenShot and it works well, but I have found that Shotcut works better for me and my needs. Other possibilities in this category are Kdenlive and LiVES, among others; I have not tried any of these.

- **Video/media playback**: My current favorite in this category is the VLC media player, but you could also try MPlayer with the mpv front end or Kaffeine.

- **Multimedia conversion**: The only real option here is the ffmpeg media converter, but many of the other multimedia tools incorporate it into their tools. The ffmpeg tool can convert many types of audio and video files to various other types. My typical uses are to convert raw MKV video files to MP4 and Apple M4A audio files to MP3. Handbrake is a good option here as a front end to ffmpeg.

- **Animation**: Blender is the tool of choice for 2D and 3D animation and rendering. I have never used it, but it gets great word of mouth and reviews.

- **Desktop**: Yes, you can even change the Linux desktop – the graphical interface with which you interact with the computer. In this book, we will us the Xfce desktop because it provides a flexible, highly configurable, yet familiar work environment. Xfce also uses fewer system resources than many of the other desktops.

Note that much of this open source software is also available for other operating systems like Windows. Try some of them and see how well they work for you on your current operating system.

By now, you get the idea, so I won't continue to bore you with the many other categories and options. Suffice it to say that the choices I have available to me mean that I can choose the best tool for a given task, even though a similar tool may do much the same thing. For example, I really like the Thunar file manager, but sometimes, for some tasks, I prefer the Xfe or Midnight Commander (MC) file managers.

Linux Is Fun

Yes, Linux is fun. Most of you probably won't think this is the case, but I do. Computers are a hobby for me, like boats, cars, and sports are for some people. I find that learning and using Linux are fun for me. And there is always more to learn about computers in general and Linux specifically.

You may have noticed that I talk about my "current favorites" for some of the application categories mentioned earlier. This is because I am always trying out new software and finding new ways to use my old favorites. All of these different software packages can co-exist side by side so that I can use the one that most meets my needs for a particular use case. You don't have to pick just one.

So – yes – Linux is fun. Perhaps you will find it so as well.

Chapter Summary

In this chapter, we have told you a bit about who we are and why we use Linux. We have also looked at some of the more common open source software applications that you will find are available for Linux and your small business.

Exercises

1. List the reasons that you are considering Linux for your business.

2. Are you considering Linux for personal use as well?

3. What applications do you use that are critical to your business?

4. What one problem are you currently having with your computer that causes you the most pain?

CHAPTER 2

A Bit of History – Becoming Linux

Objectives

After reading this chapter, you will learn

- Why a bit of history is important to your business.

- Why Windows is a closed operating system and a bit about what that means.

- A little about The Linux Philosophy.

- What it all means to you as a small business owner.

Introduction

This chapter is a brief study of how a philosophy can have a profound effect upon the software written by developers subject to its thrall.

We look at the philosophy that guided the development of Windows and how that philosophy prevents Windows from unleashing the full power of the computers on which it is used.

Exploring the philosophy that underpins the development of Linux, we discover how that ensures that Linux provides open and unfettered access to all the power of the computer and the operating system

We also look at what all this means to you as a small business owner.

© David Both, Cyndi Bulka 2022
D. Both and C. Bulka, *Linux for Small Business Owners*, https://doi.org/10.1007/978-1-4842-8264-9_2

Windows Origins

The proprietary Digital Equipment Corporation (DEC) VAX/VMS1[1] operating system was designed by developers who subscribed to a closed philosophy, that is, that the users should be protected from the internal "vagaries" of the system because they are afraid of computers.

Dave Cutler,[2] who wrote the DEC VAX/VMS operating system, is also the chief architect of Windows NT, the parent of all current forms of Windows. Cutler was hired away from DEC by Microsoft with the specific intention of having him write Windows NT. As part of his deal with Microsoft, he was allowed to bring many of his top engineers from DEC with him. Windows versions of today, however far removed from Windows NT they might be, remain hidden behind this veil of secrecy.

Operating systems that shield their users from the power they possess were developed starting with the basic assumption that the users are not smart or knowledgeable enough to be trusted with the full power that computers can actually provide. These operating systems are restrictive and have user interfaces – both command line and graphical – that enforce those restrictions by design. These restrictive user interfaces force regular users and SysAdmins alike into an enclosed room with no windows and then slam the door shut and triple lock it.

The command-line interfaces of such limiting operating systems offer a relatively few commands, providing a de facto limit on the possible activities in which anyone might engage. Some users find this a comfort. I do not and, apparently, neither do you judge from the fact that you are reading this book.

As a user of Windows, this impacts you in ways that will not truly become obvious until you install and use Linux and other free open source software (FOSS).

---

[1] Wikipedia, "VAX," https://en.wikipedia.org/wiki/VAX

[2] *ITPro Today*, "Windows NT and VMS: The Rest of the Story," www.itprotoday.com/management-mobility/windows-nt-and-vms-rest-story

Unix

The short version of this story is that in the late 1960s, the developers of Unix, led by Ken Thompson[3] and Dennis Ritchie,[4] designed Unix to be open and accessible in a way that made sense to them. They created rules, guidelines, and procedural methods and then designed them into the structure of the operating system. That collection of guidance from the originators of the Unix operating system was codified in the excellent book *The Unix Philosophy*, by Mike Gancarz, and then later updated by Mr. Gancarz as *Linux and the Unix Philosophy*.[5]

Another fine book, *The Art of Unix Programming*,[6] by Eric S. Raymond, provides the author's philosophical view of programming in a Unix environment. It is also somewhat of a history of the development of Unix as it was experienced and recalled by the author. This book is also available in its entirety at no charge on the Internet.[7]

Unix is a powerful operating system that provides the user complete access to the full capabilities of the computers on which it runs. It hides nothing from the user.

But Unix was and is a proprietary operating system, heavily licensed and restricted by those licenses in what the users can do. For example, users cannot share the Unix operating system or portions of it with others. Those with the skills are not allowed to modify it for the benefit of the community.

The Birth of Linux

In 1991, in Helsinki, Finland, Linus Torvalds was taking computer science classes using the Minix[8] operating system. This tiny variant of Unix was written by Andrew S. Tanenbaum[9] to use in the computer science classes that he taught. Torvalds was

---

[3] https://en.wikipedia.org/wiki/Ken_Thompson

[4] https://en.wikipedia.org/wiki/Dennis_Ritchie

[5] Mike Gancarz, *Linux and the Unix Philosophy*, Digital Press – an imprint of Elsevier Science, 2003, ISBN 1-55558-273-7

[6] Eric S. Raymond, *The Art of Unix Programming*, Addison-Wesley, September 17, 2003, ISBN 0-13-142901-9

[7] Eric S. Raymond, *The Art of Unix Programming*, www.catb.org/esr/writings/taoup/html/index.html/

[8] https://en.wikipedia.org/wiki/MINIX

[9] https://en.wikipedia.org/wiki/Andrew_S._Tanenbaum

not happy with Minix as it had many deficiencies, at least to him. So he wrote his own operating system and shared that fact and the code on the Internet.

Many others on the Internet became interested and began supporting the operating system by submitting code to Torvalds for inclusion. This little operating system, which started as a hobby, eventually became known as Linux as a tribute to its creator and was distributed under the GNU GPL 2 open source license.[10]

Wikipedia has a good history of Linux[11] as does Digital Ocean.[12] For a more personal history, read Linus Torvald's own book, *Just for Fun*.[13]

The Linux Truth

Unix [Linux] was not designed to stop its users from doing stupid things, as that would also stop them from doing clever things.

—Doug Gwyn

This quote summarizes the overriding truth and the philosophies of both Unix and Linux – that the operating system must trust the user. It is only by extending this full measure of trust that allows the user to access the full power made possible by the operating system. This truth applies to Linux because of its heritage as a direct descendant of Unix.

The Linux Truth results in an operating system that places no restrictions or limits on the things that users, particularly the root[14] user, can do. The root user can do anything on a Linux computer. There are no limits of any type on the root user. Although there are a very few administrative speed bumps placed in the path of the root user, root can always remove those slight impediments and do all manner of clever – and sometimes stupid – things.

---

[10] https://en.wikipedia.org/wiki/GNU_General_Public_License

[11] https://en.wikipedia.org/wiki/History_of_Linux

[12] Juell, Kathleen, "A Brief History of Linux," www.digitalocean.com/community/tutorials/brief-history-of-linux

[13] Torvalds, Linus and Diamond, David, *Just for Fun: The Story of an Accidental Revolutionary*, HarperBusiness, 2001

[14] The root user is the administrator of a Linux host and can do everything and anything. Compared to other operating systems, non-root Linux users also have very few restrictions, but we will see later in this book that there are some limits imposed on them.

Non-root users have a few limits placed on them, but they can still do plenty of clever things as well. The primary limits placed on non-root users are intended to – mostly – prevent them from doing things that interfere with others' ability to freely use the Linux host.

What It Means to Small Business Owners

In Chapter 1, we looked at the two ways in which Linux, as free open source software (FOSS), is free – as in beer and as in speech. We also looked at some of the vast array of FOSS application software available for Linux.

In this chapter, we looked at the history Windows of Linux to understand a little about how the different philosophies behind their creation affect the final products and the people who use them. But how does that translate to benefits for the small business user?

The value of any software lies in its usefulness not in its price.

—Linus Torvalds[15]

The preceding quote from Linus Torvalds, the creator of Linux,[16] perfectly describes the value proposition of free open source software (FOSS) and particularly Linux. Expensive software that performs poorly or does not meet the needs of the users can in no way be worth any amount of money. On the other hand, free open source software that meets the needs of the users has great value to its users.

Most open source software[17] falls in the latter category. It is software that millions of people find extremely useful, and that is what gives it such great value. David has only downloaded and used one proprietary software application in almost 30 years that he has been using Linux.

Linux itself is a complete, open source operating system that is open, flexible, stable, scalable, and secure. Like all operating systems, it provides a bridge between the computer hardware and the application software that runs on it. It also provides tools

---

[15] Wikipedia, "Linus Torvalds," https://en.wikipedia.org/wiki/Linus_Torvalds
[16] Wikipedia, "History of Linux," https://en.wikipedia.org/wiki/History_of_Linux
[17] Wikipedia, "Open Source Software," https://en.wikipedia.org/wiki/Open-source_software

that can be used by a small business owner acting as a system administrator to monitor and manage the following things:

The functions and features of the operating system itself:

- Productivity software like word processors; spreadsheets; financial, scientific, industrial, and academic software; and much more

- The underlying hardware, for example, temperatures and operational status

- Software updates to fix bugs

- Upgrades to move from one release level of the operating system to the next higher level

The tasks that need to be performed by the system administrator are inseparable from the philosophy of the operating system, both in terms of the tools which are available to perform them and the freedom afforded to the SysAdmin in their performance of those tasks.

Chapter Summary

Linux has a long history that, with its Unix predecessor, goes all the way back to 1969. Unix – and then Linux – were designed from the beginning to be secure, to provide multitasking and multiuser capabilities, and to allow users unparalleled access to the power of modern computers.

Linux is ideal for small businesses because of its power, flexibility, and the many choices available for any type of software. It is also free of charge.

We have skipped over much of the history of Unix and Linux for the sake of brevity. If you are interested in learning more, the footnotes in this chapter provide links to a large amount of that amazing history.

## CHAPTER 3

Using Linux – The Business Case

Objectives

After reading this chapter, you will be able to

- List and describe the typical reasons that businesses switch to Linux
- Clearly define the pain points you experience with your current computing environment
- Describe the reasons Linux might be right for you

Introduction

We both switched to Linux for our businesses, and we did it for similar as well as different reasons. Most businesses that switch to Linux do so to have some specific objectives in mind, and yours won't be the same as those of other small businesses. Your business is unique, and so is the way you use your computers.

This chapter looks at the reasons that most businesses – and sometimes individuals – switch to Linux for the operating system on their computers.

The Usual Reasons for Using Linux

Linux has many advantages over other operating systems – specifically Windows. Some of these advantages are quite obvious and others not so much.

© David Both, Cyndi Bulka 2022
D. Both and C. Bulka, *Linux for Small Business Owners*, https://doi.org/10.1007/978-1-4842-8264-9_3

Most of us who have switched to Linux do so for one or two of the more common reasons but, like Cyndi and I, end up appreciating it more for the reasons you seldom hear about.

Reliability

We both like Linux for its reliability. Although it is not true that Linux never crashes, David has had few problems over the more than 25 years he has been using it. Those few problems were usually due to his own errors such as misconfiguration of service files.

Neither of us has had a serious crash with Linux.

You might be surprised to know that most of the world's largest companies use Linux. We saw in Chapter 1 that NASA has installed a Linux supercomputer on the International Space Station and used Linux in interplanetary probes like the Mars rover and helicopter. All 500 of the world's largest supercomputers use Linux. The majority of websites you access on the Internet use Linux. The major stock exchanges and many banks use Linux in their most critical applications.

Linux is widespread in all types of applications including some of the most critical and important ones. It is telling that the most critical uses for computers on and off the planet Earth use Linux.

The reliability of Linux is one of the major reasons that we both use it.

Extensive Software Choices

In Chapter 1, we listed some of the many application programs available for Linux, including some of the specialized multimedia tools that we use to create podcasts, videos, and to do live streaming.

Many other tools are available as free open source software[1] (FOSS). In fact, Fedora has a number of "Labs[2]" that are designed for specific fields. These labs include Comp Neuro for computational Neuroscience, Astronomy, Design Suite for visual design and multimedia, Jam for audio enthusiasts and musicians, Python Classroom for teaching Python programming, Security Lab for forensic analysis security auditing and system recovery, Robotics Suite for beginning and experienced roboticists, Scientific

---

[1] Wikipedia, "Free Open Source Software," `https://en.wikipedia.org/wiki/Free_and_open-source_software`

[2] Fedora Lab downloads, `https://labs.fedoraproject.org/`

for scientific and numeric research tools, and – of course – Games for some of the best games available for Fedora; pretty cool, right?

All the tools included in these labs are also available as individual downloads for any existing Fedora computer. Fedora uses secure public repositories to make thousands of software packages safely available. The software stored in these repositories (repos) is all that most users will ever need and is easy to install with the software installer provided with Fedora.

We searched for a list of other open source software on the Internet, but the ones we found were mostly "top X open source software for doing Y." Wikipedia has a long list of FOSS, but the list is hopelessly out of date. The best thing we can recommend if you are looking for a specific type of software is to search for that type and include the words "open source" in the search. This usually turns up dozens of lists, at least some of which pertain to the software being sought. In most cases, the software we searched for was already part of one of the Fedora repos.

We recommend that you use software that is available from the Fedora repositories whenever possible. This ensures that the software is well maintained, has been inspected for malware, tested for functionality and problems, and has been electronically signed so that you will know if it has been tampered with when you install it.

Other software can be safe and effective as well. We will discuss software repositories and how to install trusted ones in a later chapter.

Security

Most people who have heard about Linux know that one of the most commonly cited reasons for using it is that it is much more secure than Windows. In our experience, this is absolutely true.

Security is a critical consideration in these days of constant attacks from the Internet. If you think that they are not after you, too, let me tell you that they are. Your computer is under constant attack every hour of every day.

Most Linux distributions are very secure right from the initial installation. Many tools are provided to both ensure tight security where it is needed as well as to allow specified access into the computer.

For example, you may wish to allow SSH (Secure SHell for remote access) access from the occasional remote host, access to the web server on your server from anywhere in the world, or to send email from anywhere in the world.

On the other hand, you may also want to block, at least temporarily, access attempts by crackers (the bad guys) attempting to force their way in. Other security measures provide your personal files protection from other users on the same host while still allowing mechanisms for you to share files that you choose with others.

Many of the security mechanisms present in Linux were designed and built into Linux right from its inception. The architecture of Linux is designed from the ground up, like Unix, its progenitor, to provide security mechanisms that can protect files and running processes from malicious intervention from both internal and external sources. Linux security is not an add-on feature; it is an integral part of Linux. Because of this, most of our discussions that relate to security will be embedded as an integral part of the text throughout this book. There is a chapter about security, but it is intended to cover those few things not covered elsewhere.

Free as in Beer

Free (as in beer) is always good, right? Yup – it is, no question.

This lack of monetary cost is usually perceived by people in a negative way. The reasoning is that "you get what you pay for" which has been drummed into us by companies wanting us to buy exorbitantly priced products – especially software. How can anything that is free be of any value?

The value of any software lies in its usefulness not in its price.

—Linus Torvalds[3]

The preceding quote from Linus Torvalds, the creator of Linux,[4] perfectly describes the value proposition of free open source software (FOSS) and particularly Linux. Expensive software that performs poorly or does not meet the needs of the users can in no way be worth any amount of money. On the other hand, free software that meets the needs of the users has great value to those users.

Most open source software[5] falls in the latter category. It is software that millions of people find extremely useful, and that is what gives it such great value.

---

[3] Wikipedia, "Linus Torvalds," https://en.wikipedia.org/wiki/Linus_Torvalds
[4] Wikipedia, "History of Linux," https://en.wikipedia.org/wiki/History_of_Linux
[5] Wikipedia, "Open Source Software," https://en.wikipedia.org/wiki/Open-source_software

Linux itself is a complete, open source operating system that is open, flexible, stable, scalable, and secure. Like all operating systems, it provides a bridge between the computer hardware and the application software that runs on it. It also provides tools that can be used by a system administrator, the SysAdmin, to monitor and manage the following things:

The functions and features of the operating system itself:

- Productivity software like word processors; spreadsheets: financial, scientific, industrial, and academic software; and much more

- The underlying hardware, for example, temperatures and operational status

- Software updates to fix bugs

- Upgrades to move from one release level of the operating system to the next higher level

The tasks that need to be performed by the system administrator are inseparable from the philosophy of the operating system, both in terms of the tools which are available to perform them and the freedom afforded to the SysAdmin in their performance of those tasks. As the owner of a small business, you are also the system administrator for your computers.

Software that does what you need it to do, easily and reliably, is worth a great deal to you as a business person regardless of its price. So when powerful, reliable, useful software is available to you for not monetary cost – free as in beer – it makes excellent business sense to use it.

The fact that Linux is free also makes it ideal for installing on older computers to make them last longer. This is important to many non-profits that rebuild old donated computers for underfunded schools and disadvantaged children who would not otherwise have access to computers of any kind.

Yes, Linux is free. We like that as one of many of its attractions. That is one of the least important reasons for us to use Linux, but it is a nice bonus.

Free as in Speech

The Free Software Definition[6] which was adopted by the Free Software Foundation (FSF) defines free software as a matter of liberty not price and defines the Four Essential Freedoms which requires the software's licensing to respect the civil liberties/human rights of what the FSF calls the software user's "Four Essential Freedoms." Yes, the numbering does start at zero.

0. The freedom to run the program as you wish, for any purpose:

1. The freedom to study how the program works and change it so it does your computing as you wish. Access to the source code is a precondition for this.

2. The freedom to redistribute copies so you can help others.

3. The freedom to distribute copies of your modified versions to others. By doing this, you can give the whole community a chance to benefit from your changes. Access to the source code is a precondition for this.

What this means to us as business owners and de facto system administrators is that I can install any open source software on as many computers as I want without the need to worry about the license policy showing up to count how many "valid" licenses I have paid for. They do that but usually with medium to large companies.

We can also make copies of that software to share with our friends. We normally don't need to do that these days because – the Internet. But still...

Another advantage of these freedoms is the cases of some large companies attempting to monopolize and monetize open source software. On more than one occasion, large software companies have tried to do that. They failed because the source code for the software was freely available and the open source developers simply renamed their software and kept on going.

Open source software can be monetized as exemplified by companies such as Red Hat. Their Red Hat Enterprise Linux (RHEL) can be downloaded quite freely. To get support, which many of their large customers need and want, paid subscription services are available. For those of us who use releases of Linux based on RHEL, such as Fedora or CentOS, well, that is supported free of charge. More on that coming up.

---

[6] Free Software Foundation website, `www.fsf.org/`

Cyndi

Using Windows as my OS, not only did I have to purchase virus and malware protection programs on a regular basis, but those programs repeatedly failed to protect me from infection.

I don't have to tell you how much of an interruption a corruption can be! I've lost important data that I had to pay to recover, and sometimes was unable to restore lost files and lists to their original integrity. Not to mention having to hand over my computer or laptop for a number of days to have the fix done. There has not been a single incidence of infection since switching to Linux. I store my clients' personal information on my computer, and with Windows, I was frequently concerned about that information being compromised. Building a trusting relationship with my clients is fundamental to my work. When I claim to not sell their information to anyone, I want to be able to back that up.

David

I have been using Linux for just over 25 years as of this writing. For most of that time, I have had anywhere from 3 to 12 computers running Linux in my home office. I use them for various things including as servers; test beds for new hardware, software, and tools; and primary workstations for my wife and myself.

Not a single computer has ever been infected with any Trojan, virus, ransomware, or other malware of any kind. They never slow down or display annoying pop-ups trying to sell me something I don't need. I never get erroneous warnings my computer is infected from sketchy people trying to steal my money or worse yet my identity.

SELinux

And if you're not convinced that Linux is secure, or you deal with highly sensitive information that requires extra protection, there is the SELinux tool which is already installed on all Linux systems right from the start. Security-Enhanced Linux is an open source security enhancement written by the National Security Agency (NSA) to tighten the security of their own Linux computers. This tool is available and already activated in warning mode. If the need is there, it just needs to be reconfigured for active protection.

Support

Support is a key consideration for small business owners.

Support is about more than just having a poorly paid, barely trained person on the phone who merely follows a script that someone else has written. Support is not about paying someone to take the blame. Unlike small business owners, many managers feel compelled to spend lots of money on products that purport support and then don't deliver. Support is about more than just rebooting the computer to temporarily circumvent the real problem which remains unresolved.

Support is about having a product with well-tested code before it is released so that it seldom breaks in the first place. Support is about having someone knowledgeable to contact when it does break. Support is about having excellent built-in help facilities that document how to perform the tasks you need.

Support is also about having a supportable product.

Proprietary Software and Maintainability

Let's look at what proprietary software means to someone trying to fix it. I will use a trivial black box example to represent some hypothetical, proprietary software, but this has happened to me, companies I used to work for, and individuals I know.

This hypothetical software generates customer invoices. It was written by a hypothetical company that wants to keep the source code a secret so that their alleged "trade secrets" cannot be stolen.

As the user of this proprietary software, I have no knowledge of what happens inside the bit of compiled machine language code to which I have access. Part of that restriction is contractual – notice that I do not say "legal" – in a license agreement that forbids me from reverse engineering the machine code to produce the source code.

After using this program for a while, I notice that some customers have complained that their invoices are incorrect. After checking them myself, I determined that the data was entered correctly in all cases, so the problem must be in the software.

So I report this problem to the vendor from whom I purchased the software. They tell me they will fix it in the next release. "When will that be?" I ask. "In about six months – or so," they reply.

I must now task one of my workers to check the results of every invoice to verify whether it is correct. If not, we must manually create a revised invoice.

After a few months with no work on a fix from the vendor, I call to try and determine the status of the fix. They tell me that they have decided not to fix the problem because only a few customers are having the problem. The translation of this is, "sorry, you don't spend enough money with us to warrant us fixing the problem." They also tell me that the new owners, the venture capital company who bought out the company from which I bought the software, will no longer be selling or supporting that software anyway.

I am left with useless – less than useless – software that will never be fixed, and I cannot fix it myself. Neither can anyone else who purchased that software fix it if they ever run into this problem.

Why? Because it is completely closed to people like you and me, and the proprietary software is inaccessible and thereby unknowable. Even the greatest software expert is left with their hands tied.

FOSS and Maintainability

Let's imagine the same software as in the previous example, but this time written by a company that open sourced it and provides the source code should I want it.

The same situation occurs. In this case, I report the problem and they reply that no one else has had this problem. In many cases, the developer asks me a few questions via email to fully understand the problem. One of the developers fixes the code within hours or days and asks me to ensure that the fix works as it is supposed to.

In one case, I could not contact the developer for a very small program. So I download the source code to fix it myself – which most people are unwilling or too intimidated to even try because of the risk of making the problem worse or not having the time in their busy day to devote. I immediately saw the problem and wrote a quick patch for it. I tested the patch – in a test environment of course – and found the results to show the problem had been fixed.

In one instance, I took over development of a program from a developer in Latvia who no longer had the time to maintain it, and I maintained it for several years.

In another instance, a large company purchased a software firm called StarOffice who open sourced their office suite under the name StarOffice. Later, a large computer company purchased the company and renamed the product to OpenOffice.org. The new organization decided they would create their own version of the software starting from the existing code. That turned out to be quite a flop. Most of the developers of the open source version migrated to a new, open organization that maintains the reissued software that is now called LibreOffice. OpenOffice now languishes and has few developers while LibreOffice flourishes.

I use LibreOffice to write all of my articles and books.

One advantage of open source software is that the source code is always available. Any developers can take it over and maintain it. Even if an individual or an organization tries to take it over and make it proprietary, they cannot, and the original code is out there and can be "forked" into a new but identical product by any developer or group. In the case of LibreOffice, there are thousands of people around the world contributing new code and fixes when they are required. In my opinion, this is a wonderful thing that we all benefit from.

Having the source code available is one of the main advantages of open source because anyone with the skills can look at it and fix it and then make that fix available to the rest of the community surrounding that software. Most small business owners have neither the time nor the skill set to do that.

In the context of free open source software – FOSS – the term "open" means that the source code is freely available for all to see and examine without restriction. Anyone with appropriate skills has legal right to make changes to the code to enhance its functionality or to fix a bug.

For one recent Linux release, over 1,700 developers from a multitude of disparate organizations as well as many individuals working around the globe contributed 13,500 changes to the kernel code. That does not even consider the changes to other core components of the Linux operating system, such as core utilities, or even major software applications, such as LibreOffice, the powerful office suite that I use for writing my books and articles as well as spreadsheets, drawings, presentations, and more. Projects such as LibreOffice have hundreds of their own developers.

This openness makes it easy for SysAdmins – and everyone else, for that matter – to explore all aspects of the operating system and to fully understand how any or all of it is supposed to work. This means that it is possible to apply one's full knowledge of Linux to use its powerful and open tools in a methodical reasoning process that can be leveraged for problem solving.

Stability

Stability can have multiple meanings when the term is applied to Linux by different people. My (David) definition of the term as it applies to Linux is that it can run for weeks or months without crashing or causing problems that make me worry I might lose data for any of the critical projects I am working on.

Linux easily meets that requirement. I always have several computers running Linux at any given time, and they are all rock solid in this sense. They run without interruption. I have workstations, a server, a firewall, and some hosts that I use for testing, and they all just run.

Another type of stability is that of continuing availability and the ability to use software that I like for decades. I use GnuCash accounting software for my personal finances, and I used it for my businesses while I had them. I have used GnuCash since 2003 and still have access to all of those old transactions.

I have already talked about LibreOffice, but the stability of still being able to use old StarOffice, MS Word, Word Perfect, and other old document and spreadsheet files after 20 years is very important to me and to any business.

Why You Should Use Linux

We can't really tell you that.

Only you as a small business owner can determine why you should switch to Linux. There are plenty of reasons to do so, but your reasons will be as different from ours as our reasons were different from each other.

But we can help you figure it out.

The Points of Pain

If you are reading this book, you probably already know that you at least want to try Linux to see what it can do for you.

Whether you have already made that decision or are still unsure, take a few minutes to list those problems that are points of pain for you. You may find them in the preceding sections of this chapter, and you may note some that are not. Either way, list them and rate each according to how much pain and disruption it causes the workflow of your business.

Consider how many times you need to reboot to "fix" a problem or how long it takes your computer to boot in the first place. Think about how slow your computer runs compared to when it was new or how much time and money you spend on antivirus and anti-malware subscriptions. Recall how much you have spent on software to do your job and then how much you spend on new versions of that software.

Pick the top two or three out of your list. These are your primary reasons for considering a switch to Linux.

Take a few more minutes to consider each of these pain points and estimate how much extra time they add to your workday. Consider how much money you spend directly and indirectly to keep your computers not just running but also running smoothly.

That is the cost of not switching to Linux. Not counting the frustration. And for most small business owners, that counts for a lot.

Of course, the reality is that Linux can't fix everything. But for many small business owners, it has already made a big impact. That can be directly to the bottom line in the form of reduced expenses, and it can be in the form of freeing up time that can be used for more productive pursuits that add directly to the bottom line.

Chapter Summary

In this chapter, we have explored many of the reasons that many organizations including small businesses choose Linux. Your reasons for exploring Linux may not match up with any of the ones we have looked at here. Determining what those reasons are really must be your starting place.

Without knowing why you should make the change, you have no way to measure success after.

CHAPTER 4

Choosing Hardware

Objectives

After reading this chapter, you will be able to

- Determine whether an old computer is worth using Linux to rescue

- Understand at least enough about hardware to knowledgeably purchase new computers on which to install Linux

- Purchase a laptop or desktop computer with Linux preinstalled from specialized vendors

Introduction

Much of the time, small business owners do not get to choose what computer hardware to use when installing a new operating system. In fact, Linux is used many times as a means to extend the working life of existing but old computers. So in a very real sense, the hardware has chosen us.

However, even Linux has its limits and not all old computers can be salvaged. In this chapter, we will look at a minimum set of hardware requirements for older computers. We need to ensure that it does, in fact, make good business sense to consider trying to use Linux to extend the lives of those older computers that might otherwise be discarded. Some computers are ready for the recycling bin, but many others are not.

We also explore various computer hardware components and discuss what to look for in each when purchasing a new computer or making a determination of whether to employ an older, used computer.

© David Both, Cyndi Bulka 2022
D. Both and C. Bulka, *Linux for Small Business Owners*, https://doi.org/10.1007/978-1-4842-8264-9_4

We will explore a reasonable set of hardware requirements for purchasing new computers. We also discuss a bit about where to purchase new computers, what to look for, and why.

This chapter is intended to advise you on many technical aspects of choosing a new or used computer. We cannot cover every possibility, but we think there is enough information in this chapter to allow you to make informed decisions about computer purchases.

However, if you have a store or person you trust to help you purchase a new computer, let them advise you. A trusted person at a local computer store can help you choose a computer or at least assist you with understanding what you need. Such a person can be very helpful and can save you some time. That does not mean that you should ignore this chapter or completely delegate responsibility for choosing a computer to someone else.

Most likely a store or person is going to try to guide you to buy and use Windows, or at least they won't understand why you intend to use Linux. That's just to be expected, so you should expect it, be OK with it, and ultimately ignore it – smile sweetly, nod, and carry on.

Even with an advisor, you should know enough to understand their advice and why what they tell you makes sense – or not.

Bottom Line

There is a lot of technical information coming, and many of you will not want to deal with all of those details. So we put the bottom line at the beginning of this chapter for those of you who just want to get going and purchase a computer:

- New computers are better than old ones and will give a better long-term ROI.

- If you have used computers available to you at no cost, they can be a good alternative for the short term. Just don't get one that "needs repair."

- Never get a so-called all-in-one computer in which the display and motherboard with the processor and memory are all part of a single unit. These may look great, and they do save desk space, but the repair parts are expensive because they are nonstandard and must be purchased from the vendor.

- Pick the processor first when purchasing a new computer. This defines memory speeds and motherboard choices. In general, the more recent Intel i5 and i7 processors at 3GHz or more will provide the best overall performance, value, and ROI for most small businesses.

- New computers should have no less than 16GB of RAM.

- Stay away from hard disk drives (HDDs) and get solid state drives (SSDs) for better performance. A 500GB SSD is more than enough for most small businesses unless the computer will be used for creation or download of large numbers of graphics, audio, or video files.

- For desktop computers, stay away from Dell and Hewlett-Packard (HP) if possible because they use nonstandard cases and parts to lock us in to their repair services and unique, proprietary hardware. Upgrades to new motherboards that take faster processors are not possible with these systems. If you do get one of these, prefer Dell over HP and be aware of the limitations.

- Dell has a good line of laptops and even has Linux available on some models. Dell uses the Ubuntu distribution which is perfectly good.

- Different Linux distributions such as Fedora, Ubuntu, Mint, and Pop_OS! are far more similar than they are different. We use Fedora in this book because it is what I started with and what we are both familiar with.

- System76 sells excellent, top-quality computers, both desktops and laptops. They design and build the desktops in the United States with some parts imported. System76 computers all ship with Pop_OS! which is a version of Ubuntu. It is OK to install Fedora, and they still support their computers. Their laptops are designed in the United States and are currently built overseas. In addition to a standard 1-year and extended 2-year warranty, System76 also provides excellent lifetime support.

- Emperor Linux sells laptops from top vendors and installs almost any popular version of Linux you want. They also provide excellent long-term support.

- Get a good keyboard for a desktop computer. They can be expensive but are well worth it.

- Get a 24" or 27" HD or 4K display with HDMI and DVI inputs. Built-in speakers are a plus. Although this would be a good primary display for a desktop, it can also make an excellent secondary display for a laptop.

Keep reading if you want to know the details and why we make these specific recommendations.

Compatibility

Linux is compatible with most computer hardware. In fact, it can support more older hardware than Windows can.

In part, this compatibility is because Linux works much better on older computers that are significantly less powerful than today's computers because it requires less in the way of hardware resources such as memory and processor power. It is also due to the fact that many vendors are working to ensure that their new hardware offerings will work well with Linux.

Another reason for this compatibility is that although a very few vendors don't even try to ensure compatibility with Linux, there are tens of thousands of programmers around the world that do work to make that so.

Viewing Information Using BIOS or UEFI

We need a reliable method for locating the information we need from a computer, especially older ones. You can find much of the important information about a computer, whether new or used, from its UEFI[1] or the much older BIOS.[2] Sound scary? It's really not.

BIOS and UEFI are usually easy to access and provide a wealth of information. In Chapter 5, we will also look at some tools that Linux provides to view the hardware components installed in a computer.

---

[1] Unified Extensible Firmware Interface. A more secure replacement for the BIOS found in older systems.

[2] Basic Input/Output System/ROM BIOS. The part of the system software of the IBM PC and compatibles that provides the lowest-level interface to peripheral devices and controls the first stage of the (bootstrap) process, including loading the operating system. FOLDOC.

UEFI is intended to be more secure for booting a computer than BIOS was. Developed by Microsoft, it helps to protect against various types of malware that can infect or circumvent BIOS in order to gain control of the system. This does not protect against malware after the computer has booted into the operating system.

Accessing BIOS/UEFI

Most computers provide access to the BIOS/UEFI through a special key on the keyboard during the initial power on of the computer. Sometimes, a message is displayed on the screen during the very earliest stages of the boot process to indicate what specific key that is. The computer documentation usually has that information as well.

Entering UEFI mode is usually simple. Hold down the designated UEFI access key when you turn the computer on. The problem is that different computer and motherboard manufacturers use mostly the same keys to access UEFI mode – but not always. Figure 4-1 shows the different keys or combinations used to access UEFI mode with a list of the vendors that use that key.

UEFI / BIOS key	Brands
F1	Lenovo desktops
Enter then F1	Lenovo ThinkPads
F2	ASUS PCs, Acer, Dell, GigaByte, Lenovo, Samsung, Toshiba
Fn+F2	Lenovo laptops (not ThinkPads)
F10	Hewlett-Packard (HP)
F12	Dell
Esc(ape)	ASUS PCs and motherboards, Dell
Del(ete)	Acer, GigaByte, MSI

Figure 4-1. *UEFI/BIOS mode access keys and the vendors that use them*

If the computer brand is not listed in Figure 4-1, the F2, F12, and Delete keys are good options to try for UEFI access.

Sometimes, it can be necessary to repeatedly press the UEFI key during the early stages of boot. The time frame for this is immediately when you power the computer on and through the display of the hardware logo, for example, the Dell logo when booting a Dell computer or the MSI logo when booting a computer with an MSI motherboard.

The website, *Tom's Hardware*, also has an excellent article[3] about how to access UEFI on different brands of computers.

System Information

When the UEFI screen is displayed, there is a menu in some format that allows selection of various aspects of UEFI. We are interested in the system information, and there may be a menu item with that exact name or something similar.

Press the appropriate key or use the arrow keys to navigate to that menu item and select it. Here again, different vendors use different methods and menu structures. Figure 4-2 shows part 1 of a fairly typical Dell version of the system information page, in this case a Dell OptiPlex 3050 desktop computer. Dell designs its own motherboards including the BIOS, so the BIOS mode is much different looking than other manufacturers.

Yes, in an older computer like this Dell, you would still encounter BIOS rather than UEFI. The information displayed will be much the same although perhaps in a graphical setting for UEFI systems.

The information on the screen in Figure 4-2 shows much of what we cover in the rest of this chapter including BIOS or UEFI date which is the date the system was manufactured. For Dell, it shows the service tag and express service code that can be used to obtain support, the amount of installed memory, the memory technology, and DIMM sizes and speed. Note that the DIMMs are of two different sizes.

---

[3] Piltch, Avram, *Tom's Hardware*, "How to Enter the BIOS on Any PC: Access Keys by Manufacturer," www.tomshardware.com/reviews/bios-keys-to-access-your-firmware,5732.html

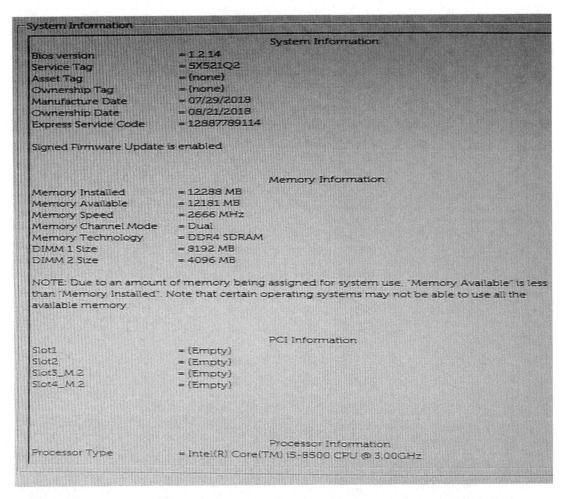

Figure 4-2. System BIOS information from an old Dell OptiPlex 3050 desktop computer. Part 1

Different Dell models will have BIOS information pages that may look significantly different from this.

Figure 4-3 shows part 2 of the Dell system information page. It includes information about the processor, installed storage devices, the MAC address for the built-in network interface card (NIC), and on-board video and audio adapters.

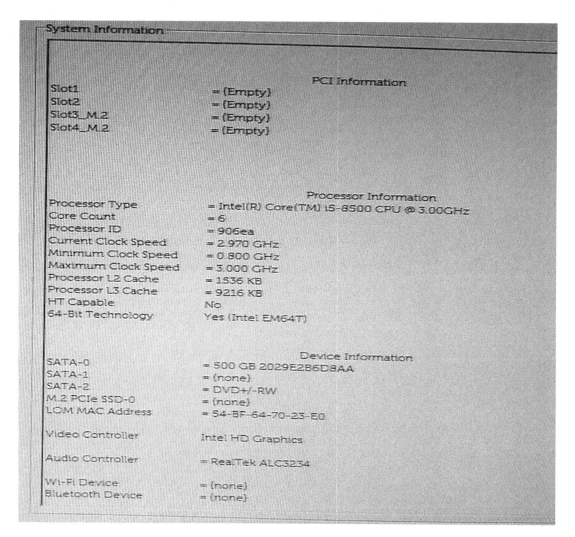

System Information

PCI Information	
Slot1	= {Empty}
Slot2	= {Empty}
Slot3_M.2	= {Empty}
Slot4_M.2	= {Empty}

Processor Information	
Processor Type	= Intel(R) Core(TM) i5-8500 CPU @ 3.00GHz
Core Count	= 6
Processor ID	= 906ea
Current Clock Speed	= 2.970 GHz
Minimum Clock Speed	= 0.800 GHz
Maximum Clock Speed	= 3.000 GHz
Processor L2 Cache	= 1536 KB
Processor L3 Cache	= 9216 KB
HT Capable	No
64-Bit Technology	Yes (Intel EM64T)

Device Information	
SATA-0	= 500 GB 2029E2B6D8AA
SATA-1	= {none}
SATA-2	= DVD+/-RW
M.2 PCIe SSD-0	= {none}
LOM MAC Address	= 54-BF-64-70-23-E0
Video Controller	Intel HD Graphics
Audio Controller	= RealTek ALC3234
Wi-Fi Device	= {none}
Bluetooth Device	= {none}

Figure 4-3. *System BIOS information from an old Dell OptiPlex 3050 desktop computer. Part 2*

This processor is an Intel i5-8500 with six cores. "HT Capable" is Hyperthreading which in this case is "no." That means that Hyperthreading is not supported, so it only has six CPUs. The text "Intel HD graphics" on the Video Controller line indicates that this is also an on-board device and not an add-in PCI card.

An Internet search can tell you a great deal more about this processor type.

Figure 4-4 shows a portion of a typical BIOS logo screen for Intel motherboards. This screen shows the key-press options available before power-on self-test (POST) starts. Intel uses the F2 key to enter BIOS mode. It also provides a method to update the BIOS code and to choose a different device from which to boot, such as a USB thumb drive.

If no key is pressed during the time the screen in Figure 4-4 is displayed, the BIOS starts power-on self-test (POST) and continues through the normal BIOS boot sequence. This screen is only shown for a few seconds, so be prepared to make your key press quickly when you need to access BIOS setup mode.

Figure 4-4. *The Intel BIOS logo screen showing that the F2 key is used to access BIOS settings*

If you do press the F2 key at the BIOS logo screen, you will see the screen in Figure 4-5. The system information shown here is not as extensive as the Dell system but still contains enough information for you to decide whether this computer will work for you. Although there is no BIOS date directly shown, the BIOS date is embedded in the BIOS version at the top. The section of the BIOS version, "2012.1105," indicates November 5 of 2012, so at nine years old, this is one of my older computers.

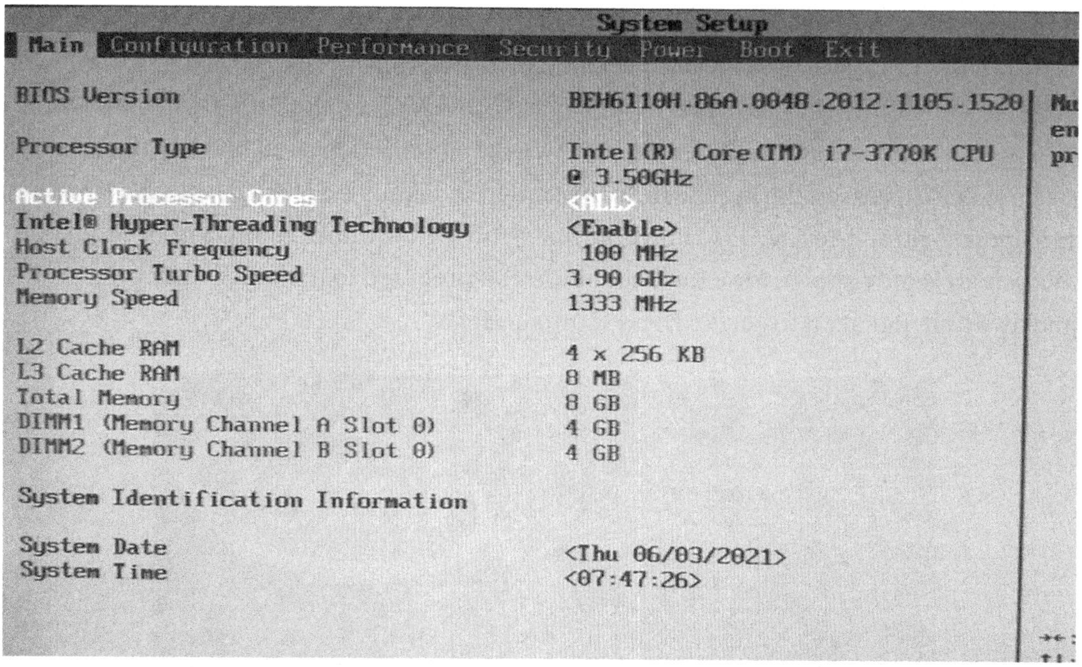

Figure 4-5. *The BIOS information screen from an Intel motherboard*

Warning   The BIOS date does not necessarily reflect the date the motherboard or the computer were built. The BIOS can be updated to a newer version, and the date in this field represents that date which may be much newer than that of the motherboard or the computer itself. Also, a new motherboard may have been installed in an older computer, thus making the BIOS date more recent than the rest of the computer.

This i7 Intel processor is designed to run at 3.5GHz but can run at 3.9GHz in turbo mode. It also supports Hyperthreading which is already enabled. We can also see that the computer has 2 DIMMS of 4GB each.

The Intel BIOS in Figure 4-5 does not specify the number of cores in the processor or the memory type (DDRX), but that information can be found by doing a search on the processor type, "Intel i7-3770K." The Intel specifications page for this processor has all the information you will need including the number of cores and much more.

Figure 4-6 shows the BIOS information page from a much newer computer that offers the option to use a BIOS boot instead of the UEFI boot. However, the user interface is the same regardless of which boot option you choose.

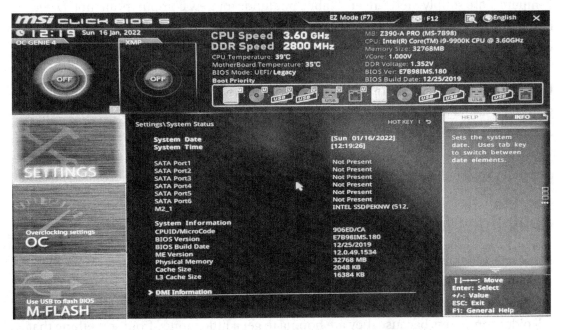

Figure 4-6. *The UEFI/BIOS interface from a newer computer shows much of the same information but in a graphical setting*

The image of the system status screen on an MSI motherboard shows information about the hardware, but it does so in a graphical environment that can be used with a mouse as well as the keyboard.

This motherboard is currently installed in one of my computers. You can (hopefully) see that this system contains a powerful i9 processor and 32GB of RAM.

You should also notice that BIOS mode is set to legacy BIOS mode. I have been experimenting with this system and have switched it between legacy BIOS and UEFI modes for my own testing purposes. Once booted, Fedora works the same regardless of which mode is used.

Rescuing Older Computers

We do not always get to choose the computers we use. In many cases, older, used computers are simply there and available, but funds for new computers are not. David found this to be true in many of the larger companies he has worked for, and we both were constrained by lack of money as small business owners.

Non-profits can also be financially unable to afford new computer equipment. David's church has had multiple computers gifted to it over the years, some of which were even usable. Because many of his friends and acquaintances are aware of David's computer skills, they also tend to gift older computers directly to him as well.

In most cases, those usable ones were between five and eight years old. By the time computers reach the age of ten, they might be salvageable but are not necessarily usable.

Guidelines for Older Computers

There are some simple guidelines you should follow with older computers. Most will seem like common sense, but others may not be so obvious.

First, don't purchase used computers for any reason. People and businesses only sell older computers because they are hoping to get a little money from something that they perceive as broken or too slow to use effectively. If you can get them to donate it to you, that is perfect. Old computers that companies discard may be usable, but that is not always the case. Don't take a chance. If a donated computer can be restored by installing Linux on it, you can use it for a few years. If not, you have not lost anything.

Second, it is not worth even attempting to restore an older computer that has a poor set of specifications. You will waste time and money if you attempt to upgrade the hardware on many older computers – even some of those you may already own.

What criteria should one look for in older computers to rescue? Here is an easy guide. Many of these criteria are by the numbers. Be sure to refer to the Glossary if necessary. The criteria listed in Figure 4-7 are important when deciding on whether a particular used computer will work for you. Much of this information can be obtained directly from BIOS as discussed earlier.

Criteria	What to look for
Age	Used computers in the five to seven year age range still have some useful life once Linux is installed. Do not accept any donated or gifted computer over 7 years of age. If you already have computers over 7 years old you might as well use them.
Case	The case – the box that contains the components – is important. A standard case that can handle standardized components allows for future growth. Some popular brands sell computers that have non-standard cases and non-standard internal components. See the discussion below.
RAM memory	16GB of DDR3[4] RAM is best but will be hard to find in a used computer. 8GB is OK. 4GB is the absolute minimum. Do *not* accept a used computer with plain DDR or DDR2 RAM.
Processor (CPU) clock speed	A minimum clock speed of 2.5GHz (2,500MHz) for a used computer is OK. 3.0GHz is a much better clock speed and 4GHz and higher is excellent for a used computer.
Processor	In general, low-end CPUs are under-powered for multimedia applications but low-end ones that are less then 3 years old might be fine for simple office work such as documents and spreadsheets. Mid- to high-end CPUs will work fine for almost any type of task you might use them for. CPUs that are more than 10 years old are not worth using under almost any conditions.
Motherboard	Any motherboard that supports the processor and memory that meets the specifications outlined for those components will work fine.

Figure 4-7. *Use this table to decide whether a specific used computer might work for you*

---

[4] Wikipedia, DDR3 SDRAM, `https://en.wikipedia.org/wiki/DDR3_SDRAM`. Also see the Glossary.

Graphics card	Many Intel processors have on-board graphics which is fine for most small business use. Other computers use add-in graphics cards and most of these should be appropriate. If the computer turns on and the display works, the graphics card is fine for most businesses.
Keyboard	Most computer keyboards are junk. The keyboard is one of the most important components of the computer because it is our primary interface to input data into the computer. Yet we use keyboards that cost $5 to $10(US). What kind of keyboard should we be using? Good ones – expensive ones. The Unicomp Model M keyboard[5] is the same keyboard that IBM made famous with its original PC in 1981. This keyboard sells for $104 and is well worth the cost. It has great tactile and audible feedback so it is clear when the keys have been pressed. This no-frills keyboard is what you want when you spend a lot of time typing and need that good, solid keyboard feel. Be sure to get the USB version. Many gaming keyboards work well, too.
Display	If a used computer comes with an old CRT display get rid of the display or just don't take it. You will save money on the power required to keep that old display turned on. Flat screens are the only way to go. They use much less power than the ancient CRTs and reduce eyestrain. They have far better resolution and brighter, more realistic colors. They also take less space. We recommend flat screen monitors that are rated at least 17" HD (High Definition) with 1920x1080 resolution and HDMI or DVI connections or both. Built-in speakers are also good and should work with both HDMI and DVI without the need for extra speaker connections. Some older computers have only VGA display connections. Some modern displays have VGA connections but many do not. If the computer has only VGA and the display does not have a VGA connector, you can use an adapter. Search Amazon for: "VGA to HDMI adapter." These adapters usually cost less than $10.

Figure 4-7. *(continued)*

---

[5] Unicomp Model M keyboard, www.pckeyboard.com/page/product/NEW_M

General Considerations for Used Computers

The basic test for a used computer is to connect it to a keyboard, mouse, and monitor. Plug it in and see if it works. Be sure to check the BIOS for the actual specifications and to determine the installed hardware components. Be sure that there are no errors displayed during the boot sequence.

But there is more to take into account.

All computers have cooling fans to dissipate the heat generated but the electronic components inside. A quick test is to feel all over the case of the computer while it is turned on and running. If the surface feels very hot, one or more fans are not working and the CPU heat sink may be clogged with dust.

In many instances, computers can be upgraded. The processor, RAM, and graphics systems can all be upgraded. With many computers, the motherboard can also be replaced. But once you start to spend money like this, you should probably just go ahead and purchase a new computer. If a used computer does not meet your needs, you should look for another or purchase a new one.

Some hardware components in used computers will eventually need to be replaced. The most common failure points in modern computers are the ones with mechanical components – cooling fans, hard disk drives, and power supplies which also have cooling fans. Be prepared to replace these components.

Purchasing a New Computer

The purchase of a new computer can be as fraught with trepidation as that of selecting a used computer. Fortunately, we can use the same criteria, along with a few more, but apply them a bit differently for a new computer.

Guidelines for New Computers

Even when you know what you need in a computer, the act of purchasing a new computer is a challenge even for those of us who are familiar with technology and know what we are doing. Even armed with the knowledge from this chapter, you should enlist a knowledgeable friend to help you choose a new computer.

This section is intended to help you understand a little about what is being offered to you off the shelf or by the sales staff when you go to purchase a computer. Figure 4-8 lists the criteria you should consider when looking for a new computer.

Criteria	What to look for
Case	The case – the box that contains the components – is important. A standard case that can handle standardized components allows for future growth. Some popular brands sell computers that have non-standard cases and non-standard internal components. See the discussion below.
Motherboard	Motherboards are not normally a discussion point when purchasing a new computer. Most computer store staff talk about processor speeds and the amount of RAM installed. Just be sure that you get a motherboard from one of the major brands, Intel, ASUS, MSI, or GigaByte. If you get the processor and memory, the motherboard that is also part of the new computer will be fine.
RAM memory	16GB of DDR4[6] SDRAM is optimal for a new computer but DDR3[7] SDRAM is also a good choice. DDR5 SDRAM Is just starting to become available but is not needed for a small business computer.
Processor (CPU) clock speed	A minimum clock speed of 2.5GHz (2,500MHz) for a used computer is OK. 3.0GHz is a much better clock speed and 4GHz and higher is excellent for a new computer.
Processor	The Intel i3 is too under-powered. Intel i5 and i7 processor families are good for small businesses with i7 being the preferred. The i9 series is considerably over-powered for most small businesses and can be quite expensive.
Power supply (PSU)	Power supplies (Power Supply Unit / PSU) are another overlooked but important part of a new computer. Good 500 Watt power supplies are available for around $50 and are sufficient for most business uses. PSUs do tend to be one of the items that fail – though not frequently – so an oversize power supply can be expected to have

Figure 4-8. *Use this table to help select appropriate components when purchasing a new computer*

---

[6]Wikipedia, "DDR4 SDRAM," https://en.wikipedia.org/wiki/DDR3_SDRAM. Also see the Glossary.
[7]Wikipedia, "DDR3 SDRAM," https://en.wikipedia.org/wiki/DDR3_SDRAM. Also see the Glossary.

	a longer life. Use a 600W, 650W, 700W, or 750W power supply for longer life.
	Somewhat more expensive, power supplies that are cited as modular have no power distribution cables connected, rather they are provided with cables that plug in so that only those cables that are required for your computer are to be installed. This keeps the case interior free of extra cables that clutter the space, restrict airflow, and make working on the interior difficult.
	Corsair, ThermalTake, and EVGA, are all good choices.
Keyboard	The keyboard is one of the most important components of the computer because it is our primary interface to input data into the computer. Yet we use keyboards that cost $5 to $10(US) and which can give us carpal tunnel syndrome as well. What kind of keyboard should we be using? Good ones – expensive ones – mechanical keyboards.
	The Unicomp Model M keyboard[8] is the same keyboard that IBM made famous with its original PC in 1981. This keyboard sells for $104 and is well worth the cost. It has great tactile and audible feedback so it is clear when the keys have been pressed. This no-frills keyboard is what you want when you spend a lot of time typing and need that good, solid keyboard feel. Be sure to get the USB version. Warning: this keyboard may sound very loud in an otherwise quiet environment.
	Many gaming keyboards work well, too, and are available at computer stores at prices ranging from about $79 to $200 and more. Unless you are into gaming (in which case you already know this) don't get a keyboard that boasts "fast" or "high speed" keys for business use. these are extremely fast and sensitive and just lightly resting your fingers on a key can cause it to activate. David prefers MX blue or MX brown keys for the best typing

Figure 4-8. (*continued*)

---

[8]Unicomp Model M keyboard, www.pckeyboard.com/page/product/NEW_M

	experience.[9] The computer store staff should know what you are talking about; if they don't find a store that has staff who do know.
Graphics card	Many Intel motherboards have on-board graphics which is fine for most small business use. Other computers use add-in graphics cards and most of these should be appropriate. When you have a choice of graphics card we recommend using Radeon cards which have better open source compatibility with Linux but NVIDIA cards also work. NVIDIA cards can have issues when upgrading to newer releases of Fedora and other distributions and this can result in the need for some knowledgeable person to help install the latest NVIDIA drivers.
Display	We recommend flat screen monitors that are at least 17" diagonal size and rated HD (High Definition) with 1920x1080 resolution and HDMI or DVI connections or both. Built-in speakers are also good and should work with both HDMI and DVI without the need for extra speaker cables or connections. Larger displays are better because they provide more screen "real estate" in which to work. Higher resolutions will also improve the quality of the display and make text easier to read. David suggests an optimum of 27" diagonal with 2560x1440 resolution. He has a 32" display using 2560x1440.
TV / Monitor	All modern flat screen TVs use HDMI input and can be used as a display for a computer that has HDMI graphics output. This is a lot like connecting a a streaming device like an HDMI Amazon Fire TV streaming box to your TV.
Printer	Yes, we do need to talk about printers. Most printers will work with Linux. In fact, many older printers work better with Linux than with Windows.

Figure 4-8. (*continued*)

---

[9] If you are interested, check out this MX switch comparison video on YouTube. `www.youtube.com/watch?v=z1SPH3HvxhQ`

Processor Details

It is important to have a basic understanding of some additional details of processors in order to ensure that you get the most processing power for your money when purchasing a new computer.

There are two vendors that produce microprocessors[10] for personal computers, Intel and AMD. Intel developed the first microprocessors suitable for use in the original IBM PC, and AMD later created a series of microprocessors that were functionally identical while offering greater power and more cores and CPUs. Intel and AMD are in a competition for the fastest and most powerful processors which is a good thing for computing in general because it ensures we have faster/better processors appearing continuously. Many gamers prefer AMD processors for their extra bit of power and speed.

In general, both AMD and Intel processors are fine for most business uses, and Linux works equally well on both. There are differences in the motherboards for AMD and Intel, so an AMD processor must be used on a motherboard designed for AMD, and an Intel processor must be used on a motherboard designed for Intel.

Let's look at some specific things to consider for each.

Intel

Intel processors fall into several families. The Intel Celeron and Pentium processor lines are targeted at very low-cost, entry-level personal computers which are not a good choice for a small business. The Xeon family of processors is most frequently found in servers and high-end workstations that may need multiple processors where each processor contains multiple cores.

For typical business and home workstations, the Intel Core[11] line of processors provides a wide range of price and performance. Intel produces two series of processors that are suitable for most businesses.

The i5 series is good for typical office tasks including video conferencing with Zoom, Jitsi, etc., and for viewing live streams. They are unsuitable for use in creating or editing videos.

---

[10] Wikipedia, "Microprocessor," https://en.wikipedia.org/wiki/Microprocessor
[11] Intel, www.intel.com/content/www/us/en/products/details/processors/core.html

The i7 series is more powerful than the i5 series and can be used for video, audio, and graphic production.

Each of the Intel Core series of processors has generational releases. The newest generation as of this writing is 11th Gen, while the 10th Gen is the most commonly available at this time. Each generation packs more processing power than the last.

AMD

Despite being our technical expert, David has little knowledge or experience with modern AMD processors. So this research is limited to what we found online.

The AMD processor lineage is newer and a bit less complex than that of the Intel processors. AMD produces two lines of processors designed for business use cases.[12] The AMD Ryzen PRO Desktop Processors and AMD Athlon PRO Desktop Processors are all suitable for business use.

Processor Comparison List

Tom's Hardware publishes an excellent list[13] that compares many AMD and Intel processors for each year.

Not all processors are listed, only the ones they were able to test. This list will provide you a good idea of the relative power and cost of many processors on the market today.

Standardization

There are also some special considerations to take into account. The primary consideration is that of longevity – do you want to fix your computer by replacing parts, or will you purchase a new computer when one part breaks? This question is one of long-term viability and requires you find computers that are completely standardized.

---

[12] AMD Processors for Desktops, www.amd.com/en/products/processors-desktop

[13] *Tom's Hardware*, "CPU Benchmarks and Hierarchy 2021: Intel and AMD Processors Ranked," www.tomshardware.com/reviews/cpu-hierarchy,4312.html

Many common computer components are standardized. For example, DDR4 SDRAM will fit in any computer of any brand designed for DDR4 memory. All hard drives and solid state drives are interchangeable and can be installed in almost any computer with few exceptions so long as you purchase storage devices that are compatible with the available SATA or M.2 connectors on the motherboard.

Cooling fans also come in a number of different standard sizes and are usually simple to replace. Even CPU fans – but not the heat sink[14] itself – can be a simple replacement.

Interestingly, the most important component for standards compliance is the case – the box that contains many of the other components such as the motherboard and power supply.

What We Have

David has a dozen computers in his home office. They range from a low-end Core i3 with 2 cores and no HT to a very high-end Core i9X with 16 cores plus HT – and pretty much everything in between. David's main workstation is the Core i9 Extreme, and he uses it for everything from video editing and processing, writing, and testing code and automation tools for system administration to more mundane tasks like writing articles and books.

Cyndi has only one computer, a Dell Inspiron laptop that she uses for all aspects of her business including Zoom yoga classes and creating audio and video sessions for teaching and meditation.

All of our computers run the Fedora distribution of Linux.

Laptops

Laptop computers are totally different from desktop or tower computers. Although memory and storage devices are mostly standard and can sometimes be upgraded, nothing else is standard. If something breaks, you will need to go directly to the manufacturer for repair or replacement.

---

[14] A heat sink is a passive radiator that pipes heat out of and away from the processor and transfers it to the air inside the computer. Fans then discharge the hot air out of the computer and replace it with cool air.

Desktop SDRAM is not compatible with that for laptops. Although the performance characteristics are essentially the same, the physical packages are different, being shaped differently for laptops. The connectors are not the same, and it is not possible to install laptop memory into a desktop motherboard or vice versa without physical damage to the DIMM, the connector, or both.

Acer, ASUS, Lenovo ThinkPad, and Panasonic are all good choices for laptops so long as they meet the hardware specifications you need.

Specialized vendors such as Emperor Linux and System76 have excellent choices for laptops. More on these two vendors in the following sections.

Where to Buy

For about 20 years after the introduction of the Apple and, a bit later, the IBM PC, computer stores and specialized computer retail chains dotted the landscape. No more. Only a few true computer stores remain, and big-box stores that sell everything from mobile phones to household appliances, and the latest OLED TVs, now dominate the scene.

Choosing a Computer Store

We are fortunate here in central North Carolina to have, in addition to those big-box stores, a small, local chain called Intrex. They require applicants to take a technical test to ensure their level of knowledge. The staff also has at least some familiarity with Linux and can help you design the computer that works best for your needs.

A custom-built computer will give you the most hardware for any given price because it will be what you need and not what a manufacturer has decided that "most people" will accept. The best part is that you can purchase only the hardware and do not need to pay the Microsoft tax. I have never asked them, but I suspect a couple of the Intrex staff use Linux and could probably install Linux.

The people at Intrex are also very good at repairs and reasonably priced, too. They are well versed in cleaning malware and nagware from Windows computers.

David purchases as much of his hardware from this chain as possible. He especially likes they can discuss his needs with them and provide recommendations for hardware. They can then build it and provide a warranty. They also have predesigned and pre-built systems that can be purchased at good prices. Most times, he already knows what he wants and gives them a list of the parts needed. He then takes the parts home and builds the new computer himself. He likes doing that, but there is absolutely nothing that says you need to do that, too.

This type of computer store – if you can find one – is the best. They can help you determine what you need. In most cases, if they don't already have it in stock, they can special order the required parts and build the computer when the parts arrive.

Search for "custom-built computer store near me" to locate stores that provide this type of service.

Big-Box Stores

Big-box stores are everywhere and most sell computers. Most have a few people on staff with some basic computer knowledge. Most of that staff cannot define the term CPU or differentiate a CPU from a core or a processor. Sometimes you get lucky and find someone on staff that really knows hardware and has heard of Linux.

The staff at big-box stores are trained to sell you whatever they have in stock at that moment and not necessarily what best meets your needs. Sometimes, you actually get what you really need if you manage to get the knowledgeable person.

The real problem with the big-box stores is that you can only purchase what they have received from the manufacturer, and that has been assembled into a few basic "one-size-fits-all" configurations that just *might* be appropriate for your business.

You will also be required to pay for a Windows license for a preinstalled copy of that OS which you do not need. That Microsoft tax runs from $99 to about $149 depending on whether it is a "home," "pro," or "server" license. It is the same basic operating system just a few different bits and a different price depending on how Microsoft expects you will use it.

Linux User Groups

Your local Linux User Group (LUG) can help you find the best place to purchase a custom-built computer. Some of the members may offer to help you. If they do, take advantage of that because LUG members are always very smart and knowledgeable.

My local group is the Triangle Linux Users Group[15] (TriLUG), and it has members across the United States in part because members move away but still like being part of this active group. Although in-person meetings were halted during the COVID-19 health crisis, TriLUG maintained communications via its mailing lists and online video meet-ups. Like many groups, it has monthly meetings with technical presentations, food when meet-ups are in person, and camaraderie.

The Fedora Project website has a list of Linux User Groups[16] that covers much of the world. If there is not a Linux User Group near you, find one on the list and get involved from wherever you are.

LUG mailing lists and meetings are excellent places to ask questions and solicit assistance.

Online Computer Stores

In general, stay away from online computer stores. In many instances, the online stores have only unused older equipment or even equipment that has been refurbished. They usually mention that, but it is not always easy to find that information.

There are some exceptions. I have purchased laptops from two different online stores that specialize in Linux.

System76

System76 is an excellent option for most desktop computers and especially laptops, a relatively new company located in Colorado that designs and builds their own line of desktops. They design the laptops, but those are still being built in other countries. They are working to change that.

System76 installs their own version of Ubuntu, "Pop!_OS!" Linux, on every computer. They do not do Windows in any form. Their support staff is smart, knowledgeable, and very helpful. The parts they use are high quality, and their laptop keyboards are excellent, they are backlit, and have a nice tactile feedback.

Because their computers are well designed and extremely well built, System76 computers tend to be expensive, but they are worth it.

---

[15] Triangle Linux Users Group (TriLUG), `https://trilug.org/`

[16] Fedora Wiki, Linux User Groups, `https://fedoraproject.org/wiki/LinuxUserGroups`

David has had a System76 Oryx Pro 4 laptop (Core i7-8750H with 6 cores with HT, 32GB of RAM, 2 500GB SSD storage devices) for about 3 years and is still very happy with it. It has had no problems of any kind so far. He did install Fedora, his preferred distribution, on it after using Pop!_OS for a few weeks. This is not a casual-use laptop. It is intended as a substitute workstation when he is traveling. He has used it for audio/video recording and editing and running multiple virtual machines (VM) during demonstrations and Linux training.

The System76 website is `https://system76.com/`.

Emperor Linux

Emperor Linux, based in Atlanta, GA, deals exclusively in laptops. They obtain laptops from quality vendors and install Linux on them. This company will install any version of Linux that you want.

David's previous laptop was purchased from Emperor, and it served him well for more than ten years. That laptop was a ThinkPad and was also used as a workstation on the go. He used it for teaching Linux classes, and it was also capable of running multiple VMs in that role.

The Emperor Linux website is `www.emperorlinux.com/`.

Our Test Computer

We obtained a pretty old ASUS laptop that we will use for a test computer in this chapter because configuration of real hardware BIOS is different from configuration of the BIOS on the virtual machines (VMs) that we use in the rest of the book.

This ASUS X550C was provided to us by a friend who no longer needs it. We are going to enter BIOS mode and look at the hardware configuration. That is all. We will not change the BIOS configuration yet.

Most computers – actually their motherboards – are not configured in BIOS as delivered from the factory to boot from a USB thumb drive. We must temporarily reconfigure the BIOS to enable that capability.

Most modern motherboards can boot from a USB device, but the BIOS must be configured to do so. The method for setting the BIOS configuration to boot from a USB device can differ widely between manufacturers and even between systems from the same vendor.

Entering BIOS Mode

To enter BIOS mode on this ASUS laptop, we first ensured that the computer was turned off and not in sleep or hibernation mode. Figure 4-1 shows a list of BIOS access keys and the brands that use each. Be sure to use the correct BIOS access key for your computer.

To enter BIOS mode for this laptop, I momentarily press the power key and then press and hold the F2 key until the ASUS/Intel logo screen appears. After that, the computer enters BIOS mode where the BIOS Information page displays information about the computer's BIOS and hardware. Figure 4-9 is a frame grab from the video, Chapt05-Video01.mp4, and shows the BIOS vendor and version information along with the processor and memory information.

```
         Aptio Setup Utility - Copyright (C) 2012 American Megatrends, Inc.
  Main  Advanced  Boot  Security  Save & Exit

  BIOS Information                                        Set the Date. Use Tab to
  BIOS Vendor                American Megatrends          switch between Date elements.
  Version                    215
  VBIOS Version              2132.I14N550.007
  EC Version                 204E150001

  Processor Information      Intel(R) Core(TM) i3-
                             3217U CPU @ 1.80GHz

  Memory Information
  Total Memory               4096 MB

  System Information
  Serial Number              E1N0CV59596904G        →←    : Select Screen
                                                    ↑↓    : Select Item
  System Date                [Sat 07/10/2021]       Enter: Select
  System Time                [09:26:38]             +/-   : Change Opt.
                                                    F1    : General Help
  Access Level               Administrator          F9    : Optimized Defaults
                                                    F10   : Save & Exit
                                                    ESC   : Exit



         Version 2.15.1227. Copyright (C) 2012 American Megatrends, Inc.
```

Figure 4-9. *The BIOS Information page of the ASUS X550C laptop*

This ASUS X550C was first released around October of 2013 and has an Intel Core i3-3217U processor running at 1.8GHz and 4GB of RAM. This is well below the minimum specifications recommended earlier in this chapter.

Not all BIOS types place all this information on one page, so you may need to explore the BIOS for your computer to obtain all the information shown in Figure 4-9. In any event, you should look at the other pages of this BIOS to see the other options available in most BIOS versions. Pay special attention to the Boot page which we will need in the next chapter.

When you are finished, you can use the last page of the BIOS to exit and reboot the computer.

Note   View the video which can be found at our Apress download site: Github.com/Apress/linux-for-small-business-owners

Chapt04-Video01: "Accessing BIOS to view hardware." This video shows how we access the BIOS on the ASUS laptop that we use as a test computer for this chapter.

Chapter Summary

We have done things a little out of order here by placing the "Bottom Line" section at the front of this chapter. It contains the summary of our recommendations without most of the reasoning behind them. But we do go on to deal with all of those recommendations along with our reasoning for both used and new computers in the rest of the chapter.

Some of the recommendations we have made in this chapter, especially with regard to keyboards and displays, are not about saving money. They are about your long-term comfort and health. Monitors and keyboards are seldom considered by most users as essential – and yet they are. Good ones will pay dividends.

We looked at places to purchase computer hardware. We also explored entering BIOS setup to verify the basic hardware components of a computer.

## CHAPTER 5

Take Linux for a Test Drive

Objectives

After reading this chapter, you will be able to

- Describe the function of a "live image USB"

- Create a live image USB device

- Configure your computer to boot from a USB device

- Test drive Fedora on your own or other used computers

- Test a new computer in the store

Note   In this chapter, the pronouns "I" and "me" refer to David.

Introduction

Like everyone else, those of us who use Linux sometimes need to purchase a new computer. Although the days of poor hardware compatibility are long gone, it is still possible to run into issues. Just going to a local store, like Intrex here in Raleigh or any of the big box stores, and watching the display models run Windows demo programs does not ensure Linux support for all aspects of their hardware.

But when I stopped to think about it, that is exactly what I am doing when I plug a Fedora Live USB thumb drive into any computer I already own to do an installation. If the Fedora Live USB works well enough to be able to even show the live desktop with its "Install to hard drive" option, most of the hardware should already be compatible, such as the motherboard, USB, graphics adapter, keyboard, hard drive, and mouse or

© David Both, Cyndi Bulka 2022
D. Both and C. Bulka, *Linux for Small Business Owners*, https://doi.org/10.1007/978-1-4842-8264-9_5

touchpad. Only a few things would remain to be tested, perhaps wired and wireless networking, the sound system, and an integrated web cam.

Even when a computer – especially a used one – looks like it has at least the minimal amount of hardware you will need, it is always a good idea to take it for a test drive. You always test drive a car, right? So we should also test drive computers whether new or used – especially used.

We know you may want to purchase from an online source such as Amazon or another hardware source. That can be a viable option, but it does not allow for a test drive before your purchase. Be sure to understand the company's return options before you purchase.

Unlike other operating systems, Linux can be taken for a test drive on the computers you use in your business. You can get first-hand experience on the hardware and with the files you use every day to see how well Linux works for you.

This is accomplished by using a "live image" of Fedora that has been installed on a USB thumb drive. The live image on the thumb drive can then be booted just as if the computer were being booted from its own hard drive. The Fedora Live USB thumb drive can be used without harming your existing hard drive or the files stored on it.

Fedora Linux can be downloaded in numerous forms including so-called spins that each provide a different desktop user workspace. It is unclear about the origin of the term "spin" in this context. Its usage may be of the form "to spin off something a bit different," or it may relate to its original usage on CDs and DVDs which would spin in the drive so that they could be read. You can view a list of the different desktop spins on the Fedora Project website.[1]

For this book, we use the Xfce spin. This spin uses the Xfce desktop because it uses fewer system resources like CPU time and memory than most of the other desktops, so it is suitable for older systems or underpowered new systems that have tight hardware resource limits.

Terms

You will encounter some terms in this chapter that are probably new to you. Take a look at those before you proceed. These terms can also be found in the Glossary at the end of this book.

---

[1] Fedora Project, *SPINS*, https://spins.fedoraproject.org/en/

Storage Device

Any type of device used for long-term storage of data such as a hard disk drive (HDD), a solid state drive (SSD), CD, DVD, or a USB thumb drive.

Live (ISO) Image

Also called an ISO image, a live image is a file that contains an exact image of Linux that can be installed on a storage device such as a USB thumb drive. This creates a bootable device that can be used to test Linux on one or more computers. After a computer is booted using the live image USB device, Linux can be tested and even installed directly from the device.

Installing an ISO image requires use of special software to create because it is not a simple copy operation.

An ISO image can be stored on a CD, DVD, or USB thumb drive. However, due to the relatively low capacity and slow speeds of CD and DVD devices compared to modern USB thumb drives, ISO images can be much larger than CD or DVD devices can contain. USB devices are also faster and provide better testing environments. Many computers no longer come with DVD/CD drives, but all come with USB connectors.

After booting your Windows computer – or any computer for that matter – from the live USB device, you will be able to test drive Linux on that computer. You can use the live USB to explore Fedora and to learn a little about the easy-to-use Xfce desktop. This will not touch or change your existing data in any way. Your data is safe unless you make some extraordinary effort to change it.

Spin

A spin is a term used to designate various types of live images that can be used to test and install specific configurations of Fedora. In addition to a basic installation of Fedora, each spin includes software designed for particular tasks or configurations.

For example, one spin installs Fedora with the KDE desktop and another installs Fedora with the Xfce desktop which is what we are using in this book. Other spins include one for software developers and one for scientists.

The Xfce spin is the one most appropriate for inexperienced users who need to be productive while becoming familiar with Linux.

Install the Linux Live Image on a USB Thumb Drive Using Your Windows Computer

Since you are just trying to get started with Linux, it is a safe deduction that your computer still has Windows on it. So this section covers creating the live image thumb drive using Windows.

The bootable ISO image files we use to create Fedora Live USB devices are designed to be less than 2GB in size. This was originally so that they would also fit on a DVD. CDs and DVDs are seldom used for software distribution anymore because they are slow and they have a strictly limited capacity compared to USB devices. Many new computers no longer even include CD/DVD drives.

The Fedora ISO image you will be using is about 1.5GB in size so that it will easily fit on a 2GB USB thumb drive, although a larger USB device would also be fine. If you ever create a live image device different from Fedora XFCE, be sure to verify that the image will fit on the device you plan to use.

Use of a relatively new USB thumb drive is preferred because newer ones are faster than older ones and will result in a better test experience.

It is not necessary to prepare the USB drive in any way. The Fedora Media Writer will do everything necessary to install the live image.

Warning   Installing the Fedora Live ISO image on the USB device will erase all the data on the drive. Be sure you have a backup of that data or that you definitely do not need it.

Download and Install the Fedora Media Writer

It is only necessary to download the Fedora Media Writer and install it in order to create the live USB device. The Fedora Media Writer allows you to select the Fedora spin image that you want and then deals with downloading and installing that image on the USB device. It is not necessary to download the ISO image separately.

Using your browser of choice – I use Firefox – download the Fedora Media Writer from https://getfedora.org/en/workstation/download. Click the Windows icon to open the dialog box shown in Figure 5-1. Then click the **Save File** button to begin the download. This file will also be saved to the Downloads directory.

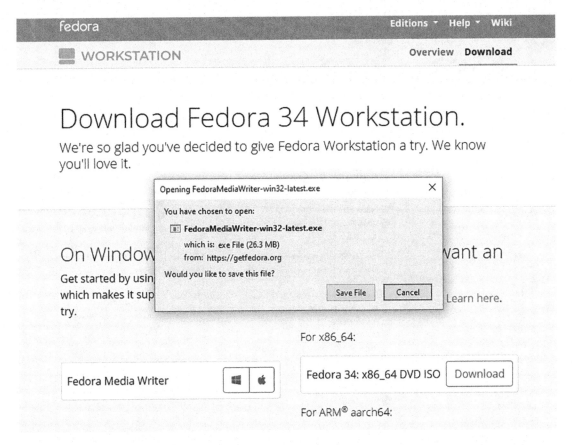

Figure 5-1. *Download the Fedora Media Writer which is used to install the ISO image to the USB thumb drive*

Even though we are installing the Media Writer from the Fedora Workstation page, we are not going to install the Workstation ISO image.

Figure 5-2 shows the Fedora Media Writer in the Downloads directory. Right-click the file and select **Run as administrator** to begin the installation of the Fedora Media Writer. Click **Yes** in the dialog that asks if you want to allow this program to make changes to your device.

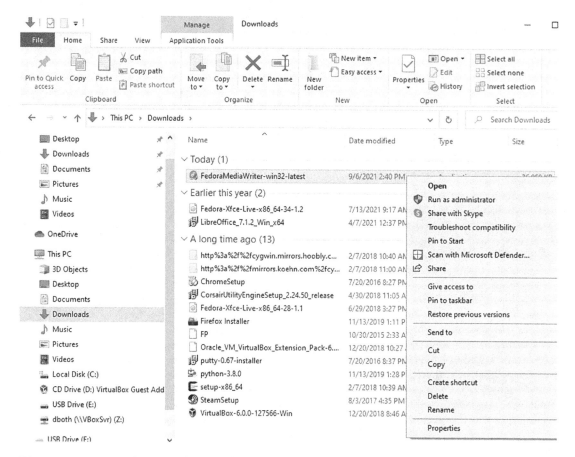

Figure 5-2. *Use the Windows File Explorer to launch the Fedora Media Writer as the administrator*

The license agreement dialog is displayed. Most people never read the Microsoft End User License Agreement (EULA), but they just scroll down to activate the button that lets you continue with the installation. Although you could just click the **I Agree** button, I suggest you read the first few paragraphs just so you know what you are getting into.

The GNU General Public License Version 2, under which this and many other open source programs are distributed, says that you are free to do pretty much anything you want with this software including giving it to your friends, viewing and changing the source software if you have the skills and the desire, and, well, pretty much anything.

Click the **I Agree** button and then the Install button. After the Fedora Media Writer is installed and the dialog says, "Installation Complete," click the **Next** button and then the **Finish** button.

At this point, the Fedora Media Writer automatically opens on the desktop. Again, click **Yes** in the dialog that asks if you want to allow this program to make changes to your device.

We are finally at the actual Fedora Media Writer dialog seen in Figure 5-3. This dialog allows selection of the Fedora version you want to install on the USB device.

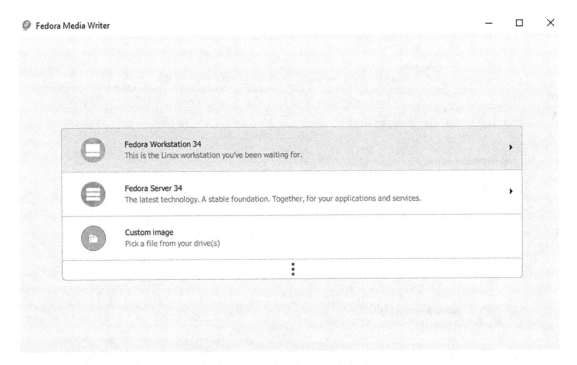

Figure 5-3. *The Fedora Media Writer main dialog*

Tip   The Fedora version used in this book is almost certainly not the one you will be using. Fedora is on a short development cycle, so the version available to download will very probably be later than the one we used. That's OK because everything important about the procedures in this book will remain consistent with only minor, if any, changes.

None of the Fedora options on this dialog are the one we want. So click the three vertical dots underneath "Custom image" to open the list of all available selections, some of which are shown in Figure 5-4. Scroll down to see the large number of options you have to choose from. At some time after you have learned more about Fedora, you may wish to experiment with one or more of these other options. They are all Fedora and all have access to the same free-as-in-beer, open source software.

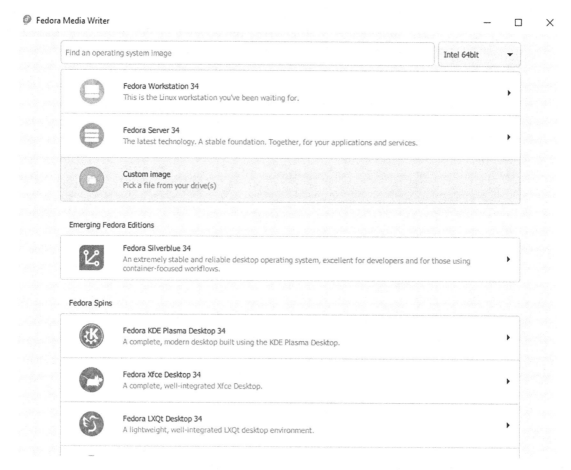

Figure 5-4. *Select the Fedora Xfce option to install on the USB drive*

Each of these different Fedora options provides a somewhat different desktop experience, but they are all the same Fedora underneath. Scroll down to look at the selections near the bottom of the dialog. Here, you will find the specialized spins that are intended for various scientific and development purposes. There is even a gaming spin – if you are into that.

When you have finished perusing the various spin options, scroll back up and select the Fedora Xfce desktop.

Figure 5-5 shows the Xfce desktop live USB creation dialog. Now is the time to insert the USB drive into your computer's USB slot if you have not already done so.

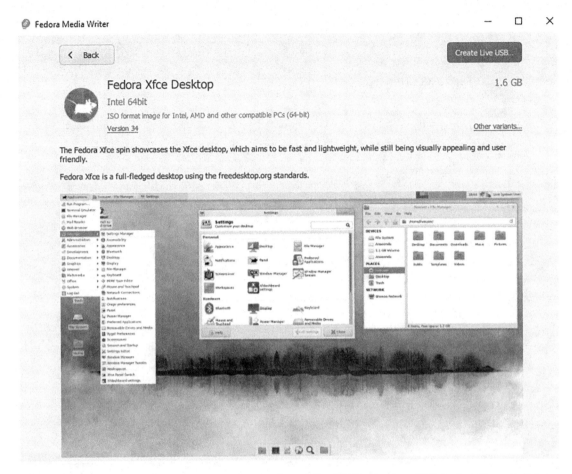

Figure 5-5. *This is the page to create a live Xfce USB device. Click the **Create Live USB...** button*

Click the **Create Live USB...** button. Verify that Fedora Media Writer has selected the correct USB device. In Figure 5-6, it has found the correct – and only, in this case – installed USB thumb drive. I found that the Fedora Media Writer finds the USB device automatically when only one is inserted into the system, but you should always verify.

Figure 5-6. *Verify that the Fedora Media Writer has selected the correct USB device*

If the wrong device has been selected, you can click the button to select a different device.

Caution!   This procedure will destroy all existing data on the USB thumb drive! Cancel if this is not what you want.

Then click the red **Write to Disk** button.

The progress bar will indicate how far the installation has proceeded. This installation is done in two passes; the first pass writes the data to the USB device, and the second pass verifies that the data was correctly written. It only took about five minutes for me when in a Windows 10 VM on my primary workstation. When the installation is complete, you can **Close** the dialog.

Testing Your Own Computers

The computers you already have are most likely the ones you will want to migrate to Linux. So begin by testing Linux on them. This test will not touch or harm the data on your computers in any way.

Boot the Live USB Device

First, insert the Fedora Live USB device created in this chapter into a USB slot of the computer you wish to test. Then boot into BIOS as described in Chapter 5.

Select the Boot page of the BIOS interface. Identify the bootable USB device in the BIOS Boot menu, and select it as the primary boot device. This is usually the hard part because the BIOS Boot menu can be quite confusing and unclear about how to make a particular device the primary boot device. I have found that it is sometimes necessary to experiment with these settings in order to determine the correct one.

The worst that can happen is that the computer will boot to Windows. Just power off the computer and start again.

Tip   An Internet search on "How do I boot to a USB device on my <use the name and model of your computer here>?" can lead you to the right method. The name and model of your computer is in the BIOS system information page that we looked at in Chapter 4.

The live USB device boots to a menu like the one shown in Figure 5-7. Remember that the Fedora version you use will very probably be more recent than Fedora 34, but the live USB devices have worked the same for as long as I have been using them.

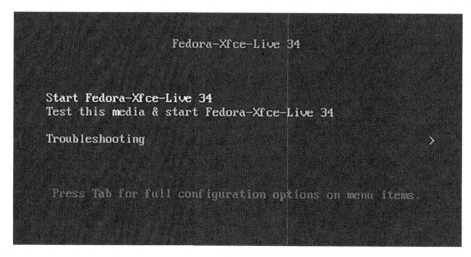

Figure 5-7. *Select **Start Fedora-Xfce-Live** and press **Enter**. The selected item is displayed with white text*

Use the up/down arrow keys to select **Start Fedora-Xfce-Live**, and press the **Enter** key. It will take a while to boot from the USB drive, but the result should look like the Fedora Xfce desktop in Figure 5-8. This is very similar to the desktop you will see after you install and boot the Xfce spin of Fedora. The exception is the number of device icons down the left side of the screen and the *Install to Hard Drive* icon in the second column of this Figure.

Figure 5-8. *The Xfce live image desktop can be used for some basic testing*

The Good News

If your computer has booted to this desktop, the good news is that your computer has already been proven to be mostly compatible with Linux. It is extremely unlikely that anything else would be the case as most motherboards and displays are well supported by Linux. Keyboards and mice are also well supported. I have never had a problem getting a desktop system to run with Linux. Only one laptop I tested in a store has not booted to Linux, and, in that particular case, it was just a test anyway, so I did not spend a lot of time with it. See the section "In-Store Testing" for more details.

Xfce Upper Panel

To ensure that all of your computer's hardware is compatible, we should do more than just look at the pretty blue wallpaper. We especially want to verify that the network, whether wired or wireless, is working, as well as the sound. To do that, we need to first explore the upper Xfce panel which is designated as panel 0.

Figure 5-9 is an annotated illustration of this Xfce panel. This is not intended to be a complete description of the Xfce desktop, so we will only cover those items necessary to ensure that the computer being tested is compatible with Linux enough to meet your needs.

Applications Menu

The first tool on the left side of the panel contains a cascading *Applications* menu that allows you to find and launch any installed applications. Click the button to open the first level of the menu tree. Select others as necessary until you find the application program you want.

The applications in the top level of this menu are organized by type such as Office, Internet, Games, and Graphics to make it a bit easier to find the type of application you need.

Window Buttons

Running applications are shown in the "Window Buttons" section. We only have one button for a terminal session shown here, but if other applications were running, their buttons would also be displayed here. I have shortened this section in order to show the entire panel on one line.

Although it is hard to discern in Figure 5-9 due to the dark colors of the panel and the fact that the printed version of this book and the contained graphics are in black and white, the workplace switcher contains four squares that represent four different workspaces. Where there is room in the workplaces in the panel, icons of the topmost open applications are displayed.

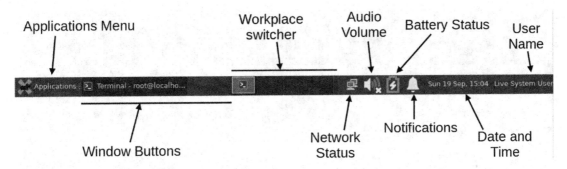

Figure 5-9. *The Xfce panel number 0 (the upper panel) contains information about your computer and running applications as well as a menu for launching applications*

I use the default workspace, which is the leftmost one, for things like dealing with email, open terminal sessions to other hosts on which I am working, and usually the Firefox web browser. The second workspace is used for my writing projects such as this one. I also have multiple terminal sessions open on this workspace, along with LibreOffice Writer, a Windows VM which is currently running the live Xfce session I am using as a model for this chapter, Spectacle which is a program that allows me to capture snapshots of all or parts of the screen, and LibreOffice Draw which I used to add text and lines to Figure 5-9.

The number of workspaces is easily configurable as we will see in Chapter 10, but I find four to be a good number for me as I am always working on multiple projects at once. And that is the best use I have found for having multiple workspaces – they help me organize multiple projects on separate workspaces with multiple open windows for each.

You should be able to see the separators between the workspaces a little better on your computer when you try this for yourself.

Network Status

The Network Status icon provides a means to view information about the existing network connections and to disconnect and disable connections. It works with both wired and wireless connections.

Right-click the Network icon to show the connection information for a wired connection on one of the VMs used in the preparation of this book. The example in Figure 5-10 lists all of the pertinent information about this connection including the IP address, default route, and DNS servers.

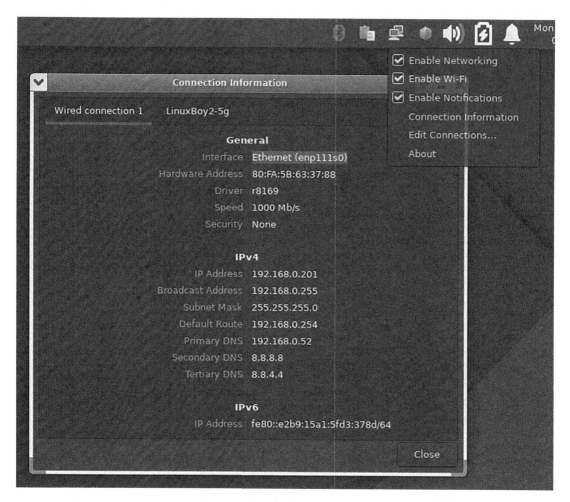

Figure 5-10. *Right-click the Network Status icon to disable networking and to check on the network information. This image, captured from my laptop, has tabs for both wired and Wi-Fi connections*

You should never need to edit the information for a network connection. Like most small business owners, if you do have a desktop computer, it should be connected directly to your ISP's router using the four-port switch built in to that router. The router will provide your computer with the correct information it needs to connect to the Internet. This is accomplished using DHCP, Dynamic Host Configuration Protocol, which makes it unnecessary to manually configure network connections.

This information might be helpful when you are trying to resolve a network problem. You can remove the check from the *Enable Networking* or *Enable Wi-Fi* check box to completely disable that type of connection.

A left-click on the Network Status icon shows both wired and wireless connections and a list of available wireless networks. Figure 5-11 shows the result on a laptop that has both wired and wireless connections. This dialog can be used to disconnect from any connected wired or wireless network without disabling networking. It can be used to select a new Wi-Fi network to connect to.

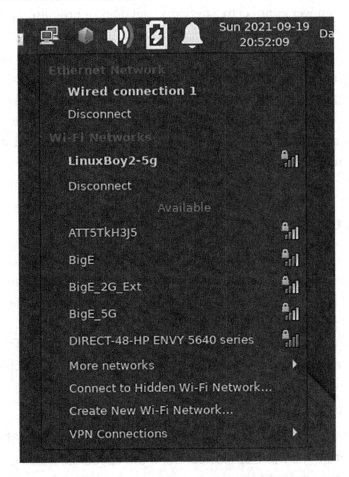

Figure 5-11. *The network status on a laptop with both wired and wireless connections*

It is not necessary to first disconnect from the current Wi-Fi network in order to select a new Wi-Fi network. Simply click the desired Wi-Fi network to connect to it and the previous network is disconnected.

When connecting to a Wi-Fi network for the first time, you will probably need to enter a password no matter how simple it may be. The Linux networking system will automatically remember passwords to all networks to which you connect. Like most tablets and cell phones, Linux will connect automatically to these known networks.

The use of passwords for wireless connections is good and indicates that there is at least some level of encryption to protect your data while it is transmitted over the air where it can be intercepted quite easily. To ensure at least a minimal level of security, we strongly suggest you never connect to a network that does not require a password.

Note that with proper hardware installed such as multiple wired and wireless network adapters, it is possible to have multiple simultaneous network connections. This includes multiple wired connections and multiple wireless connections at the same time. This is not a good thing for a laptop in a small business[2] as it could allow crackers – hackers with malicious intent – to access multiple networks without even trying hard. You should disconnect from all connections that are not being used and stick to a primary connection only, such as your main wireless router or wired connection.

It is not usually necessary to use a password to connect to wired networks.

Volume Control

The volume control can be used to adjust the volume of audio playback. To test the audio system on your computer, open Firefox web browser using the icon of the globe with a pointer that is located in the bottom panel. Figure 5-8 shows the bottom panel and the icon.

Navigate to YouTube to play a video which will demonstrate both audio and video capabilities. If your mouse has a wheel, you can hover over the volume control and use the wheel to raise and lower the volume.

Tip   Some computers I tested ran Firefox quite slowly. This is due, at least in part, to running from the live USB device. But if the speed of Firefox becomes unbearably slow, this probably is not a good computer to use for your business.

At this point, you have tested all of the major hardware systems of your computer. We will explore the desktop further in Chapter 10.

---

[2] This capability to connect to multiple networks simultaneously can be useful in a controlled environment with a well-implemented firewall because that is the basis of the ability to use Linux computers for routers. I use a Linux computer as the main router and firewall in all of the networks I manage.

In-Store Testing

From a technical standpoint, testing a computer that you want to purchase in the store is no different from testing your own computers. The social difference is that you should probably ask permission from the staff before you do. Sales staff want to sell you a computer, so I have found them to be quite helpful in most cases.

Several years ago, I performed a simple test. I took a Fedora Live USB thumb drive to Intrex, our small, local, independent computer store chain and to big box stores like Best Buy. This was not about me purchasing a computer; it was about testing the store staff to see if they would allow me to boot Linux on their demo computers.

I spoke to the sales staff in each store and told them I wanted to test Linux on their computers with my live USB drive. All were helpful and interested to see the results. I spent a good deal of time testing each computer and discussing what I was doing with the staff.

I did find that most of the computers I tested worked just fine with Fedora. One did not, but that was probably because I chose not to make any changes to the BIOS setup. If you are testing in-store with the express purpose of purchasing a new computer, you should not hesitate to make any BIOS configuration changes you need for that testing. Just be sure to reset the BIOS to factory defaults when you are finished. That is an option on every modern BIOS I have ever seen.

I spent about 20 minutes trying to coax one laptop to boot to the USB drive, but was never able to do so. In any real situation where I was looking to purchase a product, I would rule out any device that I could not get to boot to the live USB drive in that time – probably even less time than that.

Testing demo hardware in a retail store is a great way to help narrow down the choices. Just getting the live USB drive booted to the Fedora desktop is a big step in the right direction. And the tools available in the live environment allow testing of the rest of the system's peripherals. Even though I did not try to connect to the wireless access points, I could see using the desktop Networks icon, just seeing the list indicated that wireless was working.

Chapter Summary

This chapter has been all about preparing a bootable USB thumb drive with a version of Fedora Live on it so that you can test your own computers and the demonstration computers in a store.

Creating the live USB device itself is not especially difficult. Usually, getting the computer being tested to boot to the USB device is what takes the most work. It can be easy, but many times, the many different BIOS versions in computers by different manufacturers can obscure the path to take through the BIOS menus. Many BIOS versions have built-in help, so be sure to use that as well as checking the Internet for information on specific models.

You should now know enough about how Linux works on the hardware you have tested to make a well-informed decision about which computer to use or purchase.

CHAPTER 6

Finding Software

Objectives

After reading this chapter, you will be able to

- Inventory the software you use in your business

- Find equivalent open source software

- Use the live image to test the most common available open source software

- Find other places to look for open source software

Introduction

So you are close to deciding to make the switch to Linux. The big questions for most who get to this point are "can I use Microsoft Word or Office" and "where do I buy all the software to replace what I use now?"

This chapter will answer those questions and guide you through the task of identifying all of the software used by your small business. The obvious business software such as office suites, accounting, email, and web browsing will be covered. We also look at some less commonly used software such as various types of notes, multimedia playback and creation, file management, epub and PDF viewers, document scanning, and more.

© David Both, Cyndi Bulka 2022
D. Both and C. Bulka, *Linux for Small Business Owners*, https://doi.org/10.1007/978-1-4842-8264-9_6

About Microsoft Programs

Your Microsoft Office programs will not work with Linux. None of the programs you purchased for Windows will work on Linux. But, well, the long answer is that they could with some additional software and some work, but it is truly not necessary.

Your existing Microsoft Office files, Word, Excel, and others, all work with the open source LibreOffice suite. In fact, Microsoft Office programs can also use the Open Document Format (ODF) files created by LibreOffice.

Multimedia files are well standardized. File types for pictures, graphics, audio, movies, and more are all well known, and there are applications for both Linux and Windows that work with them all. Many of these applications are open source software and are available for both Windows and Linux.

Create an Inventory

You use software every time you use your computer. You likely don't think about it very much and could not easily list from memory the complete set of software that you use to operate and manage your business. Of course, the easy ones are email clients such as Thunderbird or Outlook; a web browser such as Firefox, Chrome, or Edge; accounting software; multimedia software for viewing pictures, videos, and graphics; software for creating pictures, videos, and graphics; office tools for creating documents, spreadsheets, graphics, and presentations; epub readers; PDF readers; file and disk management; and much more.

And then there are the educational and scientific tools like calculators and dictionaries, sky maps for astronomy, interactive periodic tables and molecular visualization for chemistry, math tools like LibreOffice Math, and, again, much more.

As you work through a month on your existing computer using Windows, list every task you perform and the software program you use to perform it. You will probably be surprised at the total number of different programs you use during that time.

Select New Software

Some of this software may not be new to you but most probably is. You may already use Chrome or Firefox as a browser or Thunderbird as your email client. Some of this software is not available for Windows, such as file managers and the desktops themselves.

Most open source software are available for Windows as well as Linux, and some are also available on MacOS. This means that you can install much of this software on your Windows computer so that you can try it out. There are no restrictions or limitations on any of this software, so you can install it on as many computers as you want and use it as long as you want.

Although most of the open source software in the following list can be downloaded and installed from the websites listed, it is best to install them from the Fedora repositories after the initial Fedora installation. We will show you how to do that in Chapter 13. For installation on your Windows computer, download and follow the directions on the respective websites.

We strongly recommend you try out this software on your Windows system before you switch to Linux. You should make sure it will do what you need. Over many years, now, we have both found that the open source software in this chapter – at least that which we have used – is more than capable of meeting all of our needs.

Office Suite – LibreOffice

Linux, Windows

LibreOffice is a complete, compatible replacement for Microsoft Office. LibreOffice Writer is what we used to write this book – and David's four previous books. LibreOffice Calc is a powerful spreadsheet program, and Draw allows you to create vector graphic illustrations. LibreOffice Impress creates and displays presentations. All of your existing MS Office files will work in LibreOffice.

Like many open source tools, LibreOffice has many easily installable extensions and plug-ins that can be used to add new features and functions.

There are other options for an office suite, but none are as mature, complete, well supported, or widely used as LibreOffice.

`www.libreoffice.org/`

Fedora Magazine has a good article on office suites for Linux. That article introduces LibreOffice, ONLYOFFICE, and Calligra.

`https://fedoramagazine.org/apps-for-daily-needs-part-2-office-suites/`

Accounting – GnuCash

Linux, Windows, MacOS

All businesses need to perform standard bookkeeping tasks. We took different paths for this; see the "About Choice" section in this chapter. There are many options for accounting software if you choose to use it. GnuCash seems to be the best choice for most users, and David has been using it for 20 years.

GnuCash is personal and small-business financial-accounting software that uses double-entry accounting. It is freely licensed under the GNU GPL and available for GNU/Linux, BSD, Solaris, MacOS X, and Microsoft Windows.

Designed to be easy to use, yet powerful and flexible, GnuCash allows you to track bank accounts, stocks, income, and expenses. As quick and intuitive to use as a checkbook register, it is based on professional accounting principles to ensure balanced books and accurate reports. GnuCash can import Intuit® Quicken® QIF files using a practical assistant. GnuCash is also the first free software application to support the OFX (Open Financial Exchange) protocol that many banks and financial services are starting to use. A transaction matching system ensures that duplicate transactions are accurately recognized and automatically deleted during file import.

Other options are KMyMoney, Moneydance, and Skrooge, among others.

www.gnucash.org/

https://kmymoney.org/

http://moneydance.com/

https://skrooge.org/

The FOSS Linux website has a good list of "The 10 Best Accounting Software for Linux" at www.fosslinux.com/46034/best-accounting-software-linux.htm.

Email Client – Thunderbird

Linux, Windows

Thunderbird is quite popular for email, but others are Claws, Geary, Sylpheed, and KMail. If you like the command-line text mode interface, you could also use Mutt or Alpine.

Alpine is David's current favorite for email, but Thunderbird is his favorite for a desktop GUI email client. Cyndi uses Gmail, so does not need an email client. If you use Gmail, it is web based, so you do not need to install an email client.

www.thunderbird.net

Web Browser – Firefox or Chrome

Linux, Windows

I currently prefer Mozilla Firefox for my web browser but have also used Chrome extensively. Other choices are Midori, Chrome, Brave, and Konqueror. The browsers Links and Lynx are also available if you prefer a text mode user interface. Yes, that is a thing.

```
www.mozilla.org/en-US/firefox/new/
www.google.com/chrome/
```

Fedora Magazine has a very nice article to introduce Firefox, Chrome, and two other browsers.

```
https://fedoramagazine.org/apps-for-daily-needs-part-1-web-browsers/
```

File Manager – Thunar

Linux

File managers allow you to easily navigate your home directory tree structure and view, manage, and delete files. According to one search result, there are 47 open source file managers. Thunar is the default file manager for the Xfce desktop. Others include Krusader which is the default for the KDE desktop, Gnome Files which is the default for the Gnome desktop, PCManFM, Dolphin, Xfe, and Konqueror which are also good choices. David's favorite for the text mode interface is Midnight Commander.

As far as we can tell, all of these file managers are designed for Linux only.

```
https://docs.xfce.org/xfce/thunar/start
https://computingforgeeks.com/best-linux-file-managers-you-can-use/
```

Screen Capture – Spectacle

Linux

Spectacle is easy to use, and many of the screen images in this book were captured using Spectacle. Spectacle can be used to capture images of the entire desktop, a selected window, or any arbitrary rectangular portion of the desktop. It can save in the most common image formats including PNG, JPEG, TIFF, and BMP.

```
https://apps.kde.org/spectacle/
```

Image Editor – GIMP

Linux, Windows

GIMP, the GNU Image Manipulation Program, is a great replacement for Photoshop. According to the GIMP website

GIMP is a cross-platform image editor available for GNU/Linux, OS X, Windows and more operating systems. It is free software, you can change its source code and distribute your changes.

Whether you are a graphic designer, photographer, illustrator, or scientist, GIMP provides you with sophisticated tools to get your job done. You can further enhance your productivity with GIMP thanks to many customization options and 3rd party plugins.

I use GIMP to add text to images, to manipulate color and brightness, or to overlay multiple images.

```
www.gimp.org/
https://fedoramagazine.org/apps-for-daily-needs-part-3-image-editors/
```

Audio Editor – Audacity

Linux, Windows, MacOS

We both use Audacity to edit and splice together multiple audio files into a single file while adjusting the volume and sound quality for different segments. Audacity has many filters which can be used for fade in/out, noise reduction, pop removal, and more.

```
www.audacityteam.org/
```

Audio Playback – Audacious, Juk

Linux

Audacious is an easy-to-use yet powerful media playback tool. Juk is also an excellent choice. These programs both do an excellent job at their task of playing audio files. The best way to choose between them is to install and use both for a while and then the one you prefer once you decide which that is.

```
https://audacious-media-player.org/
https://apps.kde.org/juk/
```

Video Recording and Streaming – OBS Studio

Linux, Windows, MacOS

OBS studio is our choice for video recording and live streaming. Having made some training videos while he was at IBM, David says that this software looks and feels very much like a TV studio, yet it is very flexible.

It is sponsored by YouTube, Facebook, and Twitch, among others, so it has excellent support.

`https://obsproject.com/`

Video Editing – OpenShot, Shotcut

Linux, Windows, MacOS

David has tried OpenShot and it works well, but has found that Shotcut works better for me and my needs.

`www.openshot.org/`

`https://shotcut.org/`

Other possibilities in this category are Kdenlive and Olive; I have not tried either of these.

Video/Media Playback – VLC Media Player

Linux, Windows, MacOS

The VLC media player is the outstanding player in this category. VLC is a free and open source cross-platform multimedia player and framework that plays most multimedia files as well as DVDs, Audio CDs, VCDs, and various streaming protocols. VLC media player handles almost all video formats as well as resolutions up to and including HD and 4K.

`www.videolan.org/`

Multimedia Conversion – ffmpeg, Handbrake

Linux, Windows, MacOS

The options here are the ffmpeg command-line media converter and Handbrake which is a GUI media converter.

Many other multimedia tools incorporate ffmpeg into their own software. The ffmpeg tool can convert many types of audio and video files to various other types. My typical uses are to convert raw MKV video files to MP4 and Apple M4A audio files to MP3. This is a command-line interface (CLI) program for all platforms. There is no graphical user interface for ffmpeg, but that is one of the things that enables it to convert files quickly. Despite the fact that it is a command-line program, it is easy to use and it works well in scripts.

Like ffmpeg, Handbrake converts many audio and video data formats but uses a GUI interface, so it is easier for many users.

I have used ffmpeg but not Handbrake. Our technical editor for this book, Seth Kenlon, who is an expert in multimedia, recommends Handbrake.

```
http://ffmpeg.org/
http://handbrake.fr/
```

Animation – Blender, Opentoonz

Linux, Windows, MacOS

Blender is the tool of choice for 3D animation and rendering. Neither of us has used, it but it gets great word of mouth and reviews. Blender is the free and open source 3D creation suite. It supports the entirety of the 3D pipeline – modeling, rigging, animation, simulation, rendering, compositing and motion tracking, video editing, and 2D animation pipeline.

Opentoonz is a good choice for 2D animation.

```
www.blender.org/
```

Desktop

Yes, you can even change the Linux desktop – the graphical interface with which you interact with the computer. In this book, we will us the Xfce desktop because it provides a flexible, highly configurable work environment that will be familiar to Windows users. Xfce also uses fewer system resources than many of the other desktops.

About Choice

Although there are at least a couple choices for each type of software, especially things such as accounting and office suite software. Not every small business owner does things in the same way. Your reasons and methods for doing things will vary widely. That is why open source software provides so many choices.

For one example, we chose completely different directions for dealing with our accounting needs.

Cyndi

I keep receipts and have a bookkeeper to do all the accounting work. I used to have QuickBooks years ago.

The reason I chose a bookkeeper accountant solution was because I believe one way small biz owner fail is that they try to do everything. I am not a number cruncher, so I choose to pay someone else who's an expert. I am doing that now with social media marketing.

David

I use GnuCash. I kept one set of books for my LLC when I had that, and still keep a second set for my personal accounts. GnuCash is easy for me to use, and I particularly like the ability to keep multiple sets of books.

Flexibility

Once you make a choice in many types of open source software, there is still room for flexibility. Open source does not lock you in to software.

For example, David likes Thunar as his primary file manager – for now at least. He also likes PCManFM, Krusader, Dolphin, and Konqueror for certain file management tasks. The beauty of Linux is that all of these can co-exist on his computers, and he can use whichever one I think will best perform the task at hand.

This is also true of many open source tools like office software, web browsers, email clients, and more. Multiple tools that can be used for the same or similar purpose can all be installed and used as the best fit for specific tasks.

Resources

Here are some additional resources for locating open source software on which to run your business. Remember – you can use almost all of this software on your current Windows computer even if you never make the complete switch to open source with Linux itself.

- Open source alternatives, Opensource.com, `https://opensource.com/alternatives`

- AlternativeTo website, `https://alternativeto.net/software/open-source-software-directory/`

- Wikipedia, `https://en.wikipedia.org/wiki/List_of_free_and_open-source_software_packages`

- CIO, `www.cio.com/article/2380921/open-source-tools-how-to-run-your-small-business-with-free-open-source-software.html`

Chapter Summary

There is an incredible amount of software available for Linux, most of which is open source and free of charge. This means that you can install and test most software on your Windows computer before you actually make the switch.

That software is open source and free of charge. You can download it and install it on as many computers as you want with no restrictions of any kind.

The best way to find that software when you are ready to install it on your Linux computer is to use the DNF software management tool that is already present. We explore that in a later chapter.

As we discovered for ourselves when exploring accounting options for our personal and business needs, there are many options available to small business owners. One of those options is to hire and pay an expert. Cyndi uses a bookkeeper and an accountant for that set of needs and another expert for her marketing efforts.

CHAPTER 7

Making the Decision

Objectives

After reading this chapter, you will be able to

- Understand the factors that caused the authors to switch to Linux
- List the factors that are prompting you to consider a switch to Linux
- Identify the two or three most important of those factors
- Make the decision

Introduction

No matter what has come before, the time to make a decision is here. You have explored reasons to switch to Linux and tried it out in Chapter 5 so that you can see that it is not really that different in the part that counts for everyday usage – how it looks and feels.

In this chapter, we discuss our own reasons for switching to Linux and take a look at why others have done so. We guide you through the decision process by providing a checklist as a framework in which to rate your own needs and yes even feelings as you make your decision.

Cyndi

Just so we're clear, I'm no expert when it comes to technology. Not even close.

I'm the kind of computer person that likes to just press a button and have everything work harmoniously without interruption. What I am is a creative person who writes and teaches yoga and coaches people to be healthier and happier. The last thing I want to

© David Both, Cyndi Bulka 2022
D. Both and C. Bulka, *Linux for Small Business Owners*, https://doi.org/10.1007/978-1-4842-8264-9_7

do is to spend a lot of time jousting with my computer trying to make it do something it's hell-bent on not doing. As a small business entrepreneur, I want to spend my time and energy creating content that helps my clients. Most small businesses have similar mindsets. We like to use our resources to produce products and services that people will pay for, and all that makes that possible behind the scenes is just a necessary evil. Okay, maybe evil is a strong word, but if you're reading this book, you get what I mean.

When I started my first yoga studio in 2000, computer technology was way out of my wheelhouse. In fact, for the first two years, I didn't even have a website. I did everything from scratch including collecting emails, sending newsletters, marketing events, and corresponding with my student base. And I was quite content operating my business in that way. My focus was on teaching yoga and creating community.

That was all well and good until my client base grew to the point where my very rudimentary systems were no longer manageable. It was time to systematize things to support my growing business. I chose Microsoft Windows as my operating system, not knowing there were many other options around. I purchased a product to manage newsletters and mailing lists. I hired a web designer to create an interactive website with a sales page. I thought I'd created a solid system for managing my clients, programs, and staff. And at first, all went well. Computer trouble resided as a vague fear in the recesses of my mind. I happily went about my business until my computer, operating with Microsoft and protected by antivirus software, became infected with malware. That sent everything into a hairpulling tizzy. Nothing worked. I smashed at buttons, cussed like a sailor, and nada. I called my smart computer friends, and all they could do was offer sympathy and say "I hope you backed everything up."

So I carried my desktop to a repair service where they held my computer for a solid week while they reinstalled my operating system and advised me to purchase another virus and malware protection program. My business was frozen in time while they worked. I lost some data, a lot of time, some cash, and my Pollyanna attitude toward my operating system.

The new system and software worked for a while, only to be infected again. And again. Eventually, I was advised that I needed to replace my computer. So I did. I rolled with that for a few years and managed to avoid any major crashes and snafus on my beautiful new laptop, which enabled me to set work anywhere. I religiously backed up and purchased expensive new versions of operating and protection software yearly. I naively thought all was well.

Until it wasn't. Those expensive updated software packages were crap, and I'd had enough time and experience under my belt to add it all up to conclude that operating my business as it was had become very costly, both in time and money. Not to mention my energy. Technology had become a drag and I wasn't happy.

By this time, I had met David and knew he was a computer pro. We had a friendly relationship and would often chat before or after his yoga class. In one of those conversations in which I was lamenting my computer woes, David offered to take a look to see if he could help. I jumped at the chance to have someone I knew and trusted to help me figure out the recurring quagmire of computer mishaps I was experiencing. Being the computer guru he is, David was able to fix things a few times with my Microsoft OS. Yet the problems still occurred.

The last straw on the camel's back created serious problems for my business. I had purchased an expensive software program designed for yoga studios and fitness centers to manage enrollments, payments, and payroll. When my computer locked up, I was unable to manage my daily business. It felt chaotic and I was embarrassed that I didn't know if the folks who showed up for class had paid or not.

I thought perhaps it was time to purchase a new computer and update my OS and virus protection... again. It was at this juncture that David suggested I rethink my OS and consider Linux. I'd never heard of Linux before. I was confident with my Microsoft skills, even though not at all confident with the system. It was scary to think I had a big learning curve ahead of me if I switched. Would I lose all the documents and lists created under Microsoft? Would Linux interfere with my ability to safely and smoothly send information out to my client base? I had a slew of questions!

I was shocked when David told me it wasn't time for me to replace my computer. Ka-ching! More money in my pot. Then I learned that Linux was open sourced, so no longer would I have to pay those costly fees for updates and protection. Ka-ching! More moola for me and my biz. He assured me that, in fact, the Linux system operated much like Microsoft, so my learning curve would not be so steep. That Linux was unique in that it was constantly being improved by very smart people who had no ulterior motives other than to improve functionality. I felt so relieved.

No matter all that had come before, clearly the time to make a decision was here. I took a deep breath and went for it.

David installed Linux in short order, and we spent a few hours over a few days teaching me my way around Linux. In reality – and much to my delight – it looked and felt quite similar to what I had been accustomed to with Microsoft. What a relief it was to my technology-stunted brain that I could make the transition with relative ease and nonexistent frustration.

Fast forward, I had now been using Linux for several years on the same laptop that I was sure needed to be replaced! Although I encountered a few random glitches now and then, downtime was at a bare minimum. All those times that my business had been hamstrung by computer failures and infections no longer existed.

I've never done the accurate math to calculate the financial savings that switching to Linux has afforded me. Between paying pros for the computer to be serviced every time it froze up or failed to boot, purchasing yearly updates for software, and purchasing a new computer every few years, the savings for my small business was significant. The financial savings was a blessing for sure, but the benefits of switching to Linux went way beyond that.

I no longer agonized over the threat of my studio operations and automation being suspended, and that was priceless. I'm in the business of chilling out! No one needs a stressed out yoga teacher. I had more time in my hands to create new content and programs that brought in new students. I'm in my element when I'm able to create, to write, and to teach. I can't put a price tag on that. We all want to be able to use our passion and talents to make a living, right?

What I do know is that when Linux solved my roller coaster computer drama, my business grew. I was able to streamline with ease and confidence. No longer did I worry about my client information and proprietary data being at risk. I could relax into my business knowing all was safe and that as long as I updated regularly, everything ran without a hitch. I had the time and confidence to expand my reach and began offering big ticket items like retreats and teacher training.

That takes me to more recent history. I decided, after 15 years in the yoga studio world, that I was ready for a new chapter in my life. It was time to transition to a different business model with much less management and more focus on my own creative process and having more personal contact with clients in a new context. I closed the studio and created Zakti Health. That meant a new website, new software, and the challenge of rebranding oneself, which if you've ever done that, you know it's a complex and time-consuming process. Linux was with me through all the changes. Knowing I had a stable and secure OS, I was able to turn my attention in this new direction with confidence.

All went smoothly and swimmingly well. I was happy with my new systems and livin' the life.

Then the pandemic hit and wiped out Zakti in a single day. It was time to pivot and swing in a new direction. Life can throw these kinds of curve balls to small business entrepreneurs! After careful consideration, I decided to close Zakti and rebrand my business once again. This time, I wanted to create a pandemic-proof digital business. I've created a digital course using some complex software that works like a dream on Linux. I'm now doing quite a bit of podcasting, vlogging, and live streaming, and I'm so happy to say that there is some really great open-sourced software that's making that both affordable and easy. Linux has felt like a loyal friend through all this transition in completely new territory.

My role in this book is to give you real-life evidence that Linux is not only a viable OS, but to share with you all the ways that switching to Linux has helped my business thrive. I'm the feelings gal in this book. I'm here to testify how much easier Linux has made my work life and my personal life. I rarely stress over computer issues (and I've cleaned up my sailor's mouth too).

David

My reasons for switching to Linux about 25 years ago are very similar to Cyndi's, but mine derive from a different set of needs.

First, let me make it clear that I have never used Windows as a primary operating system on any of my own personal computers – and I have had a lot of computers over the years. I started with IBM PC DOS in 1981 when I worked for IBM and wrote the training course for the original IBM PC. Even when some of the original Windows versions came out, I never used them. Instead, I went to IBM's OS/2 and I used that for many years.

I started fixing things early. When I was nine or ten, I would fix my parent's TV, radio, and stereo. I was quite good at that and eventually started doing the same for friends and neighbors. I eventually worked as service manager at a high-end audio store named Channel One (now defunct) in Toledo, Ohio.

I then spent 21 years at IBM, and I fixed computer hardware and later wrote training courses about how to fix hardware. I also spent a number of years working at the IBM PC Company's dealer support center and came to specialize in the OS/2 operating system.

I am the tech geek that, when you ask for the time, tells you how the atomic clock works and how my computers, all 12 of them, use the Internet to keep synced up with it so that they all have the correct time down to the nanosecond.

The only way to be really good at fixing things like audio equipment, computer hardware, and operating systems is to understand how they work. So I like to know how things work. And I am very good at fixing things.

Closed Box

Windows is a closed box – think of it as an abstraction of a system in which only its externally visible behavior is considered and not its implementation or "inner workings." There is no way to know what happens inside it. If it fails, there are no tools that can let you view more than a little bit of what happens inside. That'll put you in a bad spot if the you-know-what hits the fan.

Allow me a metaphor to illustrate. Windows is like the human body in the time before knowledge of viruses, germs, genetics, X-rays, CT scans, MRIs, and so on. There's virtually no knowledge of its own anatomy except what can be seen from the outside. When people (computers) got sick prior to the inception of modern medicine (Linux), the "doctors" treated things like "bad air" (malaria) with remedies that usually did more harm than good if they did anything at all. Treating the symptoms rather than the root cause of illness was the best that could be done.

When you have a problem with Windows, a reboot is usually the first thing you are told to perform no matter the problem. That reboot may circumvent the current set of symptoms, but it will never locate or fix the root cause of the problem. In large part, this is because the internals of Windows are simply not available as source code for our examination, so there's no way to know what's really going internally (except for a few programmers that work for Microsoft and good luck trying to get a hold of them). Not only that, there are no tools usable by end users or even system administrators that can provide a glimpse into its inner workings.

Microsoft keeps its code proprietary and unavailable for examination in order to protect its alleged secrets, that is, intellectual property (IP). There's no way around it.

Open Book

Linux and all open source software are an open book. Linux and all of the open source code that makes up the kernel, the operating system utilities, and the user-level application programs are well documented and available to anyone who wants to see it.

The anatomy of an operating system is documented and revealed in its source code. Programming experts can use that to resolve problems at what could be considered the "gene therapy" level, a targeted and transparent approach to healing your computer woes.

Many tools are available to a user and system administrators that provide a deep inside view of what's going on in Linux while it is up and running. Think of these tools as the X-rays, scans, and lab testing that can be used to diagnose problems. Many of those and other tools can be used to resolve problems by fixing the root cause (although sometimes treating symptoms is also called for). In a very large percentage of these instances, a reboot is never required!

Finally – Reasons

So this is why I like Linux and open source software in general – not in any particular order:

1. It is open, so I can learn and understand how it works.

2. I can easily fix problems.

3. Most of it is free of charge.

4. All of it is free as in speech and can be copied and given to other people.

5. There is always a choice of programs available to meet my needs.

6. I have never needed some type of software that was not available for Linux.

7. It is solid and dependable.

8. I don't need to pay for subscriptions or regular "upgrades."

9. It is much more secure than Windows.

10. It is far less susceptible to malware, viruses, and ransomware than Windows.

11. It never slows down.

12. Linux stays out of my way and lets me work.

13. I never need to pay to have malware removed.

14. Linux uses less system resources than Windows, so is better able to run on older hardware that is perfectly good. This makes it the ecologically sound choice.

Others

Many other people are finding reasons to switch to Linux, too. And some of those people write about their experiences or at least about why they think you should switch to Linux. I will let those people speak for themselves by simply providing you with the links to their online articles:

www.makeuseof.com/switch-to-linux-reasons-to-abandon-windows/
https://itsfoss.com/reasons-switch-linux-windows-xp/
https://opensource.com/article/21/5/switch-to-linux
www.lifewire.com/reasons-to-switch-to-linux-4583960
www.popsci.com/switch-to-linux-operating-system/

You can search for more stories of why people have switched to Linux. The search "why I switched to Linux" lists almost 19,000 links. Check out some of those links yourself. That is how we found the ones listed here.

You

You have clearly experienced some type of frustration with your current computing situation or perhaps you are just curious. That is, after all, why you're reading this book, right? You have reached the point in this book where the decision to switch to Linux is at hand.

The reasons that Cyndi and I have given here, as well as those of other people who have written about their own switch to Linux, are many and varied. Some of them will resonate with you, and you may also have your own reasons that no one else has experienced.

Whatever your reasons for considering the switch to Linux, take some time right now to list them on paper. Rank them in order, top to bottom, by how much pain or aggravation each generates for you.

Now you can make your decision.

Chapter Summary

We have shared our own reasons for switching to Linux and provided a list of links to stories about why other people switched to Linux.

If you have decided to switch to Linux, then congratulations! Let's move on to the next chapter, "Preparing for the Switch."

CHAPTER 8

Preparing for the Switch

Objectives

In this chapter, you will

- Locate the data you have that needs to be moved from Windows to Linux

- Determine how much data needs to be backed up

- Prepare a USB device for the backup

- Back up your data on a separate USB storage device from the one on which you installed the Xfce spin of Fedora

Introduction

You have made your decision to switch, and this chapter helps you prepare for the installation of Fedora. It is almost completely about identification of files and documents that need to be saved and provides directions for copying those files to a temporary storage device such as a USB thumb drive or an external USB HDD or SSD.

You will not need to copy any applications or other software or any system configuration files. The only thing that is necessary is to copy your data files such as Word documents (DOC and DOCX files), Excel spreadsheets (XLS files), and a few others. But don't worry; the procedure we will use to copy your files should copy all of them to the USB device that will be used for temporary data storage during the migration to Linux.

© David Both, Cyndi Bulka 2022
D. Both and C. Bulka, *Linux for Small Business Owners*, https://doi.org/10.1007/978-1-4842-8264-9_8

Finding Your Data

First, you need to find your data on the computer. Despite some of the really strange shortcuts that Windows uses, it is not really that hard and your data is not hidden – it may just appear to be so.

Log in to your Windows computer as the administrator. If your own user account is an administrator, that works fine.

Open the File Explorer and navigate to **Local Drive (C:)** ➤ **Users** as shown in Figure 8-1. On this Windows virtual machine (VM), my own account, dboth, is also an administrator, so I did not need to log in to the Admin account.

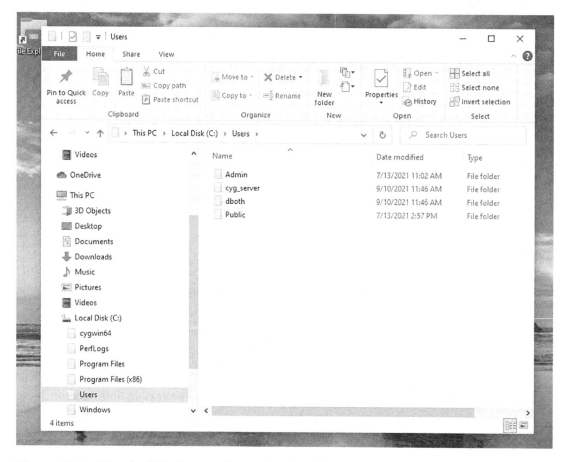

Figure 8-1. *Use the Windows File Explorer to find user data files at Local disk (C:) ➤ Users*

The subdirectories shown in the Users directory are the ones that contain all of the data that needs to be move to the computer after Linux is installed. The cyg_server folder is for an application and not a user. But the safest thing to do is to copy all of the data in the Users directory to the backup device.

You should ensure that your account can access all of the user subdirectories in the Users directory. Click each to see if you have access. All accounts should have access to the Public directory as well as their own.

You will probably not have access to all, and Windows will display a dialog like that in Figure 8-2, which indicates that you (actually the account you are logged in to) does not have access to the Amin directory. But never fear! Windows – in its extreme desire to put on a show of security yet allow anyone to access anything – allows you to give yourself access to the Admin directory. Click the **Continue** button to do just that.

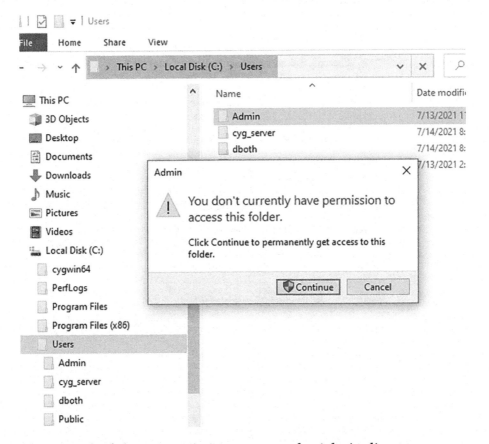

Figure 8-2. *You don't have permissions to enter the Admin directory*

After ensuring that your account has access to all of the directories in Users, it is possible to determine how much data needs to be saved now to be restored later.

How Much Data Do I have?

It is important to determine how much data is stored in the Users directory. This will help you determine how large the USB storage device needs to be in order to back up all of the data in the Users directory.

Right-click the Users directory icon where it is highlighted in Figure 8-1, and then select **Properties**. Wait for it to scan the Users directory tree and get a full count. Figure 8-3 shows a little more than 5.8GB because I don't use it for anything but testing, and I have little actual data stored on this VM.

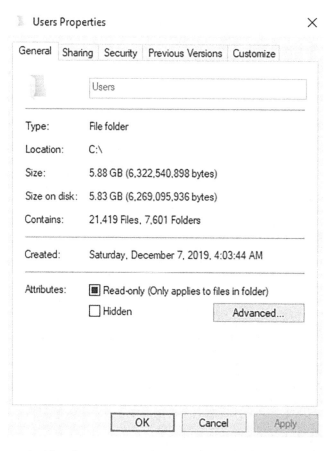

Figure 8-3. *Properties for the Users directory. Where did all those files, folders, and data come from?*

Another USB Device

You will almost certainly have more data than I do in this test system. It is likely that you will need a very large USB thumb drive or even an external USB hard drive or solid state drive.

Tip   Be careful when the size of your USB storage device is close to that of the Users directory. Filesystem metadata can take up part of the space on the storage device. Be sure to choose a storage device that will have plenty of extra space to ensure that all of your data can be stored there.

I chose an 8GB USB thumb drive for my backup device.

Insert the USB device into a USB slot on your computer. The USB device shows up in the Windows File Explorer as USB Drive E:. That may be different on your computer. Be sure to use the correct device for your computer.

This USB device actually has 7.43GB of usable space according to the Windows File Explorer as you can see in Figure 8-4.

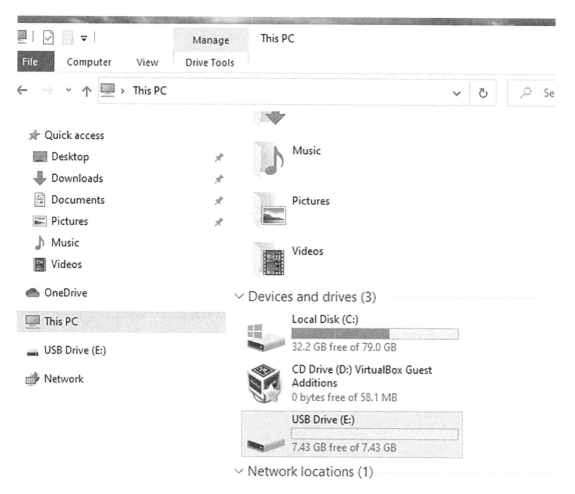

Figure 8-4. *The USB device shows up in the Windows File Explorer as USB Drive E:. That may be different on your computer*

Delete all existing files and folders from the USB device before making your backup. It may be easiest to just format the device. You can use File Explorer, right-click the USB device icon, and then select **Format**.

Back Up Your Data

The easiest way to back up all of the user's data is to copy the entire Users directory to the USB storage device.

Open a second instance of File Explorer, and arrange them like they are in Figure 8-5. The idea is to be able to see the Users directory in one dialog and the USB drive in the other.

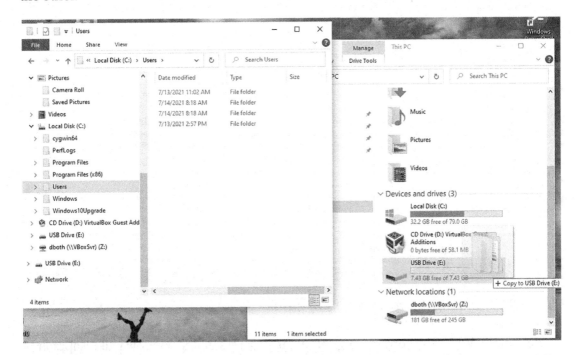

Figure 8-5. *Drag and drop the Users folder icon on the USB device to back up all of the user's data*

Then drag the Users directory from one, and drop it on the USB drive icon. This will copy the Users directory and all of the files and subdirectories contained in it to the USB drive. It took about 90 minutes to copy everything on the test system I used for testing this and capturing these graphics.

Figure 8-6 shows the copy in progress. As you can see, it took a while.

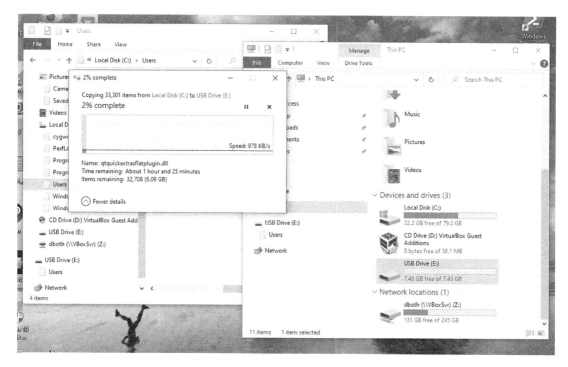

Figure 8-6. *Making the backup copy of data*

Be patient. When the copy is completed, the progress dialog window will disappear. At that point, you can right-click the USB drive icon and "eject" it so that it will be safe to physically remove from the computer.

Chapter Summary

Backing up the data from your Windows computer to be restored later is easy. We have selected and prepared a USB device. We then used a simple copy procedure to copy the Users directory to the USB device.

This procedure copies a lot of Windows and application files that won't be needed or even usable in Linux. But it did get all of your user data including documents, spreadsheets, and more. This procedure is designed to ensure that everything that might be needed for all users of the computer is saved to the USB device.

Sorting through and deciding what data files actually need to be restored is a task for Chapter 12.

CHAPTER 9

Installing Linux

Objectives

In this chapter, you will

- Boot the USB live image
- Start the installation
- Specify the host name
- Set the root password
- Create your personal user account
- Complete the installation

Note   In this chapter, the pronouns "I" and "me" refer to David.

Introduction

This chapter guides you through the process of installing Fedora directly from the live USB image device. We explore some tasks that you will perform during the installation process such as deleting the existing Windows partitions and creating a new Linux partitioning system. Network configuration should be simple in most single-computer environments in which the computer is connected directly to the ISP's modem/router. However, we briefly discuss networking and some security issues to consider.

We guide you through using Anaconda, the Fedora installation tool, to set the host name, set the root password, and to create your personal login account.

© David Both, Cyndi Bulka 2022
D. Both and C. Bulka, *Linux for Small Business Owners*, https://doi.org/10.1007/978-1-4842-8264-9_9

There are no options for selecting any additional software packages to install in any of the live images. If you want to install additional software, you must do it after the basic installation. We will explore how to do that in Chapter 13.

Boot the Fedora Live Image

Tip   The Fedora version used in this book is almost certainly not the one you will be using. Fedora is on a short development cycle, so the version available to download will very probably be later than the one we used. That's OK because everything important about the procedures in this book will remain consistent with only minor, if any, changes.

You already know how to do this because you did it in Chapter 5 when you took that test drive. So boot the Fedora Live USB image.

Installing Fedora

Installing Fedora from the live image is easy, especially when using the defaults. If you have any questions about the details of installation and want more information, you can go to the Fedora installation documentation at `https://docs.fedoraproject.org/en-US/fedora/f34/install-guide/install/Installing_Using_Anaconda/`. This URL will be different for later versions of Fedora. Just be sure to use the correct Fedora release number when you enter the URL.

Start the Installation

To start the Fedora Linux installation, double-click the **Install to Hard Drive** icon on the desktop as shown in Figure 9-1. As on any physical or virtual machine, the live image does not touch the hard drive until we tell it to install Linux.

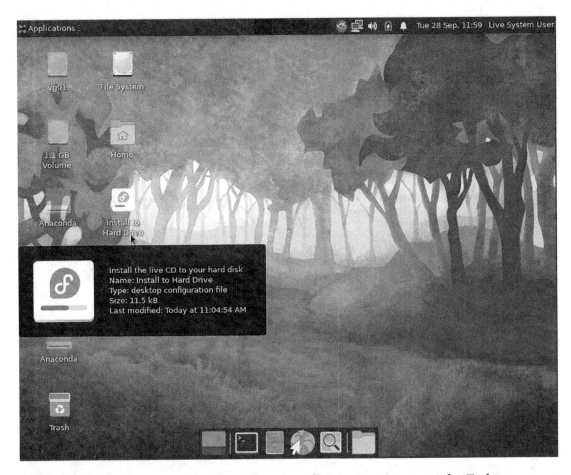

Figure 9-1. *Double-click the **Install to Hard Drive** icon to start the Fedora installation*

Double-clicking the **Install to Hard Drive** button launches the Anaconda installer. The first screen displayed by Anaconda is the Welcome screen where you can choose the language that will be used during the installation process. If your preferred language is not English, select the correct language for you on this screen. Then click the **Continue** button.

Set the Host Name

Click the **Network & Host Name** option on the **Installation Summary** dialog as shown in Figure 9-2. This host name is the one that the computer will be known to itself as. It is the host name that you will see on the command prompt line.

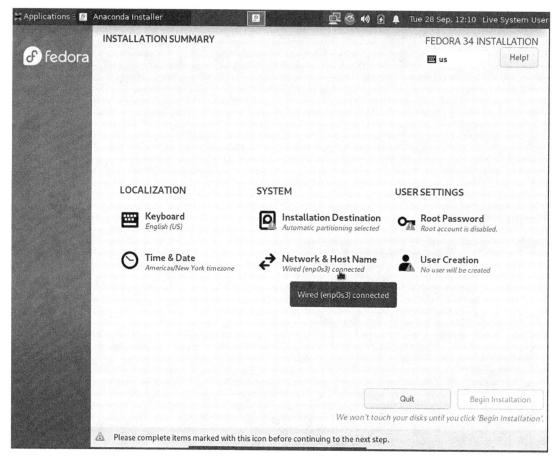

Figure 9-2. *Select **Network & Host Name** to set the host name for the computer*

By convention, computer host names are in lowercase and use only alphanumeric characters and the hyphen (-). You can name your computer anything you want within those limits. Spaces and other special characters are not allowed under any conditions.

Hostnames also have a defined syntax that – for use in a small business – is simple. You can simply use the name by itself such as mycomputer, for example, and that works fine until your business grows to the point where you have multiple computers on your internal network, and you host your own website and email system. In other words, when you need to hire a SysAdmin because you need to concentrate on the rest of your business, you can do it this way.

In the **Host Name** field shown in Figure 9-3, type the host name you want for your computer and then click **Apply**. That is all we need to do in this dialog, so click the blue **Done** button on the upper left. This will take you back to the Installation Summary dialog.

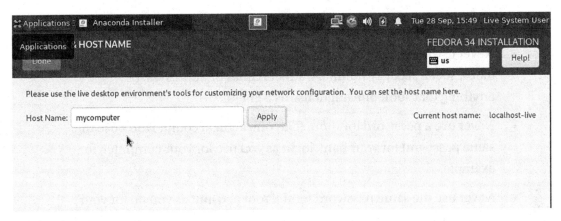

Figure 9-3. *Type the host name for the computer*

Set the Root Password

Choose a strong password but one that you can remember.[1] There are a lot of articles on the Internet about what that statement means, but I especially like the one referenced in footnote 1. That is a fairly long article, but it does have some good suggestions and a bit of humor.

Good passwords boil down to a few rules that will make them difficult for criminals to guess or discover using automated attacks or brute-force attacks:

- Passwords should be at least 12 characters in length, but 14 is much better.

- They should not be a dictionary word or based upon a dictionary word such as in substituting numeric characters for alpha characters. So p@$$w0rd is no better than password, and both really suck. The crackers know all of these substitution tricks and try them first.

- Passwords should be changed regularly – at least once a month.

---

[1] Hoffman, Chris, "How to Create a Strong Password (and Remember It)," www.howtogeek. com/195430/how-to-create-a-strong-password-and-remember-it/, How-To Geek, 2018

- Passwords should contain upper and lower case, numeric, and special characters.

- These password rules should be enforced by the appropriate Linux password settings. They should not be "optional."

Here are a few other common-sense rules:

- Never use personal information such as family names, important dates, social security numbers, street names or addresses, or anything that someone might use as a guess.

- Never use a password for more than one login account. Don't use the same password for your bank login as you use for your computer, for example.

- Never use the same password for the root account as you do for your personal account.

Yes, real password protection can be obtrusive. But if your security is not a bit of a pain for you, it won't stop a determined attack.

As root, you can choose a weak password or one based on a dictionary word. If you do, a warning will be displayed at the bottom of the **Root Password** screen. You can choose to keep the weak password, but we recommend against that. You will need to click the blue **Done** button twice if you kept the weak password to return to the main installation screen. But just don't.

Tip You should enter a strong password – one which does not generate any warnings.

Click the **Root Password** menu item in Figure 9-2 to set the root password. Type the password in the **Root Password** field in Figure 9-4 and again in the **Confirm** field. Do not make any other changes on this dialog.

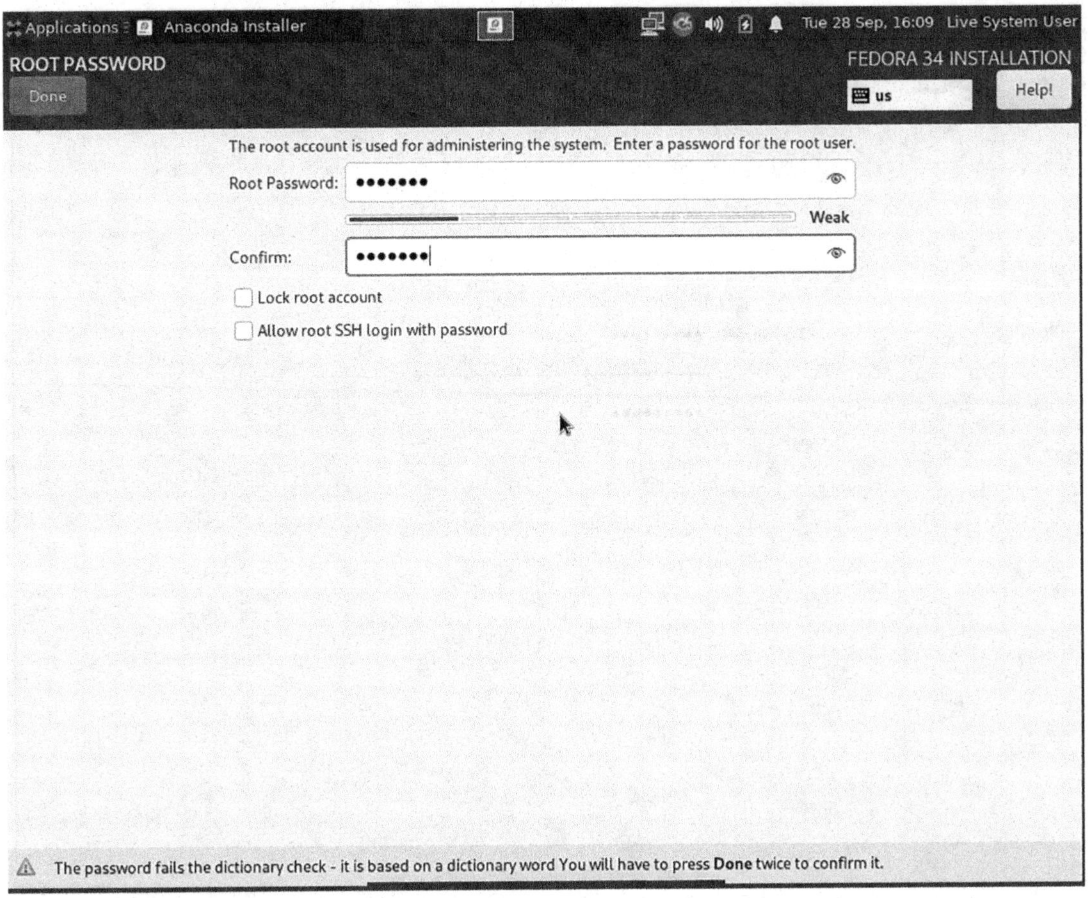

Figure 9-4. *Setting the root password. Notice the warning at the bottom that indicates a password that is based on a dictionary word*

After entering a strong password, click the **Done** button to save that password and return to the Installation Summary dialog.

Create Your User Account

Click the User Creation icon and you will enter the User Creation dialog shown in Figure 9-5.

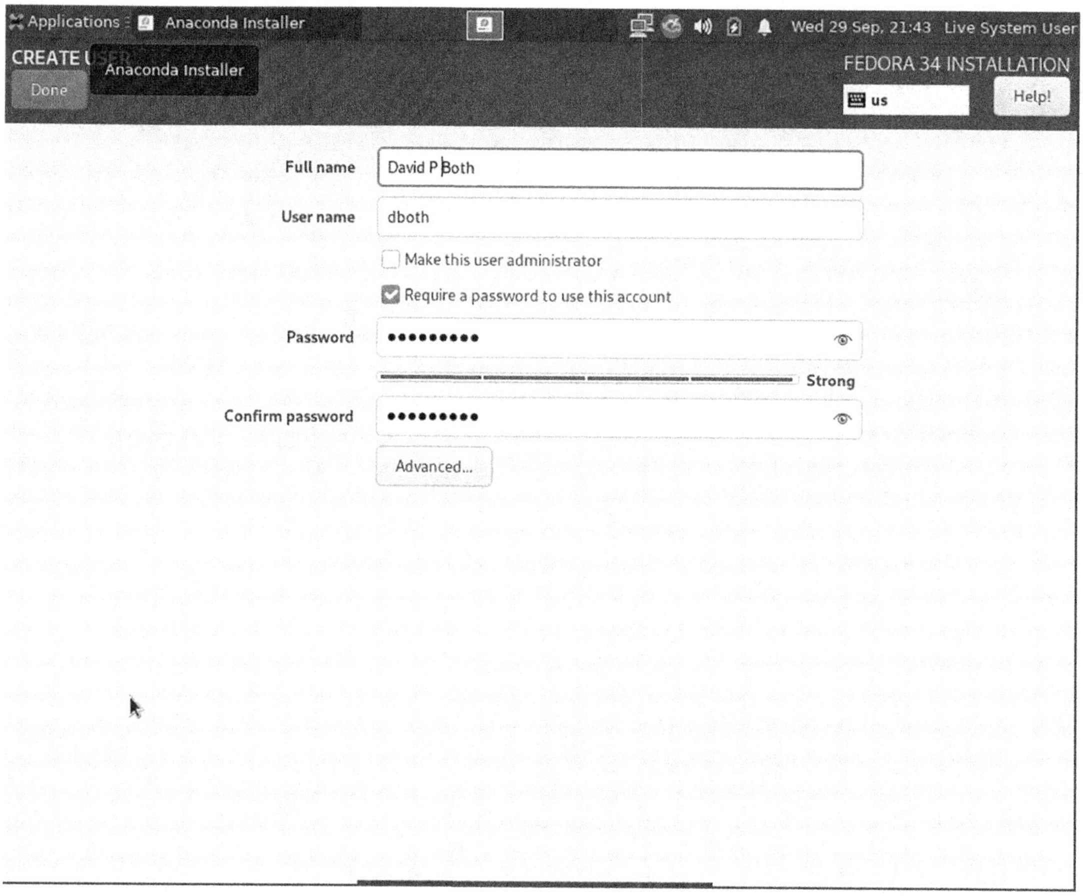

Figure 9-5. *Configure your own user account*

Enter your own data in the Create User dialog, and click the blue **Done** button. Notice that when you type your name in the Full name field, the installer automatically generates the User name. You can change the User name, but it should be all lowercase with no spaces. I suggest using the generated name which follows the standard Linux format of first initial plus the last name.

I have used my name in this example, but you should obviously use your own.

This dialog and the Root Password are the most important ones you must complete during the Fedora installation. The passwords and configuration you choose here provide the foundation for all of the security of your computer.

Here again, you can use a weak password but don't. I have entered a strong password in Figure 9-5, so there is no warning at the bottom of the screen. Do not make this user – or any user – an administrator as that weakens the overall security of the system. And always require a password for every user account.

After you complete entering the data on this dialog, click the **Done** button.

No additional accounts can be created during installation. If you want to add more user accounts, you can do that later.

Hard Drive Partitioning

The next thing we need to do is to make space available on your storage device(s) for the Linux filesystem.

In Figure 9-2, notice that the **Installation Destination** has a caution icon and the text **Automatic partitioning** in red. We do want to use automatic partitioning, but the Anaconda installer does not automatically delete existing partitions on your storage devices. This is an additional safety measure to ensure that the existing data does not get accidentally deleted – you really need to be deliberate about installing Fedora and deleting those old Windows partitions and any data in them.

Warning   If you have not backed up the data from your storage devices, you should do so now. This installation procedure will delete all existing data on your storage devices. Chapter 8 guided you through creating a backup of all your data.

Click **Installation Destination** to get the dialog shown in Figure 9-6. Place a check in the *"I would like to make additional space available"* check box, and then click **Done**.

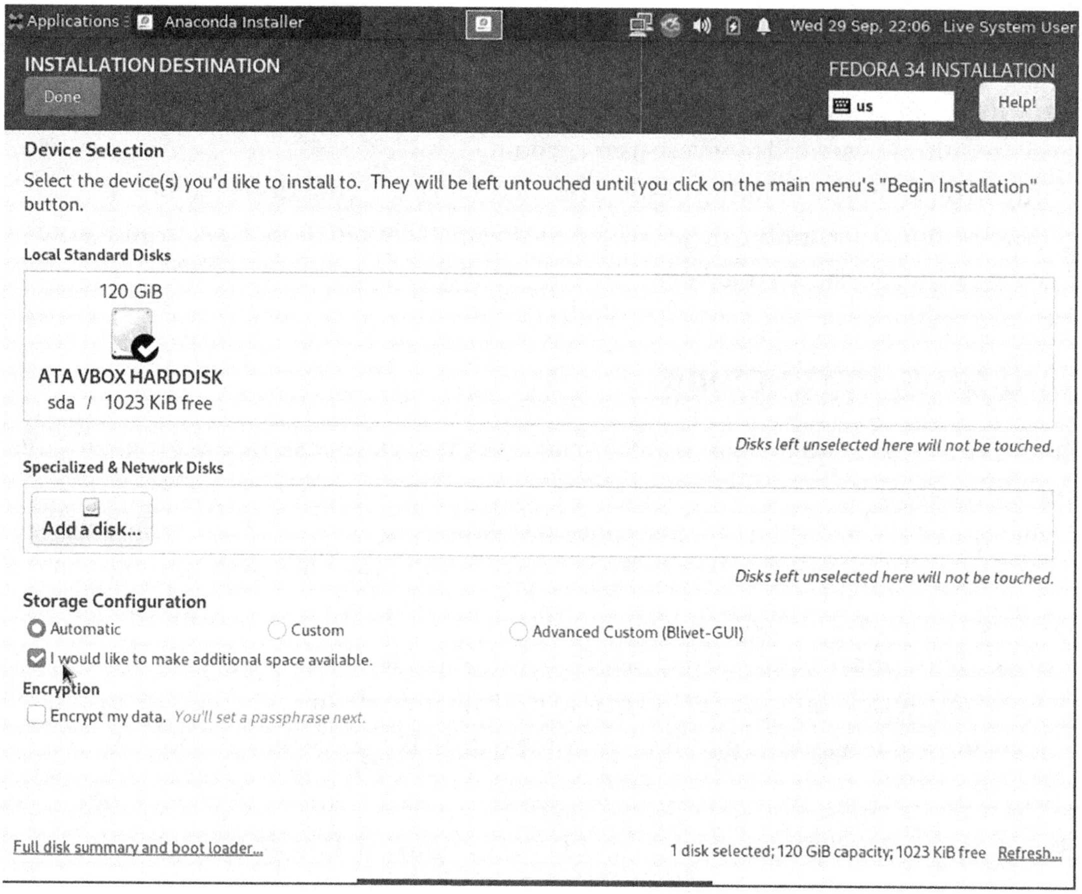

Figure 9-6. *Click the "I would like to make additional space available" check box, and then click **Done***

The Reclaim Disk Space dialog shown in Figure 9-7 displays the existing storage devices and partitions on your computer. Click the Delete all button to mark all of those existing partitions for deletion.

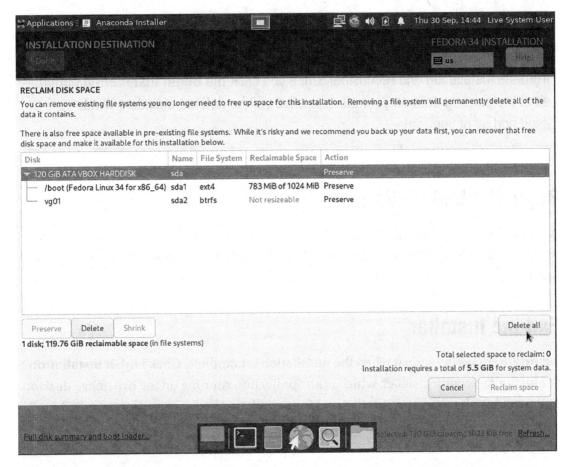

Figure 9-7. *The **Reclaim Disk Space** dialog displays the existing storage devices and partitions on your computer*

I am using a virtual machine that has Fedora already installed. The list of partitions on your computer will be different from mine, but everything else will look and work the same.

After clicking the **Delete all** button, the **Reclaim space** button will activate and no longer be grayed out. Click that **Reclaim space** button. You will be returned to the main Installation Summary dialog.

WARNING!!!   It is not too late. You can stop now and your existing Windows installation will remain untouched. If you have any doubts, now is the time to exit from the installation and reconsider. Once you click the **Begin Installation** button, all of the existing data on your storage drive will be deleted including Windows itself and all of your data.

Begin the Installation

We have now completed all of the configuration items needed to install Fedora. To start the installation procedure, click the blue **Begin Installation** button. The blue progress bar will keep you informed of the current state of the installation.

Exit the Installer

Figure 9-8 shows the screen when the installation is complete. Click **Finish Installation** to quit the Anaconda installer, which is an application running on the live image desktop. The hard drive has been partitioned and formatted, and Fedora has been installed.

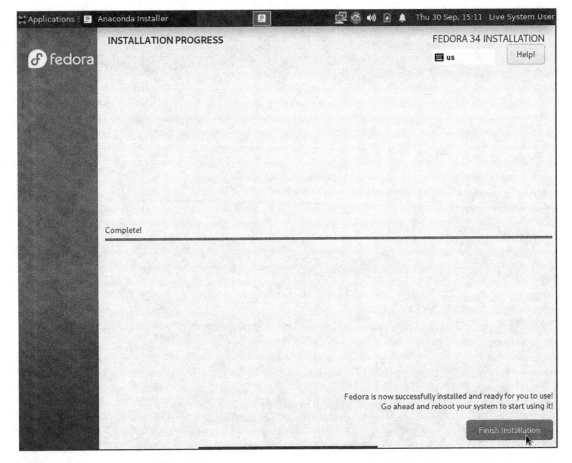

Figure 9-8. *The installation is complete*

Shut Down the Live System

Before we do anything else, look at the live system Xfce desktop. It looks and works the same as the Xfce desktop you will use when we reboot the VM using its own virtual disk instead of the live system. The only difference will be that some of the live filesystem icons will no longer be present. So using this desktop will be the same as using the Xfce desktop on any installed system.

Figure 9-9 shows how to shut down the live system. The Xfce panel across the top of the screen starts with the Applications launcher on the left and has space for the icons of running applications, a clock, the System Tray containing icons of various functions and notifications, and the User button on the far right which always displays the name of the current logged in user.

121

Figure 9-9. *Shut down the live system after the installation is complete*

Click the **Live System User** button, and then click the **Shut Down** action button. A dialog with a 30-second countdown will display. This dialog will allow you to shut down immediately or cancel the shutdown. If you do nothing, the system will shut down when the 30-second timer counts down to zero.

When the computer powers off, remove the live USB drive.

Chapter Summary

Congratulations! You have installed the latest release of Fedora Linux on your computer and are ready to get started using Fedora.

CHAPTER 10

Getting Started

Objectives

After reading this chapter, you will

- Learn why Xfce is a good desktop to use for this course as well as for regular use

- Select options on the Display Manager before login

- Perform the first login using the student account

- How to use and navigate the Xfce desktop

- How to use the Settings Manager to configure Xfce

- How to launch programs

- How to add program launchers to the bottom panel

- Basic usage of the Xfce4 terminal emulator

- The difference between various options when you are done with the computer

- Whether you should leave the computer turned on at all times or not

Introduction

In this chapter, you'll learn why the Xfce desktop is a good choice for a desktop user environment. We'll take a quick tour to learn how to log in and the basic usage of the Xfce desktop and then practice with the tools and procedures necessary to use Linux.

© David Both, Cyndi Bulka 2022
D. Both and C. Bulka, *Linux for Small Business Owners*, https://doi.org/10.1007/978-1-4842-8264-9_10

I'll show you how to manage the desktop environment and configure it to meet your own needs.

In the final installment of this chapter, will discuss the procedures and differences between power off/shutdown, sleep, hibernate, and a simple logout.

Terms

There are terms that we will use as you explore the Xfce desktop. This short list provides definitions and a contextual reference to the other terms and concepts presented in this chapter.

Account

An account on a computer is used to authenticate the user and as a means to determine what system resources, such as files and tools, that the user can have access to. This can also be called a user account or a login account.

Dialog

A dialog is a window on a computer desktop that provides a method for users to enter data of various kinds. For example, a dialog might request a user's ID and password.

Menu

A list of options from which a user can make one or more selections. The Xfce desktop has its own unique form and structure, not unlike other programs.

Context Menu

In a context menu, options for selection vary depending upon the context in which the menu was raised. For example, a right-click on the desktop brings up one set of menu options, and a right-click on LibreOffice Writer would open a menu with options needed for word processing.

Why Xfce?

Xfce seems like an unusual choice for the desktop to use in a Linux course rather than the more common GNOME or KDE desktops. I like the Xfce desktop because it is thin and fast with an overall elegance that makes it easy to figure out how to do things. Its lightweight construction conserves both memory and CPU cycles. This makes it ideal for older computers with few resources to spare for a desktop. Xfce is flexible and powerful enough to satisfy the needs of any power user.

Getting Started

Before we log in for the first time, let's take a quick look at the login screen shown in Figure 10-1. There are some interesting things to explore here.

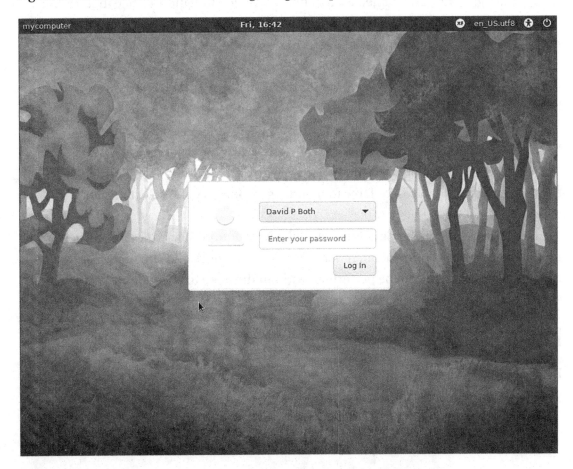

Figure 10-1. *The login screen is for more than just the login itself*

In the center of the screen is the login dialog. Your own user account is already selected because there are no other users who can log in at the GUI. The root user is not allowed to log in using the GUI. If there were other user accounts created on this host, they would be visible and selectable using the selection bar.

Note   Many of the illustrations in this chapter are from Fedora 34. If you are using later releases of Fedora, the background and other cosmetic elements may be different. However, the technical and functional characteristics remain the same.

The dark gray control panel across the top of the login screen contains information and controls. Starting from the left, first, you see the name of the host – mycomputer in this instance. In the center of the control panel is the current date and time.

On the right side of the panel, we first find – from left to right – a circle that contains "XF," which stands for Xfce. This control allows you to select any one of multiple desktops if you have more than Xfce installed. Linux has many desktops available, such as KDE, GNOME, Xfce, LXDE, Mate, and many more. You can install any or all of these and switch between them whenever you log in. You would need to select the desired desktop before you log in. For now, we only have Xfce, so there is nothing else to select here.

Next, we have language selection. This control allows you to select any one of hundreds of languages to use on the desktop. It is set for the default en_US.utf8.

Next, we have the icon of a human person with arms and legs spread wide. This allows accessibility choices for large font and high-contrast color selections for the desktop.

Last and furthest to the right is the virtual power button. Click this and you get a sub-menu that allows you to suspend, hibernate, restart (reboot), and shut down (power off) the system. These tasks can be performed without the need to log in or use a password.

Login

Before we can use the Xfce desktop, we need to log in. Type the password you chose for your user account, and click the **Log in** button.

The first time you log in to Xfce, the desktop will look like that in Figure 10-2.

Figure 10-2. *The default Xfce desktop the first time you log in*

The Xfce Desktop

The Xfce desktop has two panels that provide access to various tools, information, and applications. On the far left of the top panel is the **Applications** menu. Click this to see a menu and several sub-menus that allow you to select and launch programs and utilities. Then click the desired application to launch it.

Next is some currently empty space where the icons for running applications will be displayed. We have four squares. This is the desktop selector, and the darker one is the currently selected desktop. The purpose of having more than one desktop is to enable placement of windows for different projects on different desktops to help you keep organized. Application windows and icons are displayed in the desktop selector when

127

they are running. Simply click the desired desktop to switch to it. Applications can be moved from one desktop to another in two ways. You can drag the application from one desktop in the switcher to another, or you can right-click the application title bar to raise a menu that provides a desktop switching option.

To the immediate right of the desktop switcher is the clock. You can right-click the clock to configure it to display the date as well as the time in different formats. Next to that is the System Tray which contains icons to install software updates; connect, disconnect, and check the status of the network; and check the battery status. The network is connected by default at boot time, but you can also find information about the current connection. On a laptop, you would also have wireless information.

Soon after you log in, and at regular intervals thereafter, the dnf-dragora program – the orange hexagonal icon – will check for updates and notify you if there are any. There will very likely be a large number of updates after the installation and initial boot. For now, just ignore this. Don't try to install updates now; we will do that from the command line in Chapter 13.

Click the notification message to dismiss it. It will show up again, but until we install the updates, continue to dismiss the update notification.

The bottom panel contains launchers for some basic applications.

Figure 10-3 shows the Xfce desktop with two applications open, a terminal emulator session and the Thunar file manager.

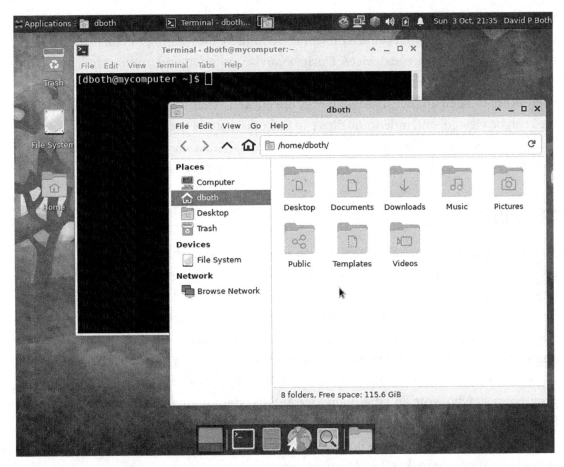

Figure 10-3.   *The Xfce desktop with the Thunar file manager and the Xfce4 terminal emulator open*

The icons down the left side of the desktop consist of Trash, home directory, and File System icons. It can also display icons for any connected pluggable USB storage devices. These icons can be used to mount and unmount storage devices, as well as to open the default file manager. They can also be hidden with the File System, Trash, and home directory icons being separately controllable. Removable storage devices can be hidden or displayed as a group.

The File Manager

Thunar is the default file manager for Xfce. It is simple, easy to use and configure, and very easy to learn. Thunar provides the capability to open multiple tabs so that multiple directories can be open at the same time. Thunar also has a nice sidebar that, like the desktop, shows the same icons for the complete filesystem directory tree and any connected USB storage devices. Devices can be mounted and unmounted, and removable media such as CDs can be ejected. Thunar can also use helper applications such as ark to open archive files when they are clicked. Archives such as zip, tar, and rpm files can be viewed, and individual files can be copied out of them.

Having used a number of different file managers, I must say that I like Thunar for its simplicity and ease of use. It is easy to navigate the filesystem using the sidebar.

Stability

The Xfce desktop is very stable. New releases seem to be on a three-year cycle. Updates are provided as necessary. The current version as of this writing is 4.16. The rock solid nature of the Xfce desktop is very reassuring if you have worked with Windows for a long time. The Xfce desktop has never crashed for me, and it has never spawned daemons or pop-up advertisements or malware that gobbled up system resources. It just sits there and works and does exactly what I tell it to do which is precisely what I want.

Xfce is simply elegant. Simplicity is one of the hallmarks of elegance. Clearly the programmers who write and maintain Xfce and its component applications are great fans of simplicity, which is very likely the reason that Xfce is so stable. It also results in a clean look, a responsive interface, an easily navigable structure that feels natural, and an overall elegance that makes it a pleasure to use.

Configurability

Within its limits, Xfce is very configurable. I found that the Settings Manager is the doorway to everything that is needed to configure Xfce. The individual configuration apps are separately available, but the Settings Manager collects them all into one window for ease of access. All of the important aspects of the desktop can be configured to meet your own personal needs and preferences.

Exploring the Xfce Desktop

Let's spend some time exploring the Xfce desktop itself. This includes reducing the annoyance level of the screensaver, doing some configuration to set default applications, adding launchers to the bottom panel to make them more easily accessible, and using multiple desktops.

Log in to the desktop.

As we proceed through this exploration of the Xfce desktop, you should take time to do a bit of exploration on your own. I find that is the way I learn best and perhaps you do too. I like to fiddle with things to try to get them the way I want them, and you should do so yourself.

Settings Manager

Let's look at how we can access the various desktop settings for Xfce. There are two ways to do so. One is to use the Applications button on panel 1, select Settings, and then select the specific setting item you want to view of change.

The other – and I think better – option is to open the Settings Manager at the top of the Settings menu. The Settings Manager has all of the other settings in one window for easy access. Figure 10-4 shows both options. On the left, you can see the Applications menu selection, and on the right is the Settings Manager.

Figure 10-4. *Launching the Settings Manager*

The settings tools in the **Applications ➤ Settings** menu are listed in alphabetical order. These same settings tools are organized in the Settings Manager alphabetically within the four categories, Personal, Hardware, System, and Other.

Changing the Wallpaper

One of the first things we all do is to change the wallpaper – a.k.a. the desktop background. The good news is that you can change the background with a few images that are already provided with the Xfce desktop or with your own images. Click the **Desktop** icon in the Settings Manager.

Figure 10-5 shows the Desktop settings with the Background tab selected; it is the default. There are only four nearly identical backgrounds there, but we can find a few more using the **Folder** selection button. Click the **Folder** button to show the default list of locations. Note that not all of these have pictures; they are just starting points such as your home directory.

Figure 10-5.   *The default Fedora wallpapers might not be right for everyone*

The default folder is **images** which is one subdirectory of the /usr/share/backgrounds directory. Select the **Other** item in the Folder menu which opens the **Select a Directory** navigation dialog. Open **/usr/share/backgrounds** and highlight the xfce directory. Then click the Open button on the upper right of this dialog. Figure 10-6 shows the contents of the /usr/share/backgrounds/xfce directory. Click one of those images to select it. The desktop wallpaper changes immediately to that image.

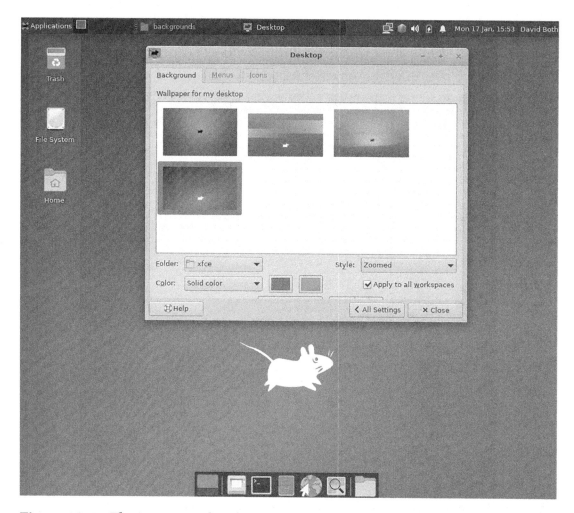

Figure 10-6. *The images in the xfce subdirectory, one of which has been selected as the new wallpaper*

The default /usr/share/backgrounds directory and its subdirectories are where the images can be accessed by all users on the system. You can access this directory and view listings of the files in its subdirectories using the Thunar file manager or the command line. Note that you can view the files in these directories, but you do not have the permissions to copy additional files to any of them unless you become root. But you don't need to do that to use your own images for the desktop wallpaper.

You can easily create a directory and store your own wallpapers using the Thunar file manager. We cover the details of using Thunar in Chapter 11.

The basic steps are to create a directory in your home directory, /home/dboth/ Wallpapers. I call mine Wallpapers, but you can use any name that makes sense to you. My home directory is dboth, but yours will be different. Copy the image files you want to use as wallpapers into that directory. Then open the Settings Manager to the Desktop Background. Use the **Folder** button like you just did here, and use the Other option to navigate to the /home/YourHomeDirectory/Wallpapers directory, and all of the files you copied there will be available.

Screensaver

Like all decent desktops, Xfce has a screensaver that can also lock the screen. This can get annoying – as it has for me while I write this. Let's reconfigure the screensaver. First, explore the screensaver, and then turn it off so it won't interfere with our work.

To launch the screensaver application, select the Screensaver icon from the Settings Manager window.

Figure 10-7 shows the **Screensaver Preferences** dialog. There are only a few screensaver choices, but go ahead and "experiment" – all right – play with this because it can be fun.

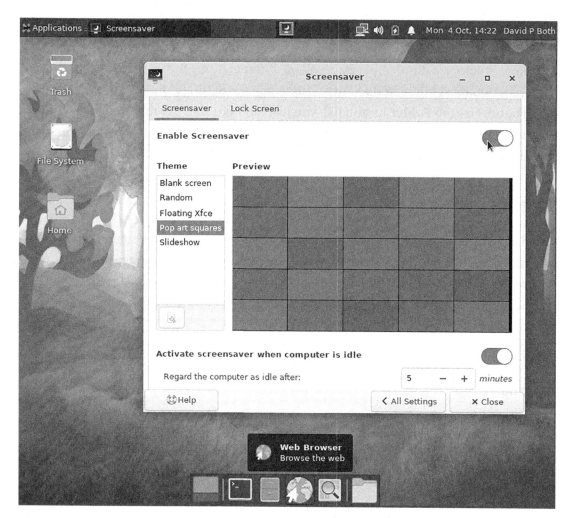

Figure 10-7. *Experimenting with the screensaver application*

Disable the screensaver when you have finished experimenting. Click the **Enable Screen Saver** slide switch to disable it. Then select the **Lock Screen** tab and disable the Lock Screen.

Return to the main Settings Manager dialog by clicking the **All Settings** button.

When I enable the screensaver, I usually select the blank screen and set the time long enough that it won't blank while I am still working but not touching the mouse or keyboard. I set the screen to lock a few minutes after that. My tolerance levels change over time, so I reset these occasionally. You can set them to your own needs.

Power Manager

The Power Manager provides a number of ways to save power by setting timeouts and specifying actions to take when the power button is pressed. It also allows setting power management options for the display. Modern flat screen displays use far less power than their ancient CRT counterparts, but they can still use 75 to 100 Watts of power when turned on.

Setting the display to go blank and ultimately turn off after a specified period of time saves a great deal of power. Figure 10-8 shows the power management dialog for the display. Set these times to best balance between your need to save energy and the irritation of having the screen blank too soon for your work style.

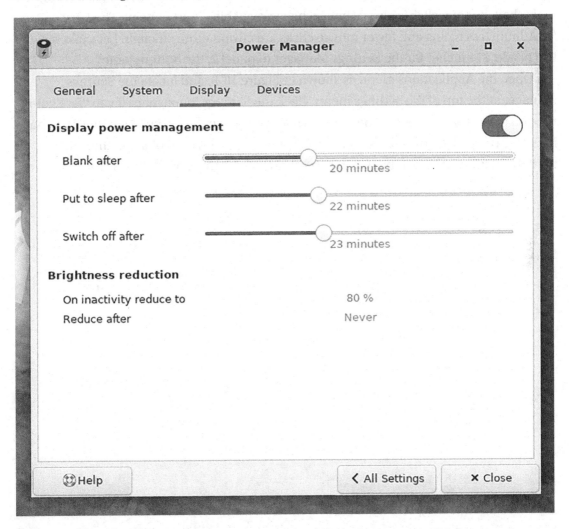

Figure 10-8. *The Power Manager provides options for power achieving savings under various circumstances*

137

The Devices tab of the Power Manager dialog will show the status of a laptop battery and a wireless mouse battery. If your computer is a desktop workstation, this tab will show the status of an external uninterruptible power supply (UPS), also referred to as a battery backup unit (BBU).

Adding Launchers to Panel 2

I prefer to use the Settings Manager for making changes as it aggregates most of the settings tools in one window. That makes it easier to access the Settings Manager itself. Not that three clicks to go through the menu tree every time I want to access a settings tool is bad, but one click is always better than three. This is part of being The Lazy SysAdmin; less typing and fewer mouse clicks are always more efficient. Let's take a side trip to add a launcher for the Settings Manager to panel 2, the bottom panel.

Open the Applications menu as shown in Figure 10-9, and locate the Settings Manager at the top of the Settings menu. Click the Settings Manager as if you were going to open it, but hold the mouse button down and drag it to the left side of panel 2 as I have in Figure 10-9. Hover over the small space just barely to the right of the leftmost icon until the vertical red bar appears. This bar shows where the new launcher will be added.

Figure 10-9. Adding the Settings Manager to panel 2

When the red bar is in the desired location on the panel, release the mouse button to drop it there. An interrogatory dialog will open that asks if you want to "Create new launcher from 1 desktop file." Click the **Create Launcher** button. The new launcher now appears on panel 2 as shown in Figure 10-10.

Figure 10-10. The new Settings Manager launcher on Panel 2

Now you can launch the Settings Manager from the panel. You could have placed the launcher anywhere on the panel where the red bar appears. That is usually next to one of the vertical gray separators. The launchers can be moved after being created on the panel. Right-click the launcher you want to move, and select **Move** from the context menu. Then use the mouse to move the launcher to the desired location.

Only one click is required to launch applications from the panel. I add all of my most used applications to panel 2 which prevents me from having to search for them in the menus every time I want to use one. As you work your way through this book, you can add more launchers to the panel to enhance your own efficiency.

Default Applications

We can now turn to setting our default applications. Default applications are choices like which terminal emulator or web browser that you want all other applications to launch when one of those is needed. You might want your word processor to launch Chrome when you click a URL embedded in the text. Xfce calls these default applications.

The icons at the bottom of the Xfce desktop, in panel 2, include a couple for which we could choose different applications, the web browser and the file manager. If you were to click the web browser icon, the Earth with a mouse pointer on it, you would be given a choice of which of the installed web browsers you want to use as the default.

Ensure the **Settings Manager** is open. Locate the **Default Applications** icon in the Settings dialog, and click it once to open it. This dialog opens to its Internet tab which allows selection of the browser and email application. At the moment, only the Firefox web browser is installed, so it is already set as the default web browser.

Currently, there isn't an email program selected because none are installed by default.

Switch to the Utilities tab of the Preferred Applications dialog shown in Figure 10-9. Notice that both items here already have selections made. Thunar is the only option available as the file manager, and the Xfce terminal is the only option for the terminal emulator. The preferred terminal emulator is already configured as the Xfce4-terminal, which you have had an opportunity to use. We will go into more detail about the Xfce4 terminal in later chapters.

The fact that there are no other options available for any of these applications is due to the basic installation that is performed by the desktop installers.

Click the All Settings button shown in Figure 10-11 to return to the main Settings Manager.

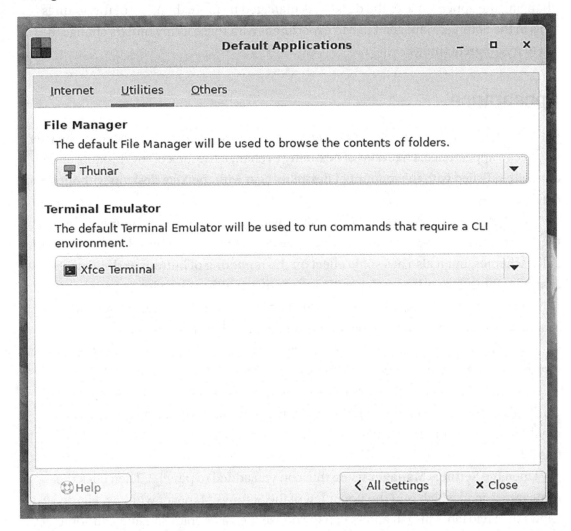

Figure 10-11. *The Utilities tab of the Preferred Applications dialog allows selection of the default GUI file manager and the default terminal emulator*

The Thunar file manager is one of the best I have used. There are many and several of them are available for Fedora Linux. The same is true of the Xfce terminal – it is one of the best of many very good options, since these are excellent options, and I don't recommend changing them. We will cover Thunar in Chapter 11.

Desktop Appearance

Changing the appearance of the desktop is managed by more than one of the settings tools in the Settings Manager. I like to experiment with these as my moods change. It is fun to try different things.

Appearance

Let's start with the Appearance tools which allow us to select various aspects of the user interface's appearance. I like a lot of flexibility to change the look of my desktop, and I am quite satisfied with the amount of flexibility I get with the Xfce desktop without being overly complex.

The Appearance tool has four tabs that provide controls to adjust different parts of the Xfce desktop. The Appearance dialog opens to the Style tab. This tab is mostly about color schemes, but it also has some effect on the rendering of buttons and sliders. For example, controls may have a flat or 3D appearance in different styles.

The second tab, Icons, allows selection of an icon theme from among several available ones. Others can be downloaded and installed as well.

The third tab, Fonts, allows the user to select a font theme for the desktop. A default variable width font can be selected as well as a default monospace font.

The fourth tab, Settings, allows selection of whether the icons have text or not and where it is located. It also provides the ability to determine whether some buttons and menu items have images on them. You can also turn sounds for events on or off on this tab.

Open the **Settings Manager** using the icon you added to panel 2. Then click the Appearance icon which is in the upper left of the Settings Manager window. Figure 10-12 shows the Style tab. This tab allows you to choose the basic color scheme and some of the visual aspects of the Xfce desktop.

Figure 10-12. *Setting the style elements of the Xfce desktop*

Click some of the different schemes to see how they look on your computer. I have noticed (at the time of this writing) that the Xfce selections look good with respect to the colors, but that the Menu bars, on windows that have them, seem to jam the menu items together, so they become difficult to read. For your new style, you might consider one of the others. I like the Adwaita-dark style.

Now go to the Icons tab and select some different icon schemes to see how they look. This is not the mouse pointer icon, but the application icons. I like the Fedora icon set.

Notice that all changes take place almost as soon as you select them.

When you have finished setting the appearance of your desktop, click the All Settings button to return to the main settings dialog. Then click Window Manager. These settings enable you to change the look of the window decorations – things like the title bar, the icons on the title bar, and the size and look of the window borders. The Settings Manager itself will not change; open the file manager so that you can see the effects of these changes on a window that is affected.

In Figure 10-13, I have chosen the B6 window decorations. Check out some of the other themes in this menu.

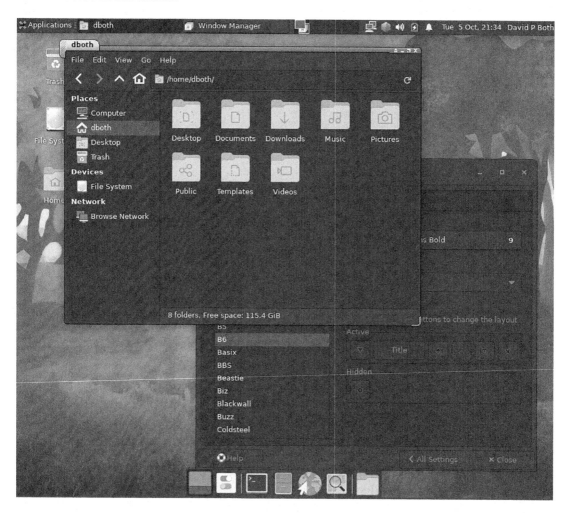

Figure 10-13. *The Window Manager settings allow you to change the look of the window decorations*

The Keyboard tab allows you to change some of the keyboard shortcuts. I never make any changes here. The Focus tab gives you the ability to determine when a window gets the focus so that it is the active window. The Advanced tab determines whether windows snap to invisible grid lines when moved and the granularity of the grid. It also allows you to configure how windows dragged to the edge of the screen act.

Leave the Settings Manager open for now.

Take a little time to explore the other tabs found in the Settings Manager. Don't forget that you can return to the Settings Manager at any time to change the appearance of your desktop. If you don't like tomorrow what you selected today, you can choose another look and feel for your desktop.

Configuring the look and feel of the desktop may seem a bit frivolous, but I find that having a desktop that looks good to me, that has launchers for the applications I use most frequently, and that can be easily modified goes a long way to making my work pleasant and easy.

Multiple Desktops

Another feature of the Xfce desktop is the ability to use multiple desktops or workspaces as they are called in Xfce. I use this feature often, and many people find it useful to organize their work by placing the windows belonging to each project on which they are working on different desktops. I have the default number of four workspaces on my Xfce desktop. My email, an instance of the Firefox web browser, and a terminal session are located on my main workspace. I have VirtualBox and all of my running virtual machines in a second workspace along with another terminal session. Writing tools are on a third workspace.

It is now time for you to practice with using multiple desktops. Your desktop should look very similar to that in Figure 10-14 to start, with the Settings Manager and Thunar file manager open. If it doesn't make it so, now.

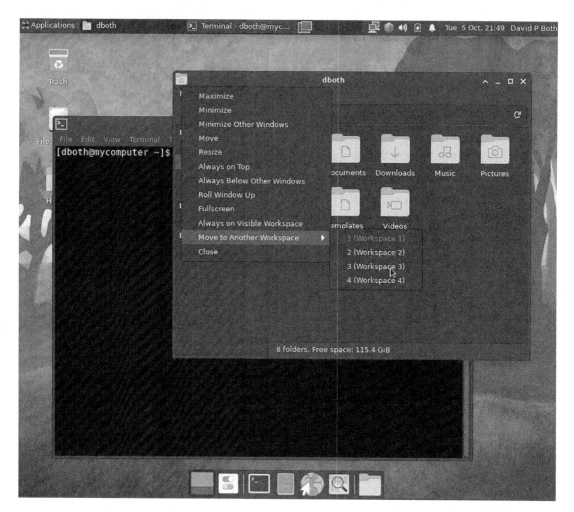

Figure 10-14. *Move the Thunar file manager to another workspace using the System menu*

Click the filing cabinet icon in the center of panel 2. If you hover the mouse pointer over this folder, the tooltip will pop up showing the title "File Manager." The default file manager is Thunar, and it can be used to explore the files and directories in your home directory as well as other system directories to which you have access, such as /tmp.

First, right-click anywhere on the file manager's title bar at the top of the window. Then select **Move to Another Workspace** as in Figure 10-12, and then click w**orkspace 3**. You could also access the same menu with a right-click on the button for the running application in the top panel, panel 1.

Tip   Some Xfce color schemes provide very little differentiation between the Workspace Switcher and the surrounding panel. This can make it very difficult to see the switcher. Use a color scheme that provides good differentiation such as the "Adwaita" scheme.

The Workspace Switcher now shows the window for the file manager in workspace 3 while the Settings Manager is still in workspace 1, as shown in Figure 10-15. You can click any workspace in the switcher to go immediately to that workspace. Click workspace 3 to go there.

Figure 10-15.   *The Workspace Switcher shows windows in workspaces 1 and 3*

Notice that the windows in the switcher are a reasonable approximation of their relative size on the workspaces that the switcher represents. Some windows in the switcher also have icons that represent the application running in the window.

If the panel size is too small, the windows may not be replicated in the desktop switcher, or just the outline of the window will be present without an icon. If there are no windows in the desktop switcher, you should skip the next paragraph.

Drag the file manager icon from workspace 3 to workspace 4 and drop it there. The file manager window disappears from the workspace, and the icon for the file manager is now in workspace 4. Click workspace 4 to go there.

As with all things Linux, there are multiple ways to manage these workspaces and the application windows in each. I find that there are times when placing windows that belong to a specific project on a workspace by themselves is a good way to simplify the clutter on my primary workspace.

When You Are Done with the Computer

You will see in the next section that I leave my computers running 24x7x365. Even after reading that, you may just decide that powering off the computer is the best thing for you. Or your laptop battery is low, and there is no place to plug in. You may want to move your desktop computer to a new location.

When you need to power off your computer, you should do so properly and not just pull the plug. Figure 10-16 illustrates how to start.

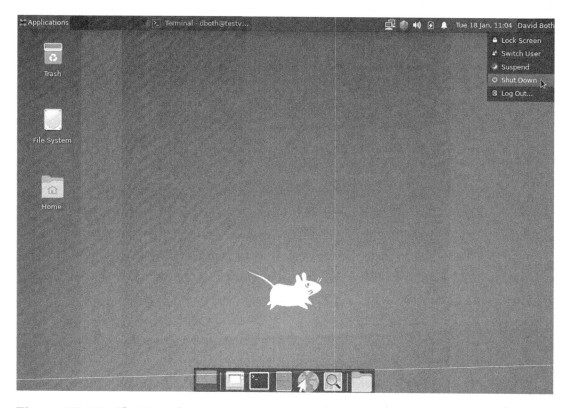

Figure 10-16. *Shutting down your computer takes just a couple clicks. Start by clicking your username in the upper right*

Click your username in the upper right corner of your screen to open the context menu. Then select the Shutdown menu item. Figure 10-17 shows the pop-up dialog that allows you to wait for the 30-second countdown to power off the system, to cancel the shutdown, or to click the red Shut Down button to perform the shutdown immediately.

Figure 10-17. *This dialog allows you to choose to cancel the shutdown or skip the remaining time on the countdown timer*

If there is no reason to wait for 30 seconds, you can click the Shut Down button to speed things up. That is what I do.

What I Do When I Am Done with My Own Computer[1]

I usually have between eight and a dozen computers in my home office, all of them running 24x7. People sometimes question me about that and tell me they think I am wasting power by doing so. Then I get another related question: is it better to run a computer 24x7 or turn it off when not needed?

In my case, the power is not wasted because my computers are always working on various projects for the World Community Grid,[2] which puts the otherwise wasted CPU cycles of home and office computers around the world to use. They use these computers as nodes in a volunteer distributed supercomputer based on the Berkeley Open Infrastructure for Network Computing (BOINC).[3] The projects include medical, genome, meteorological, and other types of calculations. I also perform backups and install updates at night, and the computers need to be on to do this.

But these functions are irrelevant to the question at hand.

---

[1] I originally wrote this section as an article for Red Hat's Enable Sysadmin website, "Should I run my desktop 24/7?", www.redhat.com/sysadmin/run-my-computer-24-7

[2] World Community Grid, www.worldcommunitygrid.org/

[3] Berkeley Open Infrastructure for Network Computing (BOINC), https://boinc.berkeley.edu/

The big question is doesn't that reduce the computer's life by wearing it out? The short answer is not necessarily; it actually may extend the life of the machine and save energy in the long run. Wait, what? How can that be?

The Light Bulb

Have you ever noticed that incandescent light bulbs[4] seem to burn out most frequently at the instant when they are turned on? Or that electronic components like home theater systems or TVs worked fine yesterday but don't today when you turn them on? I have, too.

Have you ever wondered why that happens? Me too.

Thermal Stress

Many factors affect the longevity of electronic equipment. One of the most ubiquitous sources of failure is heat. In fact, the heat generated by devices as they perform their assigned tasks is the very heat that shortens their electronic lives.

When I worked at IBM in Boca Raton at the dawn of the PC era, I was part of a group that was responsible for the maintainability of computers and other hardware of many types. Part of that task was to ensure that equipment broke very infrequently and that, when it did, it was easy to repair. I learned some interesting things about the effects of heat on the life of computers while I was there.

Let's go back to the light bulb. Every time a light bulb is turned on, an electric current surges into the filament and heats its surface very rapidly from room temperature to about 4,600°F. This thermal shock causes stress by vaporizing the filament's metal and the rapid expansion of the metal caused by the heating. When a light bulb is turned off, the thermal shock is repeated, though less severely, during the cooling phase as the filament shrinks. The more times a bulb is cycled on and off, the more the effects of this thermal shock accumulate.

The primary effect of thermal shock is that some small parts of the filament – usually due to minute manufacturing variances – tend to become hotter than other parts. This causes the metal at those points to vaporize faster, making the filament even weaker at that point and more susceptible to rapid overheating in subsequent power-on cycles.

---

[4]Wikipedia, "Incandescent light bulb," https://en.wikipedia.org/wiki/Incandescent_light_bulb

Eventually, the last of the metal vaporizes when the bulb is turned on, and the filament dies in a very bright flash.

The electrical circuitry in computers is much like the filament in a light bulb. Repeated heating and cooling cycles damage the computer's internal electronic components just as the light bulb's filament was damaged over time. Over many years of testing, researchers have discovered that more damage is done by repeated power on and off cycles than by leaving the devices on all the time.

The Energy Cost of Manufacturing

The cost of a computer that is damaged by thermal shock includes the energy cost to build a new one or to replace the damaged parts. Network World published an article in 2011, "Computer factories eat way more energy than running the devices they build."[5] In it, they cited a study showing that as much as 70% of the energy consumed by a laptop is the cost of manufacturing it and the other 30% is the cost of running it. Note: The links in that article to the cited paper are no longer valid.

Extending the useful life of a computer increases the overall return on investment. Reducing the thermal stress on the device by running it 24x7 can significantly extend its useful life.

So What Breaks?

I have been running computers of various types 24x7 for over 40 years, and some have broken. However, the interesting thing is not that they did, but that they did so infrequently and what parts broke.

I have had only one memory DIMM fail. Those components just don't fail – well except for that one!

Two motherboards failed when the Parallel ATA (a really old hard drive connection) port stopped working, but I circumvented that by installing a PATA adapter. One motherboard just quit working with no response of any kind.

I have replaced five CD/DVD drives due to broken moving mechanical parts.

---

[5] Coony, Michael, "Computer factories eat way more energy than running the devices they build," Network World, www.networkworld.com/article/2229029/computer-factories-eat-way-more-energy-than-running-the-devices-they-build.html

I have had at best estimate at least 14 power supplies fail. The frequency of these failures diminished once I started installing power supplies with significantly higher capacity than was actually required. Running a power supply near its design limit stresses it and causes it to fail sooner.

I have replaced about 30 failed hard drives over the years. Hard drives have moving mechanical parts, and those are usually but not always the failure points. I have not used SSDs long enough to have one fail.

Fans. Dozens of fans. Fans fail all the time. Sometimes they make noise when the bearings start to fail, but other times they just start slowing down as the gunk in the bearings starts to harden. This example includes case fans, CPU cooling fans, and GPU onboard cooling fans. I have not yet had a liquid cooling pump fail. Fortunately, most fans failed noisily, so I know to replace them before they stop turning completely. Bad bearings seem to be the most common cause of fan failures, and they are noisy when they do so. Accumulated gunk failures are quiet and may not be noticed until something more significant fails.

What Should You Do?

I have read many recommendations about whether to run computers 24x7. Most of them seem to be aimed at home users, and the guidance they provide is appropriate for that environment.

Based on my experiences, and this Lifewire article, "Should You Shut Down a Computer When It's Not in Use?",[6] it is clear that most devices either fail quickly or after a very long life. The "bathtub" curve shown in the article illustrates this very nicely. The author recognizes the role of power cycles in causing failures, so he recommends that you power cycle your device when it is not needed early in its life to ensure that if it fails early, it fails during the warranty. He says that once past the warranty period, computers should be run 24x7 because it is less stressful on the components than power cycling each day.

Near the end of that article, the author lists ways to extend the computer's life if it is run 24x7. This advice includes preventing the machine from entering hibernation or sleep modes as these can be almost as damaging as power cycles – which they essentially are. I would add that "wake on LAN" to do updates and backups is also a sleep or

---

[6] Nelson, Tom, Lifewire, "Should You Shut Down a Computer When It's Not in Use?", `www.lifewire.com/shut-computer-down-or-not-4135231`

hibernation mode and counts for a power cycle. It is better just to leave the computer on full rather than allow it to sleep or hibernate.

Be aware that not all failures are caused by heat and power cycling. The graph in the article shows a straight line near the bottom of the curve that illustrates "random" failures that happen equally distributed along the timeline.

What I Do

I run my computers the same way that data centers do – 24x7 for their entire lifetimes – full on power with no sleep or hibernation. I have had only one or two early-life failures. Here is what I recommend: turn it on, turn off hibernation and sleep modes, and just let it run.

Chapter Summary

This chapter is a quick look at how to log in to and use the Xfce desktop. It also explored the Xfce desktop just enough to get started. It looked at managing some desktop settings using the Settings Manager to enable you to configure the Xfce desktop to your own liking and to make some tasks easier and more efficient.

We also looked at whether a computer should be turned off and on (power cycled) regularly or left to run 24x7.

CHAPTER 11

Easy File Management

Objectives

After reading this chapter, you will be able to

- Configure the Thunar file manager

- Use the Thunar file manager to move, copy, and delete files

- Mount and unmount external USB storage devices when they are connected and disconnected

- Access the files on external storage devices

Introduction

Computers are all about files. Linux itself is a collection of many files, application programs like LibreOffice are made up of many files, and the documents, spreadsheets, financial data, photos, videos, audio, and more that you use in your business are all files. Working with files is a very important part of your work as a user.

This chapter introduces the use of the Thunar graphical file manager for managing files. Thunar is similar to the Windows File Explorer in function.

Create Some Test Files

First, you need some files to experiment with. This cannot be done in the GUI without a lot of work. But you can easily create some files for testing from the command line. Click the Terminal Emulator icon to open a terminal session on your desktop. Note in

155

© David Both, Cyndi Bulka 2022
D. Both and C. Bulka, *Linux for Small Business Owners*, https://doi.org/10.1007/978-1-4842-8264-9_11

Figure 11-1 that the Terminal Emulator icon is second from the left and looks like an old-fashioned display screen.

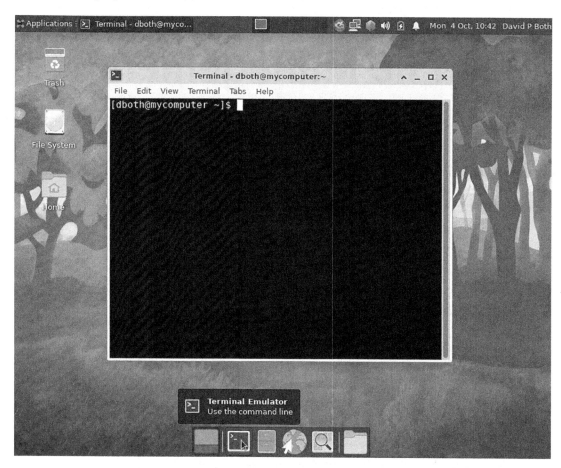

Figure 11-1. *Click the terminal icon to open a terminal session*

Enter the following command-line program[1] on one line in your terminal session. If it wraps naturally around to the next line when you are typing and it reaches the maximum width of the terminal window, that is fine; just don't press the **Enter** key until you have entered all of the program.

[dboth@mycomputer ~]$ **for I in `seq -w 20` ; do echo "Hello world" file$I >
testfile$I.txt ; done**

---

[1] Some of you are asking yourselves, "Command line WHAT??!" Yes, you are going to write a simple program.

The back ticks (`) around `**seq -w 20**` are not regular single quotes. The back tick is located on the Tilde (~) key which is usually just below the Escape key on most keyboards. Use the Shift+Tilde key combination to get the back tick.

If you have difficulty entering that command from the keyboard, you can copy and paste directly from my website at `www.both.org/?p=1912`.

Introducing the Thunar File Manager

Thunar is the default GUI file manager for the Xfce desktop. There are many other file managers for Linux, but Thunar is one of the best. A complete set of documentation for Thunar[2] is maintained at the Xfce website. You can also access the help for Thunar using the **Menu bar ➤ Help** item.

Launching Thunar

There are three ways to launch the Thunar file manager. You can click the file cabinet icon on the bottom panel (panel 2), the Home icon on the upper left side of the desktop, or the **Applications ➤ File Manager** menu sequence on the upper panel (panel 1). Figure 11-2 shows all of these options along with an open instance of Thunar.

---

[2] Xfce.org, Thunar documentation, `https://docs.xfce.org/xfce/thunar/start`

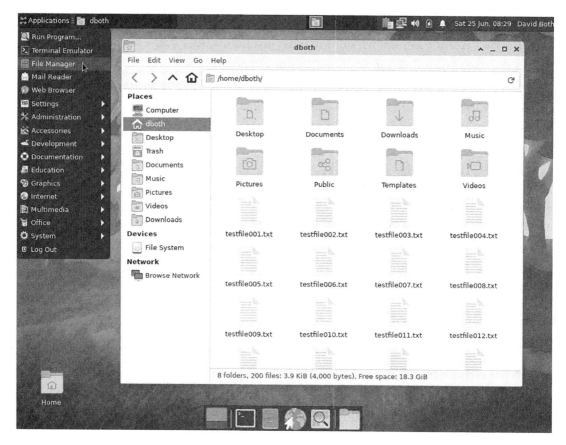

Figure 11-2. *The Xfce desktop showing all three ways to launch Thunar and one open instance of Thunar. The Home icon has been moved to the lower left side so that it will be visible instead of covered by the **Applications** menu*

Remember that the desktop icons must be double-clicked while the panel icons only need a single click.

The Thunar Interface

The view of your home directory in Figure 11-2 shows the same default directories as well as some of the files that were created earlier in this chapter. None of the so-called hidden files are displayed although that can be changed in the Thunar configuration.

The Thunar side panel, on the left, contains a Places section with icons that allow quick access to an overall view of the computer which includes the File System and all storage devices including any external thumb drives or other USB storage devices. The icon with your user ID gives immediate access to your home directory.

The Desktop icon does not really take you to the desktop. It is just a placeholder for some types of files that are related to the desktop. It may also be empty.

And, of course, the Trash icon opens the Trash bin. If you have deleted a file and not configured Thunar to delete files immediately, the deleted file or files will be located here. You can simply drag them from the Trash bin to the directory from which they were deleted. The Trash icon on the desktop also allows access to the Trash bin.

The Devices section only contains the File System. If you were to plug in an external storage device, that would also appear in this section.

The Network section will not display any locations other than Browse Network unless the host is connected to an internal network with some shared filesystems from other hosts or a Network Attached Storage (NAS) device.[3]

Note that there are multiple ways to access each of these locations using Thunar. Spend a few minutes to explore these just to familiarize yourself with them. When you have finished that, click the Home icon in the Thunar side panel.

Thunar Configuration

Let's take a few minutes to configure Thunar. Once again, there is more than one way to access the configuration options for Thunar. You can get to all of them using **Applications ➤ Settings ➤ File Manager Settings**, or you can use the Menu bar at the top of the Thunar window to access the View menu quickly. Let's start by doing that.

Location Selector

Figure 11-3 shows the View menu. I like to set the Location Selector to Toolbar Style because it changes the text mode path to a series of buttons that you can click to go immediately to that directory. Click **View ➤ Location Selector ➤ Toolbar Style** to make that change. The menus will disappear and the locations will now show in the Toolbar Style. Double-click the Documents icon and watch what happens to the location toolbar.

---

[3] Wikipedia, Network Attached Storage, `https://en.wikipedia.org/wiki/Network-attached_storage`

Notice the arrow on the left side of the location toolbar and click it. You can now see the entire path from the root (/) directory and click any button to go immediately to that directory.

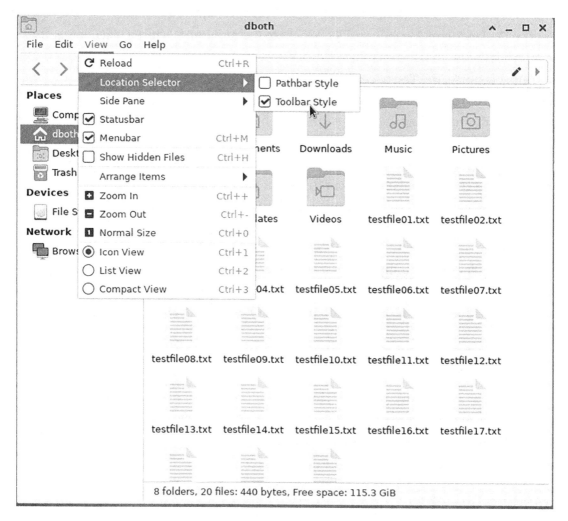

Figure 11-3. *Using the View menu from the Menu bar to change the Thunar user interface*

On the right side of the Selector is a pencil icon. Click that and you can type in any path to which you have access. Try it now with "/tmp" – without the quotes.

Make sure you are now back in your home directory.

File View

I also like to change one other thing on the View menu. I like to switch to the List view because it shows more files in a format similar to a long listing on the command line. Try that to see how it looks. Then change to the Compact view which only shows file icons and names and which lists the largest number of files in the available space.

You could also select **Show Hidden Files**, but that is not necessary. As you use more applications, they will store their configuration information in hidden files. This can add unnecessary clutter to the list of files, and you won't need to deal with these files directly anyway, so there is no point in showing them – most of the time.

File Manager Preferences Dialog

Now let's use the File Manager Preferences dialog window which provides more configuration options for Thunar. This dialog can be accessed in multiple ways also. From the Thunar Menu bar, choose **Edit ➤ Preferences**. Or you could open it from the Applications menu in the upper panel, **Applications ➤ Settings ➤ File Manager Settings**. Finally, you could also use the Applications menu to open the Settings Manager, **Applications ➤ Settings ➤ Settings Manager**, and then click the **File Manager Settings** icon.

Whichever method you use to launch it, the result will be the same. Figure 11-4 shows the File Manager Preferences dialog with its four tabs. Open the File Manager Preferences dialog now.

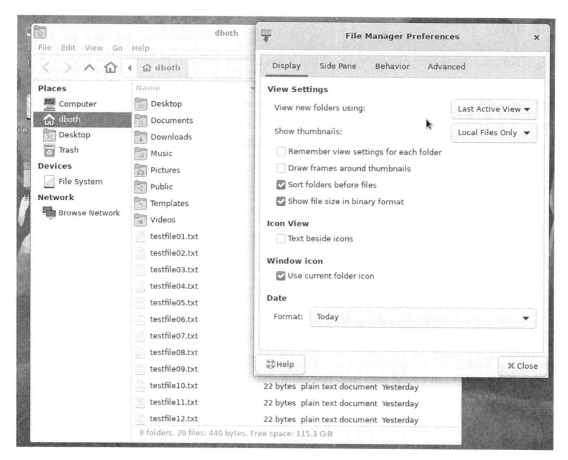

Figure 11-4. *The File Manager Preferences dialog provides additional configuration options for Thunar*

Display Tab

The Display allows setting the view options like we have already done but with a bit more choices. One example of this is the view settings in which you can also choose **Last Active View**. What this means is that if you choose a view such as List view instead of the default Icon view, that now becomes the default view. I sometimes like to use a different view, but I always prefer the List view as the default.

You may also choose to have different views for each folder. The checkbox "Remember view settings for each folder" enables you to activate that. For example, with this box checked, you can set the Icon view for your home directory and the List view for your Documents directory, and these settings will be persistent for future access to those directories.

Another default is to "Sort folders before files" which always puts folders, that is, directories at the top of the listing. I like this default because it makes it easier to find directories.

Side Pane Tab

By default, the Side Pane is in shortcut mode. The Side Pane tab allows you to set the size of the icons in the shortcuts and tree panes. It does not let you select between those two views. The only way to select the tree view for the Side Pane is from the Thunar Menu bar. Select **View ➤ Side Pane ➤ Tree** to see this. Then click the "twisty," the triangular shape next to the **Student** icon, to open the tree view of your home directory. The Side Bar now shows a tree view of your home directory. It also has sections for **Computer**, **Trash**, and **File System** and shows those directory structures in a tree view that allows you to select a needed directly quickly and gives a good overview of each of those directory structures.

For now, leave the Side Pane in the tree view because we will use that view in an upcoming section of this chapter.

Behavior Tab

This tab allows configuration of four aspects of Thunar behavior. The first is whether a single- or double-click is required to open a data file or to execute a program file. I suggest leaving this at a double-click. An accidental single-click on a file or directory can produce undesired results. You can try single-click, but it is easy to return to double-click.

The second item here is whether a folder is opened in a new window or as a new tab in the existing Thunar window when selected. I prefer new tabs to help keep the rest of the desktop from getting cluttered with Thunar windows.

Third, transferring files in parallel can make a huge difference in overall speed when moving files from one directory to another or from the home directory to an external USB device. Depending upon the speed of your network connection, it can increase overall transfer speeds there, too. The default setting of "Local Files Only" is the best setting for most users, so don't change this.

I like having the option to permanently delete files and folders without sending them to the Trash bin. So this fourth item, when selected, causes a "Delete" option to be added to the normal context menu when you right-click a file. For now, you should leave this as it is for your own account until you have more experience with Linux and file management with Thunar. Once a file is deleted, it cannot be recovered unless there is a backup. If it goes to Trash, it can be easily copied from Trash to the original directory.

Advanced Tab

This tab should not be changed because it already sets the best options for most users. In this case, it is a really good idea for Thunar to ensure that you really do want to change permissions on a directory.

Volume Management is a term used for managing storage devices when they are connected to the host. It will ask what you want to do when a new device is connected to the computer. You can use the **Configure** link to enable certain things to take place automatically such as to mount an external storage device and burn a CD or DVD when a blank one is inserted into a CD/DVD drive – even though many computers no longer come with those drives installed. It can be configured to automatically play CDs when they are inserted into a CD drive, automatically play files on a "music player," import photos from a camera, and more.

I suggest leaving these options inactive. Having those things start automatically can be the cause of some unexpected results. I prefer to do these things manually without programmatic intervention. Your needs may be different, so you should experiment when you make changes to the Advanced tab to ensure that unexpected results do not occur.

File Management with Thunar

With Thunar configured more to your liking, we can explore file management. For the most part, Thunar can do the same things in its GUI interface that can be done on the command line such as move, copy, and delete files. It does work a bit differently.

If the Preferences dialog is still open, close it now. The Thunar window should be open and your home directory should be the present working directory (PWD). There should be some files in your home directory along with the new Project directory.

Basic Navigation

Navigation around the directory tree is easy, and there are almost always multiple ways to get to the directory you want. Figure 11-3 shows most of these in one way or another.

The Side Pane should show the expanded view of your home directory. You can click any of the directory icons to navigate to that directory.

Before we do that, use the Side Pane to right-click the Public directory now to raise the context menu. The Public directory is an ancient remnant from Unix that is kept around for compatibility purposes in case the Linux host is used in an environment that might take advantage of that Public directory.

In the context menu, click **Create Folder...;** then type the name of the folder, **MyFolder**; and click the Create button. Notice what has happened to the Public icons in the Side Pane and the main window which contains the contents of the PWD. The Side Panel now shows a twisty next to the Public icon, and the main window now shows the ~/student/Public/MyFolder directory as the PWD.

There are four icons to the immediate left of the Location Selector. These icons <,>, ^, and a house are used to perform simple navigation tasks. You can navigate to the previous (<) directory displayed no matter where in the directory tree it exists relative to the PWD. You can go to the Next (>) directory. Use the up (^) icon to navigate to the parent directory of the PWD. And, of course, the house icon always takes you to your home directory.

Any time there is a directory icon in the file list pane, you can double-click that icon to navigate to that directory.

And, of course, you can always use the **Location Selector** to either click a directory button or type in a new directory path.

Selecting Files

Many times it is desirable to perform an operation on multiple files simultaneously, such as moving or deleting them. Selecting a single file is easy; just click it. Selecting multiple files is almost as easy.

To select several files that are listed sequentially in the Thunar window, select the first file in the sequence and then hold down the Shift key. Select the last file in the sequence and click it while holding down the Shift key. All of the files between the two that you clicked will be highlighted. In Figure 11-5, I have used this technique to select the highlighted files.

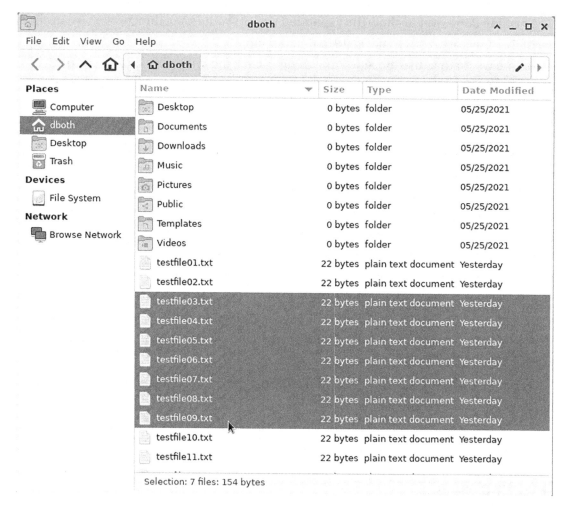

Figure 11-5. *Selecting multiple files in Thunar*

At this point, we can drag these files to move them to a different directory. Go ahead and move the selected files to the Public directory. Point to any space highlighted in blue, left-click, drag until the Public directory is highlighted, and then release the mouse button.

To copy them rather than move them, hold down the Control (Ctrl) key before you click to start the move. Double-click the Public directory to make it the PWD, and select all of the files you just moved there. Then copy them to the home directory by dragging them to the Student directory icon in the Side Pane or to the Student button in the Location Selector. Then drop the files on the Student icon or button.

You could also open a second instance of Thunar on the desktop and navigate to the target directory in that instance. It is then easy to drag files from the first instance to the PWD in the second instance.

Deselecting Files

If you need to deselect all selected files, click any empty space in the file list window. To deselect individual files from a number of selected ones, hold the Control (Ctrl) key down and click the file or files to be deselected.

Using the Context Menu

Locate testfile03.txt and right-click it to display the context menu. Although you may have configured Thunar to look differently than mine, Figure 11-6 shows the List view and the context menu for testfile03.txt.

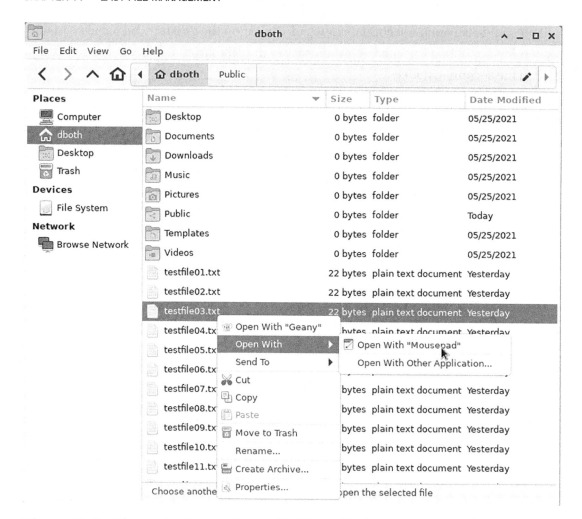

Figure 11-6.   *The context menu for testfile03.txt displays a number of common options for managing a file*

Choose the **Open With** item in the context menu, and select the **Mousepad** text editor. Figure 11-7 shows the file open in the text editor.

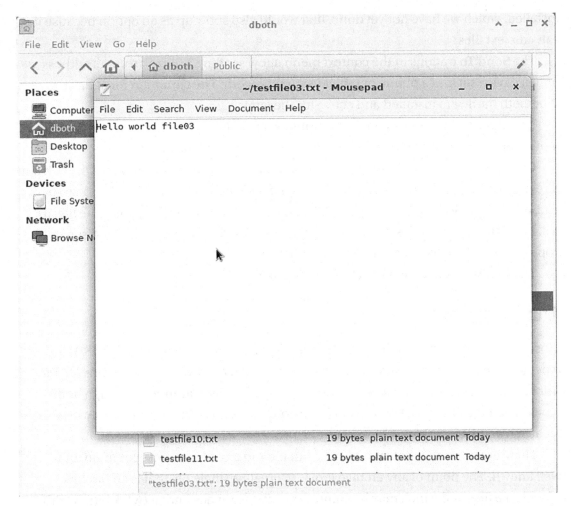

Figure 11-7. *The file testfile03.txt is opened in the Mousepad text editor*

At this point, you could edit this file to change it. Go ahead and add some text to it. It does not matter what it is; just change the file. Save the file using the **Menu bar ➤ File ➤ Save**. Then exit from the editor. If you are using the List view, you will see that the file size has changed.

Back in Figure 11-6, the default option at the top of the context menu will vary depending upon the three-character file name extension. The context menu also shows an option, **Open With**, which lists other programs that could be used to open this file. Hover the mouse over that item to see the other option at this time, Geany, an "Integrated Development Environment" (IDE) which can edit text files that are used as source code for program developers. You probably won't use Geany. If LibreOffice were installed, which we have not yet done, that would also show up as an option because it can edit text files.

The **Send To** options in the context menu allow sending a file to an email address or to a device such as a phone or tablet using Bluetooth. The computer must have Bluetooth hardware installed and active for the latter.

The **Move to Trash** menu item performs as its name implies. You can also highlight one or more files and press the Delete key to move them to Trash.

Copy performs a copy of the entire file, and **Paste** will paste the copy into the current directory (PWD) with a new name such as "testfile03 (copy 1).txt" which does use spaces and special characters. If you select a different directory into which to paste the file, it will have the same name as the original. In both cases, this is an identical and separate copy of the original file and not a link or shortcut.

The **Rename** menu item allows renaming of a file.

Archiving Files

Most of us have received or downloaded zip files. The zip format is an old DOS/Windows type of archive file. A comparable archive file for Linux is the tar file. Tar stands for Tape ARchive which gives you an idea about how long it has been around. Although both types of archive files have been around for a long time, they are still commonly used to create an archive.

There are many types of archive files, but tar and zip are the most common and well known. The point of any archive tool is to create a single file that is an "archive" of multiple files and which may be compressed to save space and network bandwidth when being transferred or downloaded.

The **Create Archive** context menu option is an easy way to create archives such as zip files and tar files of one or more files that you select. However, it is a little tricky because what you see is not exactly what you get during this process.

Start by selecting all of the files in your home directory that have the name pattern file-*.txt so that firstfile.txt and Copy-firstfile.txt are not selected. Hover over any of the selected files and right-click to raise the context menu as shown in Figure 11-8.

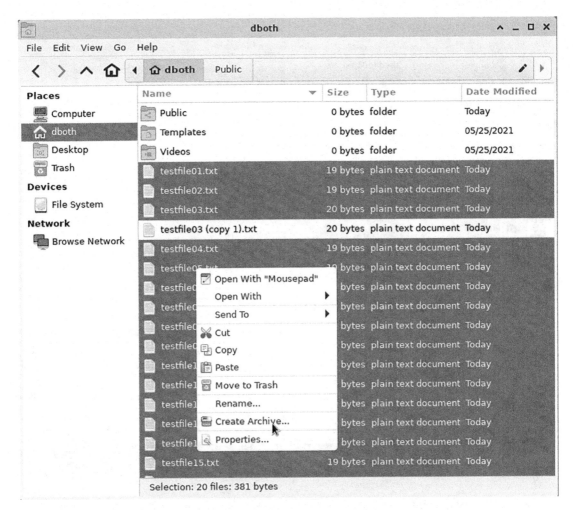

Figure 11-8. *Select files to archive and then right-click any selected file to raise the context menu*

Click the **Create Archive** menu selection to display the **Create a new archive** dialog shown in Figure 11-9. This dialog guides the process of creating and storing the archive. In Figure 11-9, I have already clicked the **Archive type** button. Do this yourself now and scroll down to find and select the **zip** option. This adds a zip extension to the file name in the **Name** text field near the top of the dialog.

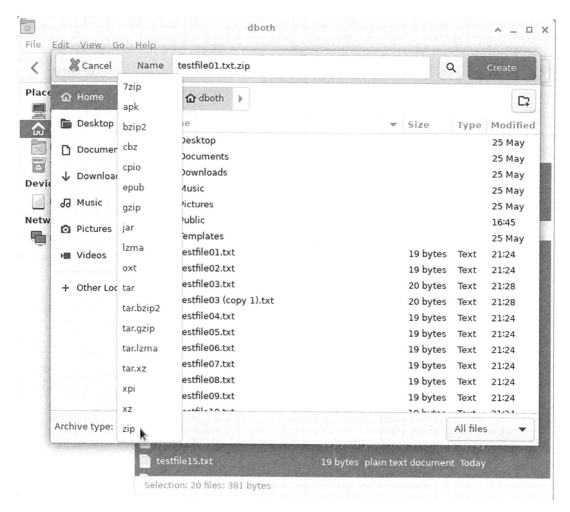

Figure 11-9. *The **Create a new archive** dialog allows selection of the archive file type to create and the location and file name for the archive*

Note that the file list does not show the selected files nor can any additional files be selected in that field. This is what I found confusing the first time I used this method for creating archive files.

Figure 11-10 shows the completed **Create a new archive** dialog. Note that I have changed the name of the archive file that will be created by this process to 2021-10-12-Files.zip. This date format YYYY-MM-DD-<filename> allows files to be automatically sorted sequentially by date when displayed in a file manager or CLI list. Using this file naming convention makes finding files like archives and date-related documents such as credit card or bank statements easy.

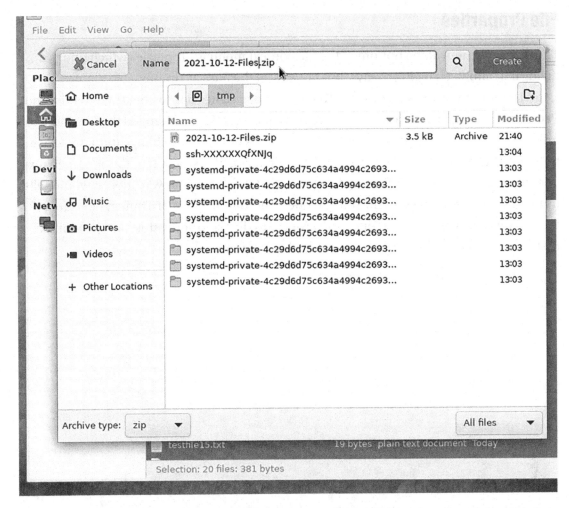

Figure 11-10. *The completed **Create a new archive** dialog showing the revised archive file name and location to store the archive*

To set the /tmp directory location, I first selected the **File System** icon in the Side Pane which listed all of the top-level directories, and then I selected **tmp** from that list.

To create the archive file, click the **Create** button and the **Create a new archive** dialog disappears. It looks like nothing has happened because there is no message to the effect that "The archive has been created." This is in line with the Linux Philosophy of "Silence is golden."

Verify that the archive was created by using Thunar to check the /tmp directory.

File Properties

The last menu item at the bottom of the file context menu is Properties which opens a dialog that allows changing many – but not all – of the file's attributes.

With your home directory as the PWD in Thunar, right-click testfile01.txt to raise the **Properties** dialog. In Figure 11-11, I have done just that. I have changed the file name to testfile01-a.txt in the Name field, but the name does not actually change until the **Close** button is clicked or another tab is selected. This dialog also shows that this is a plain text document based on the .txt file name extension. If the extension were .doc, it would tell us that this is a Word document. You can open another instance of Thunar, navigate to the Documents directory, and open the Properties dialog to verify this. Just remember that these are text files and not actually Word documents.

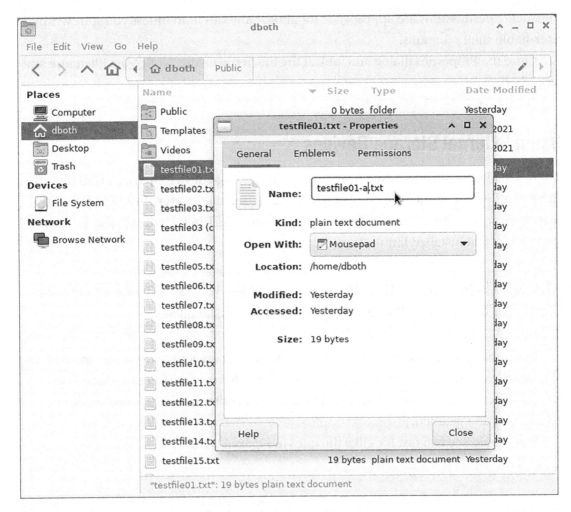

Figure 11-11. *The General tab of the Properties dialog allows changing the name of the file as well as the default application used to open it*

The General tab also shows the location of the file, its size in bytes, the last date it was modified, and the date it was last accessed. "Accessed" means that the file has been viewed using the **cat** command, a text editor, or other tools that can view the contents of the file. For a Word or LibreOffice document, that would be LibreOffice, for example.

The Emblems tab shows a list of icons from which you can choose to replace the default icon. Choose one of those icons; it does not matter which.

The Permissions tab allows you to change the permissions and the group to which the file belongs. It is unlikely that you will need to change anything on this tab. The default file permissions are appropriate for almost any situation unless you start writing executable shell programs.

Close the Properties dialog and look at the file in the listing. Notice the file name and icon change.

Do not close the Thunar dialog yet.

Using External Storage Devices

There will always be times when using an external storage device such as a USB thumb drive or other USB storage device will be useful or even necessary. Most of us have at least several USB thumb drives around, and you have the live USB device you created from which you installed Linux on your computer.

This is an important procedure to know because you will use it to restore the data from your backup USB device onto your new Linux installation.

Insert that live Xfce USB thumb drive into a USB slot on your computer. Figure 11-12 shows that you should see the new device and it should be named Fedora-Xfce-Live-XXXX. The exact sequence of numbers at the end will differ based on which Fedora release you downloaded.

You should see two text files like the ones in Figure 11-12.

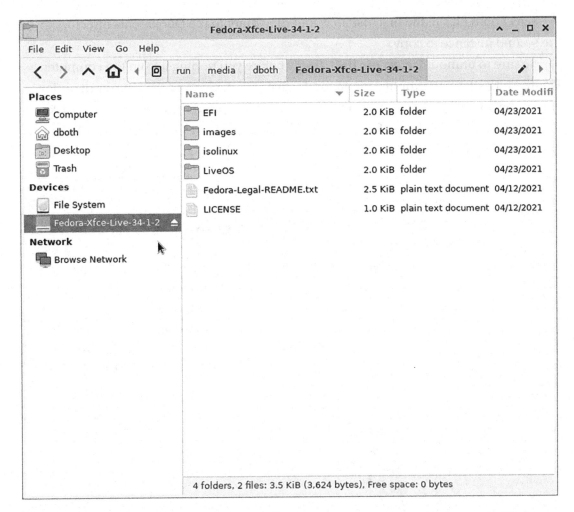

Figure 11-12. *To access an external USB storage device, insert it into a USB slot on your computer and it is automatically mounted*

Assume for learning purposes that you want to copy those two files to the home directory so you won't need to access them on the USB drive in the future. You could open the Student directory tree in the Side Pane, but let's do this a little differently. Open a second instance of Thunar and navigate to the ~/Documents directory in that second instance. Move the two instances on the desktop so that they are both visible. The first instance of Thunar can partially cover the second instance if you do not have a lot of room (real estate) on your display screen. Just be sure that the file list pane is visible in the second instance of Thunar.

Select both files in the first instance, and drag them to the Documents directory in the second instance to copy.

Be sure to unmount/eject the USB device before you unplug it from the computer. Figure 11-13 shows the context menu for the live USB device and the **Unmount** option is near the bottom of the menu. There is also an **Eject** option which is used with diskette drives (there might be a few of these around but not likely) or CD/DVD drives. As its name implies, it unmounts and then physically ejects the disk.

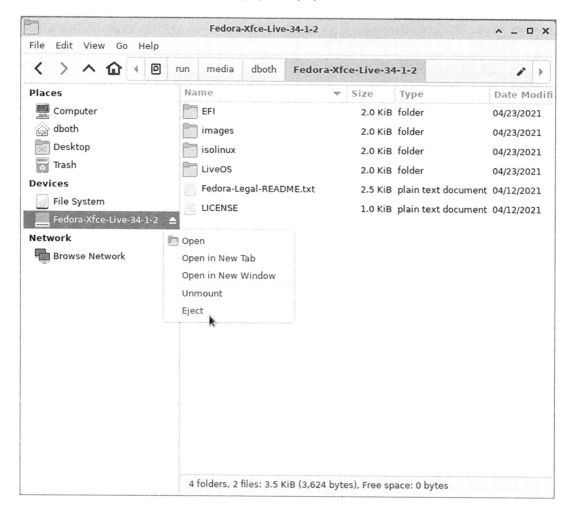

Figure 11-13. *Unmount or eject the USB device*

You can also use the **Eject** button next to the device name in the Devices Side Pane. This button looks like an underlined triangle.

Use any of these choices to unmount the device. Note that the icon on the desktop becomes grayed out and a status message is displayed in the upper right of the display. Once unmounted, you can remove the USB device from the computer.

The Trash Bin

So you have been using the Thunar file manager to move files to the Trash bin. You should use Thunar or the desktop Trash icon to check the Trash bin on a fairly regular basis, daily at best and at least weekly, to determine whether you might have accidentally deleted any files you really want to keep. The Trash bin is just like any other directory. You can move or copy files out of it and back to their appropriate locations.

After you have ensured that the files in the Trash bin are really OK to permanently delete, right-click the Trash icon, either on the desktop or in Thunar, and select **Empty Trash**. The files can no longer be recovered unless they have been backed up.

Your Storage Drive

During the installation process, we instructed Linux to perform all of the tasks necessary to prepare your storage drive or drives for use. If you did that the way we suggested, you should never need to do more maintenance other than to occasionally find and remove the cruft.

Storage Space

If your storage space totals 500GB or more as we suggested before installation of Linux, most of you will never need to add another hard drive or replace the existing one with a new, larger one.

I have been using my home directory for 25 years with Linux and moved another 20 years worth of data to my Linux host when I started using it. My data totals 52GB right now. I do clean out old files from time to time, but I also tend to keep more than I probably need to. I think most of us are like that. My point is that you should have plenty of space in which to store your data.

If your computer has one or more SSD storage devices, they do need some daily or weekly maintenance, but Linux does take care of that automatically. Some people might tell you that you need to perform certain maintenance yourself, but that is not true. Modern operating systems – both Linux and Windows – do that for you.

Storage Device Failures

Storage devices do fail. They usually work fine for years, but hard drives especially fail because they have mechanical moving parts. That is not the only reason they fail, but it is one of the most common.

In the event your HDD or SSD were to fail and you are not familiar with hardware yourself, take your computer to a professional who understands hardware and – if possible – Linux to have it physically replaced. Don't try to do it yourself.

If your professional knows Linux, they can possibly recover the data in your home directory from the old one. If not, they can restore your data from backups.

You could reinstall Linux and restore your data from a backup after the new storage drive is installed if you want to do that yourself or you can't find anyone you trust to do Linux correctly. Just install Linux on the new storage device as we did in Chapter 10. You can copy your files from a backup device just as we will do in Chapter 12 for the migration of files from your old Windows environment.

Cleanup

You no longer need the test files that you created at the beginning of this chapter. Use Thunar to delete all of the files. Use Thunar to delete these files.

You don't need to select them a few at a time. Thunar provides a tool for selecting files using what is called pattern matching. Pattern matching uses special characters * and ? to match portions of file names. This is sometimes called file globbing.

For example, you can specify testfile* which means "match every file name that begins with testfile regardless of how many additional characters there are in its name and what they are." So testfile* matches all of the file names created by the little program we used at the beginning of this chapter. It will not match any other files or directories located in your home directory.

The ? character matches any single character in the specified position. For example, you might want to only select files that start with testfile and the character "1" in the third position of the numeric portion of the file name. So testfile?1* would match all files that begin with "testfile," immediately followed by any single character and then a "1," and can have any number of characters following.

So let's experiment with this on those pesky test files we want to get rid of. Using the Thunar Menu bar, select **Edit ➤ Select by Pattern**. Type in the pattern **testfile?1*** and click the **Select** button. The Thunar dialog should now look like Figure 11-14.

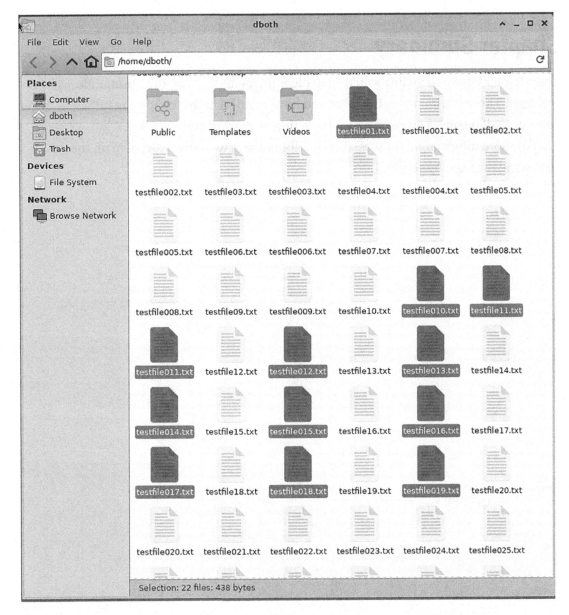

Figure 11-14. *Thunar with files matching the expression **testfile?1*** selected*

Now use the Thunar Menu bar to select **Edit ➤ Select by Pattern**. Type in the pattern **testfile*** and click the **Select** button. This should select all of the test files created earlier. Right-click any of the selected files and select **Move to Trash** from the context menu to delete all of the selected files.

Well, you actually moved them to the Trash folder. Be sure to empty that folder.

Chapter Summary

This chapter has been an introduction to file management using the Thunar file manager. There is a lot more, but what you have learned in this chapter is sufficient to get you – a small business owner who is also acting as a SysAdmin – started.

For more information on files, their attributes, and working with them on the command line, see Appendix 1.

CHAPTER 12

Restoring Your Data

Objectives

In this chapter, you will

- Locate your data on the USB device you used for backup
- Restore your data to your Documents directory
- Organize the restored data

Introduction

The next task you have to do as the SysAdmin is to restore to the computer the data you copied in an earlier chapter.

There are multiple places in which Windows stores your data, and much of it can be on your Windows desktop – which is not really a good place for it. In this chapter, you will copy the directory – the entire directory – that you saved back in Chapter 8. This will ensure that all of your files are there and allow you to organize them.

You should also retain the USB backup device for further assurance in case you later realize you missed something that Windows decided to store in a nonstandard location.

Don't panic – this is easier than you think – all of the tools and procedures to do this were covered in the last few chapters, and we describe this process in plenty of detail in this chapter.

This doesn't need to be performed as the root user; it can and should be done using your regular user account. I will use my dboth account for this to illustrate.

© David Both, Cyndi Bulka 2022
D. Both and C. Bulka, *Linux for Small Business Owners*, https://doi.org/10.1007/978-1-4842-8264-9_12

Restoring Your Files

Insert the USB thumb drive you used for your backup device into a USB slot on your computer. Next, double-click the new icon that appears on the Xfce desktop to open it in the Thunar file manager.

Now double-click the Home folder on your desktop. Then double-click your Documents subdirectory to open it. There should be no files located in your Documents directory.

Arrange the instances of Thunar so that you can see both of them – especially the Documents subdirectory in your home directory in the second instance. Your desktop should look similar to what mine does in Figure 12-1. Hopefully, you have more screen real estate than I do because I want to keep it small enough to print the whole desktop here while maintaining some level of readability.

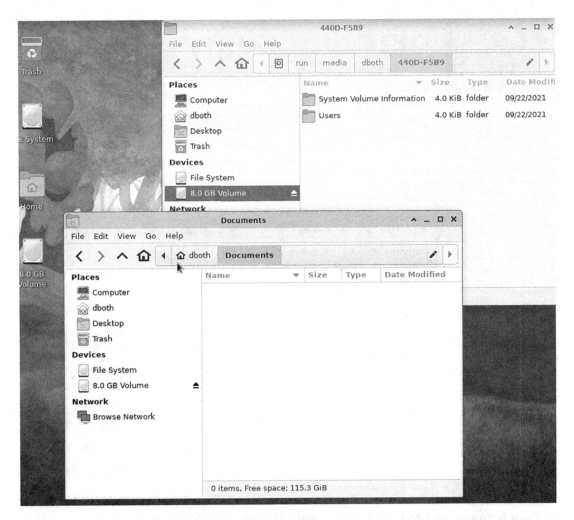

Figure 12-1. *The desktop with two instances of Thunar open and ready to copy the Users subdirectory to your Documents subdirectory*

Now drag the Users directory to the Documents directory. You can drop it anywhere in the whitespace on the right side of the target window. The Progress dialog is displayed as shown in Figure 12-2, and will provide you with a semi-accurate estimate of the amount of time needed to complete the copy.

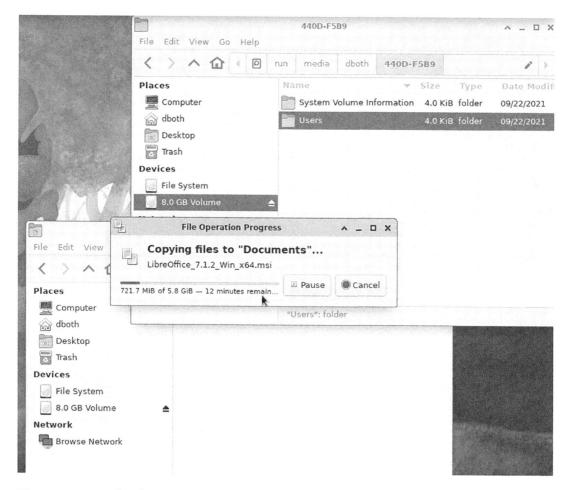

Figure 12-2. *The directory containing your backup data files – and a lot of other stuff – is being copied to the /home/dboth/Documents directory*

When the Progress dialog disappears, the copy is complete. Click the **Eject** button next to the USB device in the Devices section of either Thunar instance. This will remove the USB drive from both instances of Thunar and return the source instance of Thunar to your home directory. Be sure to physically remove the USB device from your computer.

Leave both instances of Thunar open.

Organizing Your Files

Remember that our strategy was to copy everything in the Users directory to ensure that no important data files were missed. It is easy to miss some of your data files because

Windows and some application programs store them in strange, nonstandard places. Besides that, Windows and Windows applications store huge numbers of executable files and dynamic link libraries (dll's) in what should be strictly user data storage. You'll need to sort through all of the nonessential stuff that is not needed by Linux to locate your data and move it into one or more subdirectories in the Documents directory.

With everything copied over in this manner, it ensures that all of your data has been restored – although it may take some deep exploration and a decent strategy to find all of them.

A Strategy

The strategy I like to use is to locate my data files and move them to some sort of temporary staging area just to get them out of the Users directory structure. I can further sort them into whatever categories I want later. This is just to find them all and get them into a space where I can make sense of them.

During this process, I also delete all files that are not my data documents and that Linux cannot use. These generally end in the extensions exe, dll, ini, and others and do not need to be restored. You should look for Office files with extensions of doc, docx, xls, xlsx, and pdf, to restore. Other applications will use other file name extensions that you need to restore. Northern Michigan University has a good list of the most common file name extensions as well as an explanation of file name syntax.[1]

As I empty out the directories or at least determine that there are no usable files in them, I delete them. This includes the entire directory and all unneeded files contained in it.

Doing It

Start by creating a new subdirectory in your Documents directory. One instance of Thunar should already be open to the Documents directory with the Users subdirectory there. Right-click anywhere on whitespace in the Documents directory pane of Thunar. This will open a context menu that has Create Folder as the top option. You can see this in Figure 12-3.

---

[1] IT Services, Northern Michigan University, "Common Windows file extensions," https://it.nmu.edu/docs/common-windows-file-extensions

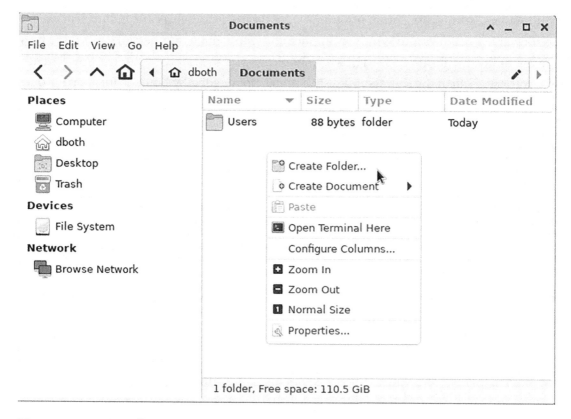

Figure 12-3. *Use the Context menu to create a temporary folder to which you can copy all of the valid data from the Users directory*

Click **Create Folder...** and type the name of the new folder. I use the name **MigratedData** to easily identify its contents.

Set up your two Thunar instances so that one is open to the MigratedData as the PWD and the other is open to the Users directory as the PWD. Your desktop should now look similar to Figure 12-4.

You can start your cleanup by deleting the desktop.ini file shown in Figure 12-4 as it is not needed. Just click the desktop.ini file to highlight it, and press the **Delete** key which moves the file to the Trash bin or use the context menu to move the file to the Trash.

Or if you added the Permanently Delete option to the context menu when you configured Thunar in Chapter 11, you can choose **Delete** instead of **Move to Trash**. Thunar does display a warning message to give you a moment to think about whether you really want to permanently delete those files or not.

Files that are deleted are not recoverable. You still have the USB device on which your backups reside. Be careful about deleting data files vs. moving them to Trash.

I also installed the Cygnus Server on my Windows host. Cygnus is a collection of tools that work like their Linux counterparts and which made it easier for me to manage the host while it had Windows on it. This directory is now irrelevant, so I can delete it and all of its contents along with the desktop.ini file.

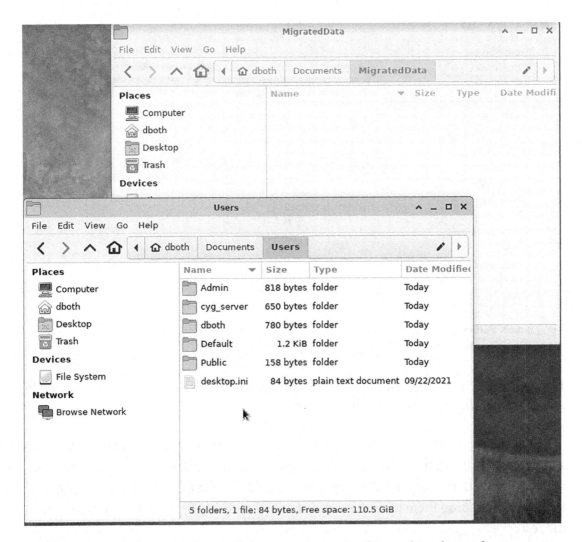

Figure 12-4. *With your Thunar instances open similar to that shown here, you are ready to start moving your data into the new MigratedData directory. Data and directories that are not needed can be deleted without moving them*

Use the Menu bar View menu to place the Side Pane into tree mode to provide an overview of the structure of the Users directory tree in Figure 12-5. I then started by deleting the desktop.ini file and the cyg_server directory as you can see in Figure 12-5. I no longer need to deal with them, so I deleted them and you should, too.

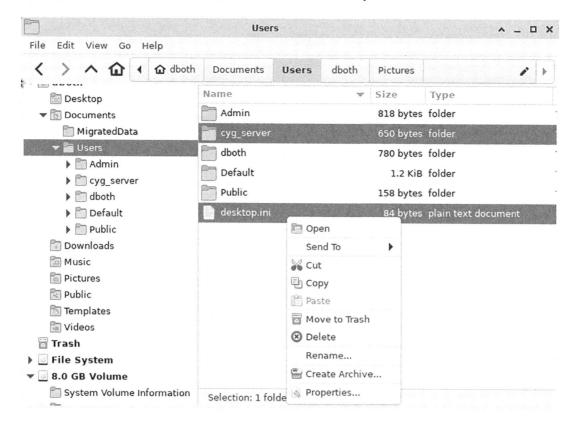

Figure 12-5. *Delete files and directories you know are no longer needed to make it easier to find those that need to be migrated*

Click the Public directory to expand the tree for that directory. Then click each subdirectory of the Public directory to verify that there are no data files you need to save in any of them. If there are any files and directories that need to be migrated, highlight them and then move them to the instance of Thunar titled "MigratedData." Delete the rest.

While you will be most concerned with your own data directory, it is important to check the other directories shown in Figure 12-5. Take some time to explore the Default and Public directories to verify that there are no data files stored there that you might need. You may have a number of different directories in this and other locations that are simply not needed. You will need to thoroughly explore the Users directory tree to find and delete them.

Figure 12-6 shows the Users/Public/Desktop directory which contains files that appeared on the Windows desktop for all users. The *.lnk files are links – shortcuts – and there are also some PDF files. The files in this directory appear on every user's desktop on the Windows computer.

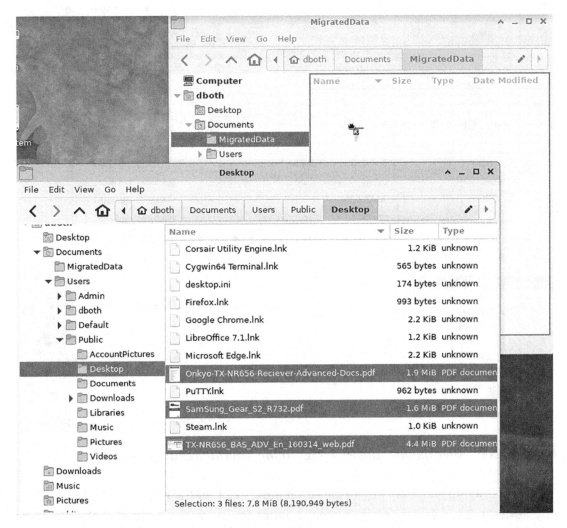

Figure 12-6. *The Users/Public/Desktop directory contains files that appeared on your Windows desktop. The *.lnk files are links – shortcuts – and there are also some PDF files*

In Figure 12-7, the PDF files have now been moved to the MigratedData folder. After migrating all of the needed files from Users/Public/Desktop, delete the Users/Public/Desktop directory so that it will no longer be cluttering up the new directory.

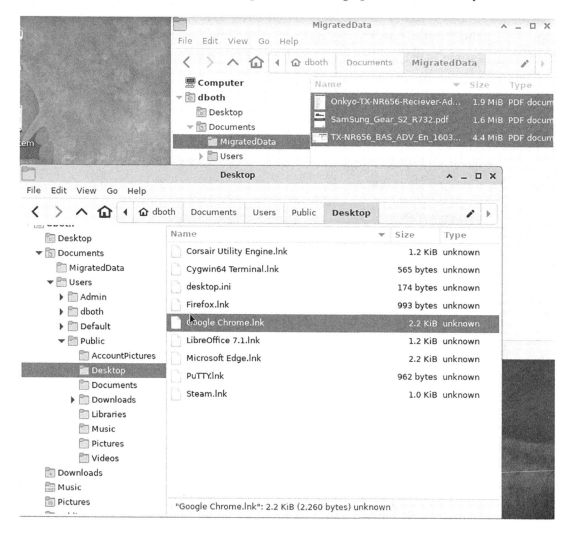

Figure 12-7. *After moving the PDF files to the MigratedData folder*

After verifying that there are no files remaining in either the Public or Default directories that you want to save, delete the entire directory tree. Right-click the directory icons and choose **Delete** or **Move to Trash** from the context menu.

The directories in which you are most likely to find your documents and other important files are in your own Users subdirectory. Use the same strategy to migrate your data files from your own Users directory to the MigratedData directory.

After migrating all of your data files, you can delete the Users directory and all files remaining in it.

Remember to label and save the USB device you used as the intermediate storage device for transferring your data from the Windows environment to your Linux home directory. That way if you missed something the USB device will always be a last resort backup of your data files as they existed on the Windows version of your computer.

Cleanup – Empty the Trash

Since you have probably moved a number of files to the Trash bin, the files are still there, so the storage space has not yet been reclaimed. You can take this opportunity to look through the Trash bin and recover any files that you think should not be discarded. Open the icon on the desktop just as you would any other folder. This opens Thunar, so you can look around. After verifying that there are no files you might need in the Trash, close this instance of Thunar.

Right-click the Trash bin and select Empty Trash from the context menu.

Organization

All of your data files are now easily accessible in the MigratedData directory. Take your time organizing those files into whatever structure makes sense to you. You can do this a little at a time so that the task does not seem so daunting if you have a large number of files.

If you need to work with one or two financial files, you could create a new directory, say, /home/<your ID>/Financial, and then move those files into that directory.

In the past, I have done this and found after many months I did not need many of those old data files that I thought were so important. I did not delete those files right away. For old financial files, for one example, I created the /home/<your ID>/Financial/Archive directory and moved those old files into it. In this way, I still have the files, but am aware that they are old and probably no longer needed due to their location in the Archive directory.

This is just one approach to organizing files. It may make sense for you to do it another way. Just use the strategy that works best for you.

Chapter Summary

Your data files have now been restored to your Fedora system! You've successfully extracted them from the Windows directory mess, and now they are easier to find.

You're ready to start the process of sorting and organizing your data files into additional subdirectories by whatever criteria and strategy works best for you.

You now have a fully functional Fedora computer.

CHAPTER 13

Software Management

Objectives

After reading this chapter, you will be able to

- Describe the tasks involved in software management

- State why you should always use the Fedora tools and repositories

- Disable dnfdragora, a low-quality software management tool with significant problems

- Search for application software and tools using dnf command

- Install and connect with additional supported repositories

- Install new software

- Remove unneeded software

Introduction

Updating existing software and finding and installing new software are important parts of administering your own computers. As a small business owner, you will undoubtedly encounter times when you need some software that may not have been included in the default installation. It's critically important to install updates when they become available in order to ensure that Fedora has all of the latest security fixes as well as functional bug fixes and feature upgrades.

195

© David Both, Cyndi Bulka 2022
D. Both and C. Bulka, *Linux for Small Business Owners*, https://doi.org/10.1007/978-1-4842-8264-9_13

This chapter looks at the use of the official Fedora software repositories (repos) which contain thousands of software tools and applications. We'll look at the installation and use of two additional repositories that contain software that is not included in the official Fedora repos. These are supported repositories, and the software is of the same high quality in addition to being open source.

DNFDragora

The dnfdragora tool, more specifically the dnfdragora-updater, is a graphical extension of the DNF command-line tool. The Xfce top panel displays an icon for the dnfdragora-updater applet that appears near the right side. This tool provides a graphical interface that allows you to install new programs, delete ones no longer needed, and install functional and security fixes (updates) for the software that is currently installed.

The dnfdragora-updater applet uses the two icons shown in Figure 13-1 as a means of indicating the availability of updates. The icon on the left is shades of orange and indicates that updates are available to be installed. The icon on the right is red with a white box in it and indicates that there are no updates available.

Figure 13-1. *The two dnfdragora applet icons indicate the availability of updates – or not*

DNFDragora Issues

Unfortunately, DNFDragora has some very serious problems. I have checked with some friends who are system administrators, developers, and writers for Opensource.com, and they have also had bad experiences with DNFDragora. It is unstable, has performance issues, and can completely lock up and is not worth using.

So we're not going to use that tool.

Deactivating DNFDragora

There are two steps required to deactivate DNFDragora. First, you remove it from panel 1. Right- or left-click the DNFDragora icon in the panel. The context menu shown in Figure 13-2 is displayed. Left-click the **Exit** selection to terminate the running DNFDragora program.

Figure 13-2. *Click* ***Exit*** *on the DNFDragora context menu to terminate the program*

The second step is to prevent DNFDragora from restarting the next time you log in. Using the Applications menu, open the **Applications ➤ Settings ➤ Session and Startup** dialog. You could also open the **Applications ➤ Settings ➤ Settings Manager** and then the **Session and Startup** dialog.

Remove the check mark from the **dnfdragora-updater** application shown in Figure 13-3 to prevent it from starting every time you log in.

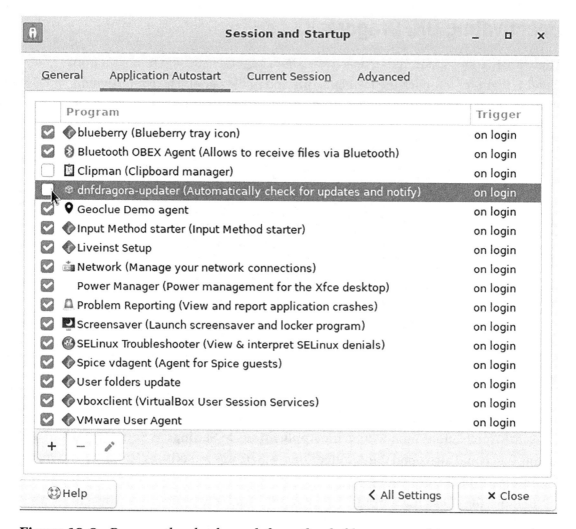

Figure 13-3. *Remove the check mark from the dnfdragora-updater to prevent it from starting when you log in*

Click the **Close** button to close this dialog.

RPMs

All software available from the Fedora Project is packaged in files called RPMs. RPM stands for "Red Hat Package Management" which is a system for managing installation and maintenance of software. RPM files are also called packages, and they have the "rpm" file name extension.

Each RPM package contains all of the files and instructions required to install the software contained in it. Each package also contains a list of other packages upon which it is dependent. This makes it easy for advanced tools to perform all the work of finding and installing those dependencies for us.

Many companies and developers package their applications in RPM format so that they can be easily installed on Red Hat and Fedora.

Repositories

All of the RPM packages required to install and maintain Fedora are located in secure official repositories (repos) at the Fedora Project[1] on the Internet. The Fedora Project maintains multiple repositories for each release of Fedora, and each repository serves a specific purpose.[2] Understanding this can save some confusion when installing new software.

There is one set of main repositories on the Internet, but there are many mirrors around the world so that the main ones are not overloaded.

There are only two Fedora repositories for each release that are of concern to users such as ourselves, and they are already configured properly, so there is nothing we need to do to make this work properly.

The fedora Repository

The fedora (yes – lowercase) repository is used to store all of the packages that make up the Fedora distribution. The packages are placed into this repository in a separate directory for each new release and made available to the world from there.

This repository never changes regardless of updates and changes to any of the packages contained in it. This repository represents a snapshot of all the software that makes up Fedora at the moment of its release.

---

[1] Fedora Project, `https://fedoraproject.org/wiki/Fedora_Project_Wiki`
[2] Fedora Project, "Repositories," `https://docs.fedoraproject.org/en-US/quick-docs/repositories/`

The updates Repository

The updates repository is used to store the most recent version of each package that has had any updates, fixes, or changes. These updates can include fixes that are merely functional, changes that add new features, or security updates that are needed to fully protect the Fedora system.

How It Works

Immediately after installing Fedora from the live USB, you'll need to install all of the available updates. The tool, called DNF, checks the updates repository for updates to the packages installed on your computer and installs any that are required. This will happen whenever you initiate updates.

Using the DNF tool, you can install an entire office suite, a word processor, accounting software, or even games. Select the software to install and initiate the process. The DNF tool checks the both repositories and lists the most recent and up-to-date package in either of them.

Together, the fedora and update repos represent the most current and stable release of Fedora. This ensures that you always have the most current software installed on your computer.

DNF

The DNF[3] facility is a powerful command-line tool that provides for management of RPM packages from remote repositories like the Fedora ones and deals with dependencies as required. DNF's handling of dependencies includes the ability to recursively determine all dependencies that might prevent the target package from being installed and to fulfill them. For example, if the target package has 25 packages on which it depends, DNF will identify them all, determine whether they are already installed, and mark them for installation if they are not. It will check those dependencies for further dependencies and mark them for installation. It will continue to recurse through all newly marked packages until no further dependencies are found. It then downloads all of the marked packages and installs them.

---

[3] Wikipedia, "DNF," https://en.wikipedia.org/wiki/DNF_(software)

DNF can install and remove packages. It can also install updates and provide us with information about installed packages and packages that are available in the repositories and which have not been installed. DNF allows packages that have been signed to be automatically checked to prevent counterfeit packages from installing malware on your Fedora system.

DNF automatically downloads the GPG signing keys from the configured repositories and checks the RPM packages for authenticity after they are downloaded and before they are installed. This helps to prevent counterfeit packages from being installed and significantly improves the security of installing software from the Fedora repositories.

Although many Linux tool names have some meaning, DNF officially stands for nothing.

Updates

After any new installation of Fedora, there are always updates to install, so this is the first task we will perform. This usually consists of one or more updated RPM packages that contain bug fixes, security fixes, documentation updates, and sometimes software version upgrades.

The number of updates that are available will vary widely depending upon how new the ISO image is and how many updates have been released since the ISO was created.

This procedure does not install a complete upgrade from one release of Fedora to another, such as from Fedora 34 to Fedora 35. It only installs updates to the current release of Fedora. We'll cover upgrades to new Fedora releases in Chapter 15.

Update Philosophy – Windows vs. Linux

There is a significant difference between the Windows and Linux update philosophies.

Force

Most of us have seen people in the middle of a presentation or trying to start a presentation but had to wait for updates to complete. And many of you have experienced having to wait for Windows updates to install before beginning work or when trying to shut down at the end of the day. I have seen customer kiosks at gas stations, gyms, and large organizations' front lobbies stuck seemingly forever in the BSOU – the blue screen of updates – which is very much like the BSOD, the blue screen of death. Both mean that you can't get any work done.

We discussed the reason for the Windows design philosophy back in Chapter 1. The bottom line of that philosophy is that users are afraid of computers and want as little to do with them as possible. That philosophy extends to performing updates by assuming that users will keep putting them off as long as possible. Although this can be true, in my experience, it seems to be more about the organizationally inevitable resistance to any change whatsoever – the "if it ain't broke, don't fix it" style of system maintenance, which, by the way, never works for computers.

Microsoft decides what is best for you and uses some seemingly random process to determine that *RIGHT NOW* is the time your updates *MUST* be installed regardless of whatever else you are trying to do.

Linux will never force your computers to install updates no matter how long it's been since the last updates were installed or how many are lined up in the queue. *You* get to choose.

It's critically important that security updates be installed as soon as they become available. Other updates should be installed as quickly as possible, too, although not installing non-security updates won't leave your system vulnerable to attacks by crackers.

The Update Stream

Another important philosophical difference is the availability of updates.

Microsoft (MS) usually releases all of its updates once a month on what is typically called "Patch Tuesday.[4]" For various reasons, this once-a-month approach can leave Windows systems open to attack against security vulnerabilities that have not been fixed. The length of time that those systems are vulnerable could range up to a month *after* the patch is available.

Linux, on the other hand, releases update patches as soon as they are ready. So we have a constant stream of fixes for Linux as opposed to weekly at best, semimonthly, or monthly for Windows. Because Linux updates become available as soon as they are ready, it has happened that new updates became available within minutes of my finishing previous updates.

Linux gives you choices – a choice of when to perform updates and a choice of when to reboot. This puts *you* in control.

---

[4]Wikipedia, "Patch Tuesday," https://en.wikipedia.org/wiki/Patch_Tuesday

Checking for Updates

I check frequently to see whether any updates are available, usually every day.
I determine the types of updates that are available because that informs me whether or
not a reboot is required. It is time for you to do your first update, so start there.

Open a terminal session and switch user to root. Then use the command
dnf check-update to list all available updates. The first column is the package name, the
second is the version and Fedora release, and the last column is the repository in which
the update is found. I have cut out large portions of the output to save space.

```
dboth@mycomputer ~]$ su -
Password: <Enter the root password>
[root@mycomputer ~]# dnf check-update
Last metadata expiration check: 1:58:22 ago on Mon 08 Nov 2021
05:37:11 AM EST.

NetworkManager-l2tp.x86_64                  1.20.0-1.fc34       updates
NetworkManager-l2tp-gnome.x86_64            1.20.0-1.fc34       updates
<SNIP>
kernel.x86_64                               5.14.16-201.fc34    updates
kernel-core.x86_64                          5.14.16-201.fc34    updates
kernel-modules.x86_64                       5.14.16-201.fc34    updates
kernel-modules-extra.x86_64                 5.14.16-201.fc34    updates
<SNIP>
samba-common-libs.x86_64                    2:4.14.9-0.fc34     updates
selinux-policy.noarch                       34.22-1.fc34        updates
selinux-policy-targeted.noarch              34.22-1.fc34        updates
spice-vdagent.x86_64                        0.21.0-4.fc34       updates
strongswan.x86_64                           5.9.4-1.fc34        updates
strongswan-charon-nm.x86_64                 5.9.4-1.fc34        updates
unicode-ucd.noarch                          14.0.0-1.fc34       updates
virtualbox-guest-additions.x86_64           6.1.28-1.fc34       updates
webkit2gtk3.x86_64                          2.34.1-1.fc34       updates
webkit2gtk3-jsc.x86_64                      2.34.1-1.fc34       updates
[root@mycomputer ~]#
```

You can see there is an update to the kernel in the preceding list which is one of the circumstances that require a reboot after the updates are installed. Other packages that will necessitate that you perform a reboot when they are updated are systemd and glibc.

The next command shows you a summary of the various types of fixes. In this case, there are four security notices, one of which is critical. There are 13 bug fixes and some enhancements as well.

```
[root@mycomputer ~]# dnf updateinfo
Last metadata expiration check: 2:05:57 ago on Mon 08 Nov 2021
05:37:11 AM EST.
Updates Information Summary: available
    4 Security notice(s)
        1 Critical Security notice(s)
        1 Important Security notice(s)
        1 Moderate Security notice(s)
        1 Low Security notice(s)
   13 Bugfix notice(s)
    4 Enhancement notice(s)
    1 other notice(s)
[root@mycomputer ~]#
```

Tip   The number of updates listed by the **dnf check-update** command will not be the same as those summarized by the **dnf updateinfo** command. The **dnf check-update** command lists all packages that are currently installed on your host that have updates available. The **dnf updateinfo** command is only a summary of the updates that have notices. Many updates do not have any type of notice associated with them so they do not appear in the summary.

This next command provides more detailed information by listing all packages that have a notice of some type associated with them along with the type of update:

```
[root@mycomputer ~]# dnf list-updateinfo
Last metadata expiration check: 2:22:12 ago on Mon 08 Nov 2021 05:37:11 AM
EST.
FEDORA-2021-09d25b60dd enhancement    NetworkManager-l2tp-1.20.0-1.fc34.x8
6_64
<SNIP>
FEDORA-2021-bdd146e463 Important/Sec. kernel-5.14.16-201.fc34.x86_64
FEDORA-2021-bdd146e463 Important/Sec. kernel-core-5.14.16-201.fc34.x86_64
FEDORA-2021-bdd146e463 Important/Sec. kernel-modules-5.14.16-201.fc34.x86_64
FEDORA-2021-bdd146e463 Important/Sec. kernel-modules-extra-5.14.16-201.fc3
4.x86_64
FEDORA-2021-49a33e790f bugfix         pipewire-0.3.39-1.fc34.x86_64
FEDORA-2021-49a33e790f bugfix         pipewire-alsa-0.3.39-1.fc34.x86_64
FEDORA-2021-49a33e790f bugfix         pipewire-gstreamer-0.3.39-1.fc34.x86
```

Your list of available updates will probably be different from mine. You now know that updates are available, which ones are security or bug fixes, and about how many there are in total.

Installing Updates

The task of installing the updates is just as easy – a single command. I have reduced the font size and snipped out thousands of lines of the output data stream from this command to give you a more comprehensive view of the sections in this data.

```
[root@mycomputer ~]# dnf -y update
Last metadata expiration check: 0:01:46 ago on Wed 10 Nov 2021
08:42:32 AM EST.
Dependencies resolved.
```

```
================================================================================
Package                              Arch    Version
            Repository               Size
================================================================================
Installing:
 kernel                               x86_64  5.14.16-201.fc34
            updates                  66 k
 kernel-modules                       x86_64  5.14.16-201.fc34
            updates                  32 M
 kernel-modules-extra                 x86_64  5.14.16-201.fc34
            updates                  2.0 M
Upgrading:
 ModemManager                         x86_64  1.16.8-4.fc34
            updates                  1.0 M
 ModemManager-glib                    x86_64  1.16.8-4.fc34
            updates                  277 k
 NetworkManager                       x86_64  1:1.30.6-1.fc34
            updates                  2.3 M
 NetworkManager-adsl                  x86_64  1:1.30.6-1.fc34
            updates                  26 k
 NetworkManager-bluetooth             x86_64  1:1.30.6-1.fc34
            updates                  52 k
 <SNIP>
 mozilla-openh264                     x86_64  2.1.1-2.fc34
            fedora-cisco-openh264     432 k
 python3-simpleaudio                  x86_64  1.0.4-3.fc34
            fedora                   1.8 M
 tpm2-tools                           x86_64  5.1.1-1.fc34
            updates                  722 k

Transaction Summary
================================================================================
Install   38 Packages
Upgrade  647 Packages
```

This command first lists all of the packages being installed or updated. Note that the kernel packages are installed rather than updated. This is intended to allow you to boot to an older kernel if a new one fails for some reason. I have had this occur, so this is a good option to have. The Fedora boot menu allows you to select one of these older kernels, but the newest is the default. This section ends with a summary.

The second section of this output lists each upgrade package as it is being downloaded, and it shows a progress bar on the screen for each package:

```
Total download size: 973 M
Downloading Packages:
(1/685): PackageKit-1.2.4-2.fc34.x86_64.rpm      1.8 MB/s | 601 kB      00:00
(2/685): ghostscript-tools-fonts-9.55.0-1.fc34.  467 kB/s |  12 kB      00:00
(3/685): ghostscript-tools-printing-9.55.0-1.fc  365 kB/s |  12 kB      00:00
<SNIP>
(10/685): kernel-5.14.16-201.fc34.x86_64.rpm      2.3 MB/s |  66 kB      00:00
(11/685): kernel-modules-5.14.16-201.fc34.x86_6   25 MB/s |  32 MB      00:01
<SNIP>
(685/685): zram-generator-defaults-1.0.1-2.fc34  153 kB/s | 9.1 kB      00:00
-----------------------------------------------------------------------------
Total                                             33 MB/s | 973 MB      00:29
```

This next section shows the progress of the actual upgrade:

```
Running transaction check
Transaction check succeeded.
Running transaction test
Transaction test succeeded.
Running transaction
  Running scriptlet: selinux-policy-targeted-34.22-1.fc34.noarch          1/1
  Running scriptlet: firefox-94.0-1.fc34.x86_64                           1/1
  Running scriptlet: alsa-sof-firmware-1.9-1.fc34.noarch                  1/1
  Preparing        :                                                      1/1
  Upgrading        : libgcc-11.2.1-1.fc34.x86_64                       1/1335
  Running scriptlet: libgcc-11.2.1-1.fc34.x86_64                       1/1335
  Upgrading        : linux-firmware-whence-20210919-125.fc34.noarch   2/1335
<SNIP>
```

```
Verifying          : zram-generator-1.0.1-2.fc34.x86_64                  1332/1335
Verifying          : zram-generator-0.3.2-3.fc34.x86_64                  1333/1335
Verifying          : zram-generator-defaults-1.0.1-2.fc34.noarch         1334/1335
Verifying          : zram-generator-defaults-0.3.2-3.fc34.noarch         1335/1335
Upgraded:
  ModemManager-1.16.8-4.fc34.x86_64
  ModemManager-glib-1.16.8-4.fc34.x86_64
  NetworkManager-1:1.30.6-1.fc34.x86_64
  NetworkManager-adsl-1:1.30.6-1.fc34.x86_64
  NetworkManager-bluetooth-1:1.30.6-1.fc34.x86_64
<SNIP>
  zram-generator-defaults-1.0.1-2.fc34.noarch
Installed:
<SNIP>
  kernel-5.14.16-201.fc34.x86_64
  kernel-core-5.14.16-201.fc34.x86_64
  kernel-modules-5.14.16-201.fc34.x86_64
  kernel-modules-extra-5.14.16-201.fc34.x86_64
  libcloudproviders-0.3.1-3.fc34.x86_64
<SNIP>
  xlsfonts-1.0.6-2.fc34.x86_64
  xprop-1.2.3-2.fc34.x86_64
  xvinfo-1.1.3-2.fc34.x86_64
  xwininfo-1.1.5-2.fc34.x86_64
Complete!
```

This is a lot of data despite the fact that I have cut out large portions, but this gives you a good idea of what to expect. The upgrade process can take from 15 or 20 minutes to a couple hours depending upon the speed of your Internet connection and the speed of your computer.

I strongly recommended that you close all running applications and do not use it until the update is complete.

Rebooting After Updates

Now that the updates have been installed, reboot your computer so that some of the new packages like the kernel and some others can take effect. The old kernel and other system-level software will continue to be used until the computer is rebooted.

Although you have the choice of when to perform the reboot after doing an update, you should still reboot the computer as soon after installing updates as possible to ensure the greatest level of security and system stability:

```
[root@testvm1 ~]# reboot
```

After rebooting, your computer is fully updated and ready to work.

Installing New Software

Installing new software is the first thing most of us do after installing Linux on a new system. Most of the software we will use in our daily tasks needs to be installed after the initial installation of the operating system.

GnuCash

Let's install some useful software. Most businesses need accounting software, and even if you do not plan to use accounting software, this is a good illustrative exercise.

I have used GnuCash for both personal and business use for over 20 years. It is stable and well supported with updates and occasional new features. All 20 years of my data is still immediately available and easily accessible. GnuCash is easy to use, looks and works using standard accounting double-entry procedures. It can produce a number of standard accounting reports such as trial balance, profit and loss, and income and expense reports as well as custom reports that you can design or download.

Searching for Software

Since you likely won't know the names of specific software to begin with, you can start with a general search for accounting and personal finance software. The Fedora repositories provide several options for this type of software – you just need to find it.

Enter the following command to locate all packages that contain the word "finance." The gnucash package is listed among the results.

```
[root@testvm1 ~]# dnf search finance
Last metadata expiration check: 3:18:43 ago on Mon 15 Nov 2021
08:50:47 AM EST.
===================== Name & Summary Matched: finance ====================
perl-Finance-YahooQuote.noarch : Perl interface to get stock quotes from
Yahoo! Finance
python3-yfinance.noarch : Yahoo! Finance market data downloader
===================== Name Matched: finance ==============================
perl-Finance-Quote.noarch : A Perl module that retrieves stock and mutual
fund quotes
sugar-finance.noarch : Financial planning for Sugar
===================== Summary Matched: finance ===========================
QuantLib.i686 : A software framework for quantitative finance
QuantLib.x86_64 : A software framework for quantitative finance
gnucash.x86_64 : Finance management application
gnucash-docs.noarch : Help files and documentation for the GnuCash personal
finance manager
grisbi.x86_64 : Personal finances manager
kmymoney.x86_64 : Personal finance
skrooge.x86_64 : Personal finances manager
[root@testvm1 ~]#
```

This command results in three sections of output. First is a list of all packages
in which the search term "finance" was found in both the package name and in the
description. Next is a section listing matches that only occurred in the package name,
and the third section lists matches found in the summary section of the package. Also,
try the search command using the term "accounting" just to see what you get.

Before you install the GnuCash financial software, use this next command to view
the complete description and summary of the software, along with some additional
useful information:

```
[root@testvm1 ~]# dnf info gnucash
Last metadata expiration check: 3:41:28 ago on Mon 15 Nov 2021
08:50:47 AM EST.
Available Packages
Name        : gnucash
```

```
Version      : 4.6
Release      : 2.fc34
Architecture : x86_64
Size         : 11 M
Source       : gnucash-4.6-2.fc34.src.rpm
Repository   : updates
Summary      : Finance management application
URL          : https://gnucash.org/
License      : GPLv2+
Description  : GnuCash is a personal finance manager. A check-book like
               register GUI
             : allows you to enter and track bank accounts, stocks, income
               and even
             : currency trades. The interface is designed to be simple
               and easy to
             : use, but is backed with double-entry accounting principles
               to ensure
             : balanced books.
```

To install GnuCash, just use the following command:

[root@testvm1 ~]# **dnf -y install gnucash**

The DNF tool will download the required files and install them. GnuCash will also be added to the application launcher. Click **Applications ➤ Office**.

Tip   Did you notice that a reboot was not required? Installing new software for Linux does not require a reboot.

Program and Package Names

You may have noticed in the dnf search list results earlier that the package names usually have some numbers attached to them. These are version and release numbers that help identify the newest releases. Those numbers are used by DNF to determine which packages need updates. An installed package with a lower number than an available package needs to be updated with the available package because it is newer.

Another bit of information you can see is related to the architecture of the package. Older computers are 32 bits and use i686 packages. Newer computers are 64 bits and use the x86_64 packages. Some packages are designated as noarch, which means that they can be used in either 64- or 32-bit environments. Any modern computer you purchase will be 64 bits. Only very old computers would be 32 bits.

When installing software, just use the package name and DNF will automatically install the latest version and the correct architecture. If you have any question about the name to use when entering the dnf install command, you can first use the dnf info command. The Name field is exactly what you need to use. The DNF command will do the rest for you.

About Groups

There are many complex software systems that require many packages – sometimes hundreds – to be fully complete. LibreOffice, for example. It is a large and complex software system rather than a single program. It requires many separate packages to be fully functional.

DNF has a "group" capability that allows packagers to define all of the individual packages that are required to create a fully functional system such as a desktop like Xfce or LXDE, LibreOffice, educational software, electronic lab, Python classroom, and more.

However, many packages do not belong to a group. Groups are a means to manage complex software systems that require many packages. Packages that are members of one or more groups may be installed without installing the entire group.

We start by listing all groups:

```
[root@testvm1 tmp]# dnf grouplist
```

The groups in the resulting list are separated into categories. The groups listed in the *Available Environment Groups* category tend to be desktop environments. The *Installed Groups* category is just what the title implies. There should be only one group listed in this category. The *Available Groups* category consists of groups that have not been installed and that are not desktops.

Look at the information about the groups. The use of quotes around group names that have spaces in them is required for all DNF group commands.

Installing LibreOffice

We've already discussed LibreOffice in this book as an excellent suite of standard office applications. It is not installed by default because it is not part of the Xfce ISO image. Office suites are one of the most common needs of any business.

Let's install a group that might be useful for you in real life. I use the LibreOffice suite to write my books and to create spreadsheets and presentations. LibreOffice uses the widely accepted Open Document Format (ODF) for its documents, and it can also create and use Microsoft Office documents, spreadsheets, presentations, and more.

First, use DNF to view the group information for LibreOffice, and then install the LibreOffice group.

```
[root@testvm1 ~]# dnf group install -y LibreOffice
```

Depending upon the speeds of your Internet connection and computer, this should take a couple minutes to download and install a complete office suite. If you have a very fast Internet speed, the download of 73 packages will take very little time. The VM I am using has 8 CPUs running at 2.8GHz which is pretty average these days.

Fonts

One of the things that many people like to do is to install additional fonts on their computers. Fedora provides a large number of fonts that can be used both in the user interface itself and in documents, spreadsheets, and other applications.

There are thousands of fonts available for free. Many fonts are provided by the Fedora repository, but many are available elsewhere.

One of the largest sources of free and open source fonts is Google at `https://fonts.google.com/` which contains over 1000 font families in more than 135 languages. By some accounts, Google fonts are now the international standard because they are freely usable on websites and can be downloaded from the Internet by any browser. This means that fonts for use in websites need not be installed on the local computer but are instead loaded directly from fonts.google.com as they are needed by the browser. This ensures the look of a website is consistent on all computers and other devices.

The Fedora repository contains many Google fonts, and some of those are installed as part of the basic Fedora Xfce image. There are fonts for many languages to support the wide internationalization of Linux.

Font Compatibility

Linux can install and use the three most common types of fonts including True Type, OpenType, and Adobe Postscript (Type 1). This provides for excellent font compatibility between Linux, Windows, and Mac since the same fonts can be used with all three operating systems.

The three main font families used in early Windows and Office are Arial, Arial Narrow, Times New Roman, and Courier New and are still used today. Unfortunately, they are distributed under a license with those products that makes them illegal to use without getting permission from Microsoft.

To circumvent this legal issue, Red Hat obtained licenses for a set of fonts that are now known as the Liberation fonts[5] and which were designed to be metrically compatible with the Microsoft fonts. These fonts are distributed with all Red Hat distributions including Fedora.

The Liberation Sans, Liberation Sans Narrow, Liberation Serif, and Liberation Mono fonts are free and compatible substitutes for Arial, Arial Narrow, Times New Roman, and Courier New, respectively. Programs such as LibreOffice use the Liberation fonts by default and automatically use the Liberation fonts as substitutes when displaying and printing MS Office documents. The Liberation fonts are slightly different from the original MS fonts.

The bottom line here is that any documents you created with MS Office can be used in LibreOffice and will look good in both.

Listing Fonts

Before installing new fonts, it can be a good idea to list the ones that are already installed.

The **dnf** command lists all currently installed fonts, and the **less** command allows you to page through the lengthy results. The asterisks, which can also be referred to as

---

[5] Wikipedia, "Liberation fonts," https://en.wikipedia.org/wiki/Liberation_fonts

"splats," are used in the same way that globbing is used for file names. It simply means to "find everything that contains the string 'font.'"

```
[root@testvm1 ~]# dnf list installed *font* | less
Installed Packages
aajohan-comfortaa-fonts.noarch          3.101-1.fc34              @updates
abattis-cantarell-fonts.noarch          0.301-2.fc34             @anaconda
adobe-source-code-pro-fonts.noarch      2.030.1.050-10.fc34      @anaconda
dejavu-sans-fonts.noarch                2.37-16.fc34             @anaconda
dejavu-sans-mono-fonts.noarch           2.37-16.fc34             @anaconda
<SNIP>
urw-base35-gothic-fonts.noarch          20200910-6.fc34          @updates
urw-base35-nimbus-mono-ps-fonts.noarch  20200910-6.fc34          @updates
urw-base35-nimbus-roman-fonts.noarch    20200910-6.fc34          @updates
<SNIP>
xlsfonts.x86_64                         1.0.6-2.fc34             @updates
xorg-x11-fonts-misc.noarch              7.5-31.fc34              @updates
(END)
```

Now you can explore the long list of available fonts:

```
[root@testvm1 ~]# dnf list available *font* | less
Last metadata expiration check: 0:30:06 ago on Tue 16 Nov 2021 07:24:47 AM EST.
Available Packages
PersonalCopy-Lite-soundfont.noarch      4.1-23.fc34              fedora
R-fontBitstreamVera.noarch              0.1.1-10.fc34           fedora
R-fontLiberation.noarch                 0.1.0-9.fc34            fedora
R-sysfonts.x86_64                       0.8.3-2.fc34            fedora
R-systemfonts.i686                      1.0.2-2.fc34            updates
R-systemfonts.x86_64                    1.0.2-2.fc34            updates
R-systemfonts-devel.i686                1.0.2-2.fc34            updates
R-systemfonts-devel.x86_64              1.0.2-2.fc34            updates
adf-accanthis-2-fonts.noarch            1.8-24.fc34             fedora
adf-accanthis-3-fonts.noarch            1.8-24.fc34             fedora
<SNIP>
```

Viewing Fonts

There are two ways that you can see what a font looks like. Do an Internet search and there will usually be one or more websites devoted to that font which will have samples of what the font looks like. I have found that Wikipedia has entries for most fonts that also include a sample.

Another option is to install the font you are interested in and then open a session of LibreOffice Writer. Pull down the font selector to view all installed fonts with a short sample of each.

Installing New Fonts

It is easy to install fonts directly from the Fedora repository, being the same procedure as installing any new software. To practice installing fonts, find the bitstream-vera fonts[6] which are a common font.

```
[root@testvm1 ~]# dnf install bitstream-vera*
Last metadata expiration check: 0:16:22 ago on Wed 17 Nov 2021
08:32:48 AM EST.
Dependencies resolved.
================================================================
 Package                    Arch     Version       Repository  Size
================================================================
Installing:
 bitstream-vera-fonts-all   noarch   1.10-41.fc33   fedora      7.1 k
 bitstream-vera-sans-fonts  noarch   1.10-41.fc33   fedora      126 k
 bitstream-vera-sans-mono-fonts noarch 1.10-41.fc33 fedora     99 k
 bitstream-vera-serif-fonts noarch   1.10-41.fc33   fedora      75 k

Transaction Summary
================================================================
Install  4 Packages

Total download size: 307 k
Installed size: 619 k
<SNIP>
```

---

[6]Wikipedia, "Bitstream Vera," https://en.wikipedia.org/wiki/Bitstream_Vera

Fonts do not normally change from one release to the next. Fonts are not dependent upon whether the host is 64- or 32-bit architecture.

Try opening an instance of LibreOffice and pull down the font selector to view the newly installed font. Figure 13-4 shows LibreOffice and the bitstream-vera font sample along with some other fonts I have installed.

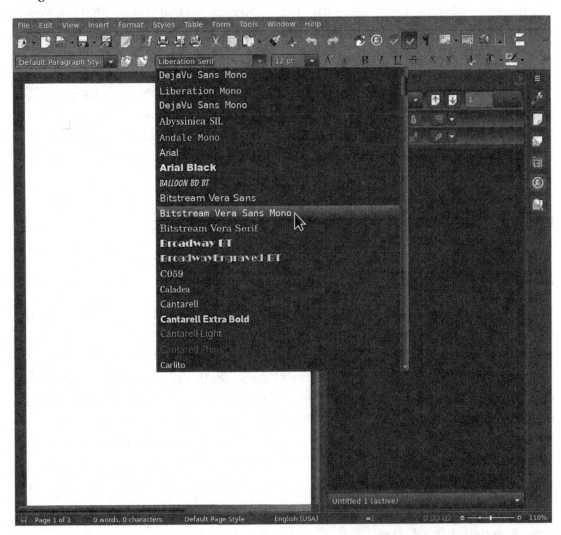

Figure 13-4. *Using LibreOffice to view a sample of the newly installed font*

Removing Software

The DNF tool can also remove software and the dependencies that were installed with that software. It will check to ensure that other software packages don't also require those dependencies.

You installed GnuCash earlier in the chapter, so suppose that you decided that you want to remove it. To remove GnuCash, just use the following command:

[root@testvm1 ~]# **dnf -y remove gnucash**

There are some files that are not removed with the software. When you use many programs, they create a default set of configuration files somewhere in your home directory. These can be a single "hidden file" where its name starts with a period or multiple configuration files for complex programs can be stored in a directory for those programs. Data files in your home directory are not removed.

These configuration files are not touched. This means that you can reinstall the program, and both your data and configuration are retained.

Adding Repositories

Not all of the software you might need when using Fedora is located in the standard Fedora repositories. Adding other repos, particularly a trusted repo like RPMFusion, can make adding new software that is not part of the Fedora distribution much easier and faster.

The RPMFusion repositories contain many packages that are not provided with the official Fedora distributions. The RPMFusion repos and the packages in them are well maintained, signed, and can be trusted. If you wish, use your browser to explore the RPMFusion website at `www.rpmfusion.org`. Installation of the two RPMFusion repos is straightforward. We will download the RPMs for the RPMFusion-free and RPMFusion-non-free repositories and install them.

Make /tmp the PWD.

[root@testvm1 ~]# **cd /tmp**

Use the **wget** command to download the RPMFusion RPMs into /tmp. Enter each of the following two commands. Each command should be on a single line. They are split here due to space issues.

Be sure to use the correct release number for your Fedora system. We use 34 here because that is what is installed on the host I am using to create this experiment.

```
[root@testvm1 tmp]# wget http://download1.rpmfusion.org/free/fedora/
rpmfusion-free-release-34.noarch.rpm
--2021-11-17 13:27:24--  http://download1.rpmfusion.org/free/fedora/
rpmfusion-free-release-34.noarch.rpm
Resolving download1.rpmfusion.org (download1.rpmfusion.org)...
193.28.235.60, 2001:67c:1740:8005::60
Connecting to download1.rpmfusion.org (download1.rpmfusion.
org)|193.28.235.60|:80... connected.
HTTP request sent, awaiting response... 200 OK
Length: 11532 (11K) [application/x-rpm]
Saving to: 'rpmfusion-free-release-34.noarch.rpm'

rpmfusion-free-release-34.noarc
100%[======================================================>]  11.26K
   --.-KB/s    in 0.001s

2021-11-17 13:27:25 (21.3 MB/s) - 'rpmfusion-free-release-34.noarch.rpm'
saved [11532/11532]

[root@testvm1 tmp]# wget http://download1.rpmfusion.org/nonfree/fedora/
rpmfusion-nonfree-release-34.noarch.rpm
--2021-11-17 13:29:13--  http://download1.rpmfusion.org/nonfree/fedora/
rpmfusion-nonfree-release-34.noarch.rpm
Resolving download1.rpmfusion.org (download1.rpmfusion.org)...
193.28.235.60, 2001:67c:1740:8005::60
Connecting to download1.rpmfusion.org (download1.rpmfusion.
org)|193.28.235.60|:80... connected.
HTTP request sent, awaiting response... 200 OK
Length: 11597 (11K) [application/x-rpm]
Saving to: 'rpmfusion-nonfree-release-34.noarch.rpm'
```

```
rpmfusion-nonfree-release-34.no
100%[======================================================>]  11.33K
  --.-KB/s      in 0.001s
```

```
2021-11-17 13:29:13 (11.9 MB/s) - 'rpmfusion-nonfree-release-34.noarch.rpm'
saved [11597/11597]
```

Install these two RPMs locally with the following command.

```
[root@testvm1 tmp]# dnf -y install ./rpmfusion*
```

Change to the /etc/yum.repos.d directory and list the files there. You should see several RPMFusion repositories. You should also see the default fedora and fedora-updates repository configuration files.

```
[root@testvm1 tmp]# cd /etc/yum.repos.d/
[root@testvm1 yum.repos.d]# ll
total 52
-rw-r--r--. 1 root root  728 Apr 28  2021 fedora-cisco-openh264.repo
-rw-r--r--. 1 root root 1302 Apr 28  2021 fedora-modular.repo
-rw-r--r--. 1 root root 1239 Apr 28  2021 fedora.repo
-rw-r--r--. 1 root root 1349 Apr 28  2021 fedora-updates-modular.repo
-rw-r--r--. 1 root root 1286 Apr 28  2021 fedora-updates.repo
-rw-r--r--. 1 root root 1391 Apr 28  2021 fedora-updates-testing-
                                          modular.repo
-rw-r--r--. 1 root root 1344 Apr 28  2021 fedora-updates-testing.repo
-rw-r--r--. 1 root root 1248 Apr 24  2021 rpmfusion-free.repo
-rw-r--r--. 1 root root 1264 Apr 24  2021 rpmfusion-free-updates.repo
-rw-r--r--. 1 root root 1324 Apr 24  2021 rpmfusion-free-updates-
                                          testing.repo
-rw-r--r--. 1 root root 1312 Apr 24  2021 rpmfusion-nonfree.repo
-rw-r--r--. 1 root root 1309 Apr 24  2021 rpmfusion-nonfree-updates.repo
-rw-r--r--. 1 root root 1369 Apr 24  2021 rpmfusion-nonfree-updates-
testing.repo
[root@testvm1 yum.repos.d]#
```

Now you can install software like Shotcut, a powerful video editing tool, that is not in the standard Fedora repositories:

```
[root@testvm1 ~]# dnf list shotcut
Last metadata expiration check: 0:14:46 ago on Mon 22 Nov 2021 09:42:49 AM EST.
Available Packages
shotcut.x86_64              21.03.21-2.fc34             rpmfusion-free
[root@testvm1 ~]#
```

The best part of these new repositories is that DNF will find the packages for you regardless of the repo in which they are located. You do not need to be concerned about which repository a particular might be found in.

Other Software

There is very little software that you might need that is not found in one of the Fedora or RPMFusion repositories. Others can be downloaded for installation just like you did for the RPMFusion repository packages.

Just to clarify, however, if you download a file that has an EXE extension it will never work on Linux. You must download RPM packages that will work on Fedora.

Zoom is one example of this. You can go to the Zoom website and download the RPM for Fedora. Store it in the /tmp directory and use the dnf command to install Zoom, just like you did with the RPMFusion repository packages.

Chapter Summary

Updating software and installing new software is easy with tools like DNF. DNF offers advanced features such as the ability to provide automated handling of dependencies; it will determine the dependencies, download them from the repository on the Internet, and install them.

DNF uses the concept of groups to enable installation and removal of large numbers of related packages such as would be used by complex software systems. Using groups to define things like desktops, development environments, office suites, scientific, and related technology packages makes it easy to install complete systems with a single command.

You installed some additional repositories beyond the default repos provided by Fedora. These additional repos make it easier to install software that is not part of the Fedora distribution.

CHAPTER 14

Backups

Objectives

After reading this chapter, you will be able to

- State at least three reasons why you should make backups
- Describe what constitutes a good backup
- Decide what needs to be backed up
- Select the best backup medium for today's high-capacity systems
- Configure a backup tool, rsbu, written by one of the authors
- Configure your computer to use rsbu for backups
- Create your first backup
- Test restoring a file from the backup to verify that it works as expected

Introduction

I'm about to explain in detail how to configure and set up for regular backups. The details are probably most important to system administrators, but for those who are independent business owners and the less technically oriented, most of this chapter is only the information you will need to make backups. Here is a quick synopsis to get you started.

Backups are an incredibly important aspect of a system administrator's job. Without good backups and a well-planned backup policy and process, it is a near certainty that sooner or later some critical data will be irretrievably lost.

223

© David Both, Cyndi Bulka 2022
D. Both and C. Bulka, *Linux for Small Business Owners*, https://doi.org/10.1007/978-1-4842-8264-9_14

All companies, regardless of how large or small, run on their data. Consider the financial and business cost of losing all of the data you need to run your business. There is not a business today ranging from the smallest sole proprietorship to the largest global corporation that could survive the loss of all or even a large fraction of its data. Your place of business can be rebuilt, and your computers can be replaced using insurance, but your data can never be recovered unless it is backed up.

After looking at some of the dangers to your data, some expected and some not, I will discuss how to choose the data to be backed up and why external USB hard drives are the best data storage medium for your backups.

I will introduce you to a program that I wrote that creates daily backups and that can provide you with archival backups for a period of weeks. This backup program is already configured to work well for a small businesses when used with an external USB hard drive of at least 500GB. All that you will need to do is to download and install an RPM package that contains the backup program and a setup program. I then show you how to run the setup program to prepare the external hard drive. Complete instructions for all of this are included in this chapter.

If you are interested and have the background, I do go into some advanced technical detail about how the backup program works. That section is entitled 'rsync as a Backup Tool.' You can skip that section without worry as it is not necessary for you to actually perform your backups. You can always come back to it later or just ignore it altogether.

The Dangers

There are many dangers to your data that can cause its loss. By loss, here, I don't mean stolen data; that is an entirely different type of disaster. What I mean here is the complete destruction of the data. There are lots of ways in which that can happen.

When I say "file" here, I mean "important file." All files are important, or there would be no reason to keep them.

- Everyone who has ever worked with computers has accidentally deleted a file. I certainly have done that – many times.

- The file you deleted today, fully knowing that it will never be needed again, will suddenly be needed next week.

- The storage device – hard disk drive (HDD) or solid state device (SSD) – suddenly fails completely leaving all your data inaccessible.

- A disgruntled employee deletes all of the data to which they have access as their last act before walking out the door.

- A power failure results in the loss of some files you were editing.

- Despite the fact that it is far less likely on Linux than it is on Windows, your computer becomes infected with ransomware, and you can no longer access your data.

- Your computer is destroyed in a fire or a natural disaster such as an earthquake.

- Your child and their friends find your computer unlocked and manage to destroy some or all of your data.

- Radiation from contaminated metal used in the assembly of your storage device damages the data on the device. Yes, this happened while I was working at IBM. That problem was determined to be due to slightly radioactive solder.[1] That was easily resolved, but the point is that even very unlikely things do happen.

- Your computer is stolen.

Even if you are an individual or a small business owner and not running a large corporation, backing up your data is very important. I have almost three decades of personal financial data as well as that for my now closed consulting businesses, including a large number of electronic receipts. I also have many documents, presentations, and spreadsheets that I have created over the years. I really don't want to lose any of that.

Backups are imperative to ensure the long-term safety of my data. And yours, too.

Actual Events

I have had a number of the things in that list happen to me, and I have encountered other people with some interesting stories. Here are a couple.

Let's start with the professor at a local university here in Raleigh about 30 years ago. Their computer with all of the data required for their research project was stolen. They did have a backup – but it was on a different hard drive in the same computer that was stolen. That computer and the data on it were never recovered.

---

[1] Wikipedia, "Solder," https://en.wikipedia.org/wiki/Solder

While working at the IBM Dealer Support Center, I was frequently asked to help customers recover files that had been erased accidentally or otherwise. Some of those people were quite insistent that it could be done very easily. There were some tools such as the Norton Utilities that could help recover deleted files, but they were never guaranteed to work and many times did not. Somehow, a few of these customers thought that we were withholding information about simple recovery techniques in the hope of extorting large sums of money from them to recover their files.

As a person known by friends and neighbors to work with computers, I am asked frequently to help resolve their computer problems. In one case, a person came to me and asked if I could recover the data on their old hard drive and restore it to their new computer. The computer had crashed with no warning and could not be restarted. I removed the hard drive from their computer and inserted it into the desktop hard drive docking station I keep for just this purpose and attempted to locate their data, any data. That hard drive had crashed catastrophically and, if there were any data left on it, was not recoverable. Of course, they had no backups.

In a similar situation, the user of one computer said they had backups. I suspect that the backup system they had was either not set up correctly or just flawed. I found no data of any kind on the alleged backup device.

Personally, I have experienced events of many different types that have required that I recover my data from a backup. The most recent was just yesterday as I write this. I was just sitting down to work on this chapter on, yes, backups when my primary workstation crashed beyond recovery and started emitting a very nasty burning smell. There were no flames, but it *smelled* very hot. Based on my assessment of the symptoms, I ordered a new motherboard.

In order to keep working while I wait for a new motherboard to arrive, I switched over to my laptop. Since I do not keep all of my current files on that laptop, I needed to restore a few files from the latest backups of my primary workstation. Because I am very strict about creating daily backups, the ones I had on hand were only a few hours old and nothing had changed on any of the files I needed during that time. It was easy to locate and copy the files I needed, including the LibreOffice file for this chapter, from my external backup drive to the home directory on my laptop so I could keep working.

After I resolved the problem with my primary workstation, I was able to copy the files I had worked on while it was out of commission back to their proper locations.

It turned out that the problem with my workstation was not the motherboard but rather a front panel media dashboard that had short-circuited which made it look as if the power supply and motherboard were the culprits.[2]

Choosing What to Back Up

This is actually a simple decision. The easiest form of backup is to back up the entire /home directory because it is where all of your data and personal configuration files are stored. It is also a good idea to back up the /root directory because you will probably find yourself storing useful administrative files and RPM packages there.

After losing some or all of your data, it is a simple matter to replace a single file or your entire home directory. If you had a serious crash and had to reinstall Linux, you may also need to reinstall any application programs like GnuCash and LibreOffice.

You could also make backups of other system directories such as /etc and /var, but that is not worth the trouble or disk space unless you have someone on staff who knows what files to restore when necessary.

Backup Requirements

The primary objectives for backups are simple. You may have others, but these are a good start and can help you sort through the options that are available for backup solutions.

- Create daily backups.

- Backups should be maintained for a configurable number of days.

- Backups must provide an easy means to restore any file from any day that still remains in the backups.

- Create backups from which users can easily locate and restore files.

- Minimize the amount of time taken to create the backups.

- Minimize the amount of space required to maintain the backups.

---

[2] Both, David, Opensource.com, "How curiosity helped me solve a hardware problem," https://opensource.com/article/22/1/troubleshoot-hardware-sysadmin

Backup Medium

Choosing the right backup medium is easy these days. Despite the fact that some tools like Amanda claim to be "tape backup solutions," they all deal easily with more modern media such as external hard drives. I have used many types of backup media during my career, and tape was always difficult to work with. Don't go there.

The best media by far – as well as the least expensive on a per megabyte basis – is the simple USB external hard drive. Be sure to use spinning hard disk drives (HDDs) and not solid state drives (SSDs). Hard drives can store data for many years sitting on the shelf while the data on SSDs begins to degrade at around the one year mark of being stored without power applied.

The HDD should be about 500GB capacity which will provide plenty of space for storing two or three months worth of daily backups.

Typical Backup Solutions

There are a large number of backup solutions available for Linux. For example, TecMint has an article entitled "25 Outstanding Backup Utilities for Linux Systems in 2020,"[3] and the FOSS Linux website contains the article "The 10 Best Linux Backup Tools".[4]

There is some overlap in these lists, but there are plenty of options from which you can choose. I do not have a particular recommendation; your needs should determine the backup tools you use. All of these backup solutions are worth exploring. My only suggestion is that, as a small business, you should try to go with the simpler tools.

My Backup Solution

Several of the advanced backup solutions listed in those articles use the Linux **rsync** command as their engine for determining which files need to be backed up and doing the backup itself. They use this tool which is distributed with Fedora because of its speed, efficiency, and elegance.

---

[3] Kili, Aaron, "25 Outstanding Backup Utilities for Linux Systems in 2020," TecMint, `www.tecmint.com/linux-system-backup-tools/`, February 17, 2020

[4] Jones, Brandon, FOSS Linux, "The 10 Best Linux Backup Tools," `www.fosslinux.com/44619/best-linux-backup-tools.htm`, January 11, 2021

In fact, the tools that use rsync are just GUI wrappers around this powerful CLI command. To be sure, many Linux administrative tools that run as GUI programs on the desktop are simply graphical wrappers around the real tools that run on the command line.

Because rsync is so powerful, I have written my own rsync-based backup program as a Bash shell script. The Bash shell program I use to perform my backups is easy to use and takes all of the guesswork out of doing it yourself. This section is intended to describe my own use of rsync in a backup scenario and to help you get started using my script.

It is perfectly fine to skip this next section. I have set it apart in the next section to make it easy to skip. But if you want to understand how these backup applications use rsync, it is a good read.

rsync as a Backup Tool

The rsync command was written by Andrew Tridgell and Paul Mackerras and first released in 1996. The primary use case for rsync is to remotely synchronize the files on one computer with those on another. Did you notice what they did to create the name there? rsync is open source software and is provided with all of the distros with which I am familiar.

The rsync command can be used to synchronize two directories or directory trees whether they are on the same computer or on different computers, but it can do so much more than that. rsync creates or updates the target directory to be identical to the source directory. The target directory is freely accessible by all the usual Linux tools because it is not stored in a tarball or zip file or any other archival file type; it is just a regular directory with regular files that can be navigated by regular users using basic Linux tools. This meets one of my primary objectives.

One of the most important features of rsync is the method it uses to synchronize preexisting files that have changed in the source directory. Rather than copying the entire file from the source, it uses checksums to compare blocks of the source and target files. If all of the blocks in the two files are the same, no data is transferred. If the data differs, only the blocks that have changed on the source are transferred to the target device. This saves an immense amount of time and network bandwidth for remote sync. For example, when I first used my rsync BASH script to back up all of my hosts to a large external USB hard drive, it took about three hours. That is because all of the data had to be transferred. Subsequent syncs took between three and eight minutes of real time, depending upon how many files had been changed or created since the previous sync. I used the **time** command to determine this, so it is empirical data. Last night, for example, it took 5 minutes and 35 seconds to complete a sync of approximately 750GB of data from 8 remote systems and the local workstation. Of course, only a few hundred megabytes of data were actually altered during the day and needed to be synchronized.

The following simple rsync command can be used to synchronize the contents of two directories and any of their subdirectories. That is, the contents of the target directory are synchronized with the contents of the source directory so that at the end of the sync, the target directory is identical to the source directory.

```
rsync -aH sourcedir targetdir
```

The -a option is for archive mode which preserves permissions, ownerships, and symbolic (soft) links. The -H is used to preserve hard links.[5] Note that either the source or target directories can be on a remote host.

Now let's assume that yesterday we used rsync to synchronize two directories. Today, we want to synchronize them again, but we have deleted some files from the source directory. The normal way in which rsync would do this is to simply copy all the new or changed files to the target location and leave the deleted files in place on the target. This may be the behavior you want, but if you would prefer that files deleted from the source also be deleted from the target, you can add the --delete option to make that happen.

Another interesting option, and my personal favorite because it increases the power and flexibility of rsync immensely, is the --link-dest option. The --link-dest option allows a series of daily backups that take up very little additional space for each day and also take very little time to create.

Specify the previous day's target directory with this option and a new directory for today. rsync then creates today's new directory, and a hard link for each file in yesterday's directory is created in today's directory. So we now have a bunch of hard links to yesterday's files in today's directory. No new files have been created or duplicated. Just a bunch of hard links have been created.

Wikipedia has a very good description of hard links. After creating the target directory for today with this set of hard links to yesterday's target directory, rsync performs its sync as usual, but when a change is detected in a file, the target hard link is replaced by a copy of the file from yesterday and the changes to the file are then copied from the source to the target.

---

[5]Wikipedia, "Hard link," https://en.wikipedia.org/wiki/Hard_link

Now our command looks like the following:

```
rsync -aH --delete --link-dest=yesterdaystargetdir sourcedir todaystargetdir
```

There are also times when it is desirable to exclude certain directories or files from being synchronized. For this, there is the --exclude option. Use this option and the pattern for the files or directories you want to exclude. You might want to exclude browser cache files, so your new command will look like this:

```
rsync -aH --delete --exclude Cache --link-dest=yesterdaystargetdir
sourcedir todaystargetdir
```

rsync can sync files with remote hosts as either the source or the target. For the next example, let's assume that the source directory is on a remote computer with the hostname remote1 and the target directory is on the local host. Even though SSH is the default communications protocol used when transferring data to or from a remote host, I always add the ssh option. The command now looks like this:

```
rsync -aH -e ssh --delete --exclude Cache --link-dest=yesterdaystargetdir
remote1:sourcedir todaystargetdir
```

rsync has a very large number of options that can be used to customize the synchronization process. For the most part, the relatively simple commands that I have described here are perfect for making backups for my personal needs.

The rsbu Backup Script

I automated my backups because "automate everything" is one of the basic tenets of the Linux Philosophy.[6] I wrote a Bash script named **rsbu** that handles the details of creating a series of daily backups using rsync. This includes ensuring that the backup medium is mounted, generating the names for today's backup directory, creating appropriate directory structures on the backup medium if they are not already there, performing the actual backups, and unmounting the medium.

Just in case you are wondering, "rsbu" stands for **rs**ync **b**ackup.

My script creates a file structure on the target backup medium that looks like Figure 14-1, which is similar to my own backups.

---

[6] Both, David, *The Linux Philosophy for SysAdmins*, Apress, 2018, 165–192

```
/media/
├──── Backups
│     ├──── Backups
│     │     ├──── server1
│     │     │     ├──── 2021-10-03-RSBackup
│     │     │     │     ├──── etc
│     │     │     │     ├──── home
│     │     │     │     ├──── local
│     │     │     │     ├──── root
│     │     │     │     └──── var
│     │     │     ├──── 2021-10-04-RSBackup
│     │     │     ├──── 2021-10-05-RSBackup
│     │     │     ├──── 2021-10-06-RSBackup
│     │     │     ├──── 2021-10-07-RSBackup
│     │     │     ├──── 2021-10-08-RSBackup
│     │     │     ├──── 2021-10-09-RSBackup
<snip>
│     │     │     ├──── 2021-12-01-RSBackup
│     │     │     └──── 2021-12-02-RSBackup
│     │     ├──── server2
│     │     │     ├──── 2021-10-03-RSBackup
│     │     │     ├──── 2021-10-04-RSBackup
│     │     │     ├──── 2021-10-05-RSBackup
│     │     │     ├──── 2021-10-06-RSBackup
│     │     │     ├──── 2021-10-07-RSBackup
│     │     │     ├──── 2021-10-08-RSBackup
│     │     │     ├──── 2021-10-09-RSBackup
<snip>
│     │     │     ├──── 2021-12-01-RSBackup
│     │     │     └──── 2021-12-02-RSBackup
│     │     ├──── workstation1
│     │     │     ├──── 2021-10-03-RSBackup
│     │     │     ├──── 2021-10-04-RSBackup
│     │     │     ├──── 2021-10-05-RSBackup
│     │     │     ├──── 2021-10-06-RSBackup
│     │     │     ├──── 2021-10-07-RSBackup
│     │     │     ├──── 2021-10-08-RSBackup
│     │     │     ├──── 2021-10-09-RSBackup
<snip>
```

Figure 14-1. *A sample of the directory structure created by the rsbu script on the backup target medium. The top-level directories that were backed up from server1 are shown for illustrative purposes*

This directory structure makes it easy to find any file for any computer on any date within the age range specified in the rsbu.conf configuration file. You can use Thunar or any file manager to navigate this directory structure. This software can perform backups of many computers but can also do backups of a single computer which is a much more likely use case for small businesses.

The script runs daily on my primary workstation. It is triggered by a timer early every morning to ensure that I never forget to perform my backups.

Installing rsbu

The rsbu RPM package file contains everything you will need to manually perform a backup or to automatically perform backups using a timer. The timer is not enabled by default, so you will need to do that if you want your backups to automatically run each day.

It is necessary to perform all of these tasks as the root user. Installing the rsbu package, running the setup script, and performing the backups must all be done as root. You will only need to perform the first two tasks once, but you will run the rsbu backup script each day, and it must always be run as the root user.

Start by opening a terminal session on the desktop and switch user (**su -**) to escalate your privileges to root.

Download the RPM Package

To install my rsbu backup system, you can download the rsbu RPM package from Github.com/Apress/linux-for-small-business-owners. You could download the package as yourself using the web browser and store it in the /tmp directory since your non-root account does not have access to the /root directory.

The other – and easier – option is to do the download as root since you need to be root anyway to do the installation.

The **wget** command makes it easy to do this from the command line:

```
[root@testvm1 ~]# wget http://www.both.org/downloads/
rsbu-2.4.0-0.1.noarch.rpm
```

This downloads the package and stores it in /root from where you can easily install it.

Install the RPM Package

Installing the RPM package is just as easy:

```
[root@testvm1 ~]# dnf -y install rsbu-2.4.0-0.1.noarch.rpm
Last metadata expiration check: 0:46:48 ago on Wed 08 Dec 2021
02:21:27 PM EST.
Dependencies resolved.
================================================================================
 Package      Architecture    Version         Repository             Size
================================================================================
Installing:
 rsbu         noarch          2.4.0-0.1       @commandline           14 k

Transaction Summary
================================================================================
Install  1 Package

Total size: 14 k
Installed size: 36 k
Downloading Packages:
Running transaction check
Transaction check succeeded.
Running transaction test
Transaction test succeeded.
Running transaction
  Preparing        :                                1/1
  Running scriptlet: rsbu-2.4.0-0.1.noarch          1/1
  Installing       : rsbu-2.4.0-0.1.noarch          1/1
  Running scriptlet: rsbu-2.4.0-0.1.noarch          1/1
  Verifying        : rsbu-2.4.0-0.1.noarch          1/1

Installed:
  rsbu-2.4.0-0.1.noarch

Complete!
[root@testvm1 ~]#
```

And that is all there is to it. Your new **rsbu** backup program has been installed.

The rsbu-setup Program

There are two important tasks that need to be performed in order to prepare the computer for backups using rsbu. First, the external hard drive you will use to store your backups needs to be prepared, and your host needs to be configured to properly recognize that storage drive as the backup device.

Second, the rsync command used by the rsbu script uses SSH[7] and a public/private keypair[8] (PPKP) to securely connect with all computers including the local host on which it is running. SSH stands for Secure SHell and is a protocol that provides secure, encrypted connections between computers when using tools like rsync even on a standalone host. The data stream is encrypted by SSH even when the backup source and the backup storage medium are both on the same host. This is how the rsync command was designed to work.

But SSH must be properly configured to make this happen.

Note   Although SSH encrypts the data stream while it is being transmitted, it does not encrypt the data on the hard drive.

The **rsbu-setup** script that was installed by the rsbu RPM does most of the work to perform these two configuration tasks. You will need to enter some information when it is required. The **rsbu-setup** script will prompt you for specific information when it is needed. It will also request that you verify certain information and give your permission to continue at multiple places in the process.

Caution!!   *Be sure to follow the directions mentioned later exactly or your backups will not work or you may accidentally delete all of the data on your hard drive.*

---

[7] Kenlon, Seth, "A beginner's guide to SSH for remote connection on Linux," https://opensource.com/article/20/9/ssh
[8] Wikipedia, "Public-key cryptography," https://en.wikipedia.org/wiki/Public-key_cryptography

What You Will Need

You will need an external USB hard drive as discussed in the backup media section of this chapter. You will also need the root password.

It is very important that you know some unique identification information about the external USB storage device in order to prevent the possibility of deleting important data or the operating system itself from the internal storage device(s).

If you have already connected the external USB hard drive to your computer, disconnect it now. Look at the label on the device. All external storage devices have a label on the case with at least some identifying information. You should look for the label and identify at least two of the following three things:

1. First, look for a brand name such as Western Digital, My Passport, SeaGate, Samsung, SanDisk, and etc.

2. Second, you may find a model number. Most of my devices do not have a model number printed on the case, but you may find one on the original packaging material if the device is new.

3. The device serial number. This is the single most important bit of data you can use to identify the device. The serial number will always be unique.

These three items of data are permanently stored in the storage device and cannot be modified or deleted. The rsbu-setup program will display these three items and ask you to verify that rsbu-setup, and you are both working with the same physical device. If nothing else matches, the serial number always will.

If the serial number displayed by the program does not match that printed on the device label, do not continue. Terminate the program and start from the beginning by disconnecting and then reconnecting the USB storage device to your computer. If that does not change the results, obtain a different external storage device to try.

Run the rsbu-setup Program

The rsbu-setup program is interactive and requires input from you at a number of points during its run. This is to provide you with information that allows you to verify the setup program is working on the correct storage device. It also allows you to change your mind and terminate the setup program if you have any doubts about the program using the correct storage device.

Part of the setup for the rsbu backup program is to create and install a public/private keypair (PPKP) that provides encrypted communications between the program and the computer being backed up. This allows the backup program to run without requiring you to enter a password.

Caution   Be sure to carefully read and follow the onscreen prompts as you proceed through this procedure.

Enter the data requested by the program when prompted. Other than the root password you will need to enter, this will consist of typing the letter y for yes, or n for no, or q for quit, and then pressing the Enter key. In some instances, you will just need to press the Enter key. Your responses are highlighted in bold in the following output from the program when I ran it on my test system. Instructions such as when you need to enter the root password are contained in angle brackets like this, **<Enter root Password>** and **<Press Enter>**.

Enter the following command to run the setup program:

```
[root@testvm1 ~]# rsbu-setup -v


############################################################################
#                             ATTENTION!!!                                 #
#                                                                          #
#  Plug in the external USB hard drive you will be using for your backups. #
#                                                                          #
############################################################################

Have you plugged in the external USB hard drive? (ynq) y <Press Enter>


############################################################################
#                                                                          #
#    Please be patient while we identify this new USB hard drive.          #
#                                                                          #
############################################################################
```

```
###############################################################################
#                                                                             #
#                  A new device has been plugged in.                          #
#                                                                             #
###############################################################################
###############################################################################
#                                                                             #
# Verify that the information on the external storage device, especially      #
# that the device serial number matches that printed below.                   #
#                                                                             #
###############################################################################
###############################################################################

###############################################################################
#                                                                             #
#     WARNING!!   Be sure that this information is correct!   WARNINIG!!       #
#                                                                             #
#-----------------------------------------------------------------------------#
#                                                                             #
# The new storage device is:                                                  #
#                                                                             #
#     Model Family:     Western Digital Elements / My Passport (USB)
#     Device Model:     WDC WD5000BMVV-11GNWS0
#     Serial Number:    WD-WX71A30P3470
#                                                                             #
#-----------------------------------------------------------------------------#
#                                                                             #
# WARNING!!!    If the serial number printed above does not match that         #
#               printed on the physical label on the storage device, DO NOT   #
#               CONTINUE this procedure. Enter n or q below.                   #
#                                                                             #
#                                                                             #
```

```
#                                                                              #
################################################################################
Are you POSITIVE that the device shown above is the correct one for your
backups? (ynq) y <Press Enter>

################################################################################
#   WARNING!!    WARNING!!    WARNING!!    WARNING!!    WARNING!!    WARNING!!   #
#                                                                              #
#                                                                              #
#     !!THIS PROCEDURE WILL DELETE ALL OF THE DATA ON THE USB HARD DRIVE!!     #
#                                                                              #
#                   ARE YOU REALLY SURE YOU WANT TO CONTINUE?                  #
#                                                                              #
#                                                                              #
#   WARNING!!    WARNING!!    WARNING!!    WARNING!!    WARNING!!    WARNING!!   #
################################################################################
ARE YOU REALLY SURE YOU WANT TO CONTINUE? (ynq) y <Press Enter>

################################################################################
#                                                                              #
# Please be patient.                                                           #
#                                                                              #
# This may take a few minutes depending upon the size of the backup           #
# device being prepared.                                                       #
#                                                                              #
################################################################################

The partition table has been altered.
Calling ioctl() to re-read partition table.
Syncing disks.
Creating new partition on sdb
Checking that no-one is using this disk right now ... OK

Disk /dev/sdb: 465.11 GiB, 499405291520 bytes, 975400960 sectors
Disk model: My Passport 070A
Units: sectors of 1 * 512 = 512 bytes
Sector size (logical/physical): 512 bytes / 512 bytes
```

I/O size (minimum/optimal): 512 bytes / 512 bytes
Disklabel type: dos
Disk identifier: 0x38b9bf1c

Old situation:

>>> Created a new DOS disklabel with disk identifier 0x917beade.
/dev/sdb1: Created a new partition 1 of type 'Linux' and of size 465.1 GiB.
Partition #1 contains a ext4 signature.
/dev/sdb2: Done.

New situation:
Disklabel type: dos
Disk identifier: 0x917beade

Device   Boot Start   End   Sectors   Size Id Type
/dev/sdb1   2048 975400959 975398912 465.1G 83 Linux

The partition table has been altered.
Calling ioctl() to re-read partition table.
Syncing disks.
mke2fs 1.45.6 (20-Mar-2020)
/dev/sdb1 contains a ext4 file system labelled 'MyBackups'
        last mounted on Sun Dec 19 16:43:43 2021
Creating filesystem with 121924864 4k blocks and 30482432 inodes
Filesystem UUID: 7d1a7eab-1ec0-4157-9c8d-df8d28554885
Superblock backups stored on blocks:
        32768, 98304, 163840, 229376, 294912, 819200, 884736, 1605632,
        2654208,
        4096000, 7962624, 11239424, 20480000, 23887872, 71663616, 78675968,
        102400000

Allocating group tables: done
Writing inode tables: done
Creating journal (262144 blocks): done
Writing superblocks and filesystem accounting information: done

```
total 0
drwxr-xr-x. 1 root root 0 Dec 20 21:25 MyBackups
Creating fstab entry

############################################################################
#                          !!!ATTENTION!!!                                 #
#                                                                          #
#  During this portion of configuration you need to create a Public/Private #
#  KeyPair (PPKP) to provide encrypted communication during the backup     #
#  procedure.                                                              #
#                                                                          #
#  You will be asked to enter a file name in which to save the RSA key.    #
#  DO NOT enter a name for the file. Just press the Enter key to accept     #
#  the default file name.                                                  #
#                                                                          #
#  You will be asked twice to enter a passphrase. Do not enter a passphrase. #
#  Just press the Enter key for an empty passphrase.                       #
#                                                                          #
# Refer to Wikipedia for details of PPKP.                                  #
#  https://en.wikipedia.org/wiki/Public-key_cryptography                   #
#                                                                          #
############################################################################

Generating public/private rsa key pair.
Enter file in which to save the key (/root/.ssh/id_rsa): <Press Enter>
Enter passphrase (empty for no passphrase): <Press Enter>
Enter same passphrase again: <Press Enter>
Your identification has been saved in /root/.ssh/id_rsa
Your public key has been saved in /root/.ssh/id_rsa.pub
The key fingerprint is:
SHA256:6thExA+Vr028udidtJA5ckRH16zHLYrjEKzMszNCTaM root@testvm1.both.org
The key's randomart image is:
+---[RSA 3072]----+
|       .. .. .o  |
|      . .. . ..  o|
|       +. + .  o.|
```

```
|      .ooo =   o +|
|      *.oS* * . o |
|     E.*.+ % o    |
|     .  oo B B o  |
|      .=+ . + +   |
|      ..oo        |
+----[SHA256]-----+
```

```
#################################################################
#                                                               #
# We now need to install the public key for this computer. You will first   #
# need to respond with 'yes' and press the Enter key when asked if you      #
# want to continue connecting to the host. Be sure to use the word 'yes'    #
# not just 'y'.                                                 #
#                                                               #
# Next enter the root password when requested.                  #
#                                                               #
#################################################################
```

/usr/bin/ssh-copy-id: INFO: Source of key(s) to be installed: "/root/.ssh/
id_rsa.pub"
The authenticity of host 'testvm1.both.org (fe80::373b:a342:48dd:a99b%en
p0s3)' can't be established.
ED25519 key fingerprint is SHA256:FhOUkKOOIX88o3ivTMkUYE8O/
bjNG6CuCR54MkvjPLg.
This key is not known by any other names
Are you sure you want to continue connecting (yes/no/[fingerprint])? **yes**
<Press Enter>
/usr/bin/ssh-copy-id: INFO: attempting to log in with the new key(s), to
filter out any that are already installed
/usr/bin/ssh-copy-id: INFO: 1 key(s) remain to be installed -- if you are
prompted now it is to install the new keys
root@testvm1.both.org's password: **<Press Enter>**

Number of key(s) added: 1

Now try logging into the machine, with: "ssh 'testvm1.both.org'" and check to make sure that only the key(s) you wanted were added.

```
################################################################
#               Backup partition space usage data              #
################################################################
# Device label =    MyBackups
# Mount Point =     /media/MyBackups
Filesystem      Size  Used Avail Use% Mounted on
/dev/sda2       119G  3.0G  116G   3% /
Filesystem      1K-blocks      Used Available Use% Mounted on
/dev/sda2       124779520 3051152 120936784    3% /
################################################################
Program terminated normally
[root@testvm1 ~]#
```

Test the Encrypted Connection

Test the SSH PPKP encrypted connection. You log in to your own computer to perform this test. It should not require a password for this.

The first time you log in to your own computer this way, you will be asked to verify that you want to continue. You must perform this step for your backups to work. This step is only required prior to the first time you perform a backup.

Enter the following command and, when requested, type **yes** and press **Enter**:

```
[root@testvm1 ~]# ssh testvm1
The authenticity of host 'testvm1 (192.168.0.101)' can't be established.
ED25519 key fingerprint is SHA256:FhOUkKOOIX88o3ivTMkUYE8O/
bjNG6CuCR54MkvjPLg.
This host key is known by the following other names/addresses:
    ~/.ssh/known_hosts:1: testvm1.both.org
Are you sure you want to continue connecting (yes/no/[fingerprint])? yes
<Press Enter>
Warning: Permanently added 'testvm1' (ED25519) to the list of known hosts.
Last login: Wed Dec  8 21:41:49 2021 from 192.168.0.1
[root@testvm1 ~]#
```

Type **exit** and press the **Enter** key to exit from this SSH connection. If this works as shown earlier, the setup is properly completed.

Configuration

The rsbu program has one configuration file, /usr/local/etc/rsbu.conf. The rsbu.conf configuration file has already been configured to perform backups of the /home, /usr/local, and /root directories. Those are the locations that contain the important files on your computer. Obviously, the /home directory contains your personal and business files. The /root directory contains files you use as root such as the one used to install the rsbu backup system.

The /usr/local directory contains two files that are also important, /usr/local/bin/rsbu and /usr/local/etc/rsbu.conf – the rsbu backup system.

Tip   You should not make any changes to the rsbu.conf configuration file. It is already configured to perform backups of all the files you would need to recover in case of a disaster.

If you ever need to change the rsbu configuration to back up additional directories or additional computers on your network, you can use a text editor to modify the /usr/local/etc/rsbu.conf file. For now, you should not change the rsbu.conf file because it is already set to back up the files you would need to recover your business in the event of disaster.

Warning!!   Do not make any changes to the rsbu program itself. There are no configurable items located in that program file.

Getting Started with rsbu

Before making your first backup, you'll need to become familiar with the rsbu program. The best way to do this is to first run the program using the -h option to display the help.

[root@testvm1 ~]# **rsbu -h <Press Enter>**

rsbu - Performs backups of local and remote hosts using rsync.
It also uses the link capability of rsync to minimize storage usage
for unmodified files for series of daily backups.

Syntax: rsbu -[l|L|c|b|h|u]vd <Device number> s <host number> f <file name>
options:

b   Backup data to the selected Backup Media.
c   Check the contents of the Backup Media.
d   The number of the backup device. Use -l to list devices by number.
f <filename>   The fully qualified path to an alternate configuration file
                You are not likely to need the -f option.
h   Print this help.
l   List the backup devices and their respective numbers.
L   List the hosts to be backed up and their respective numbers.
p   Prepare the backup device. Requires device number and device name.
t   Test mode. Performs all functions except the actual backups. Does
       NOT create backup directories.
u   Unmount the backup device after completing backup or check.
v   Verbose mode.
V   Print version number and exit.

The configuration file is /usr/local/etc/rsbu.conf. Make all configuration
changes in that file.

Setting a 1 day retention in this file creates a single
backup of each host without dates. Additional backups simply update the
existing set of backup files and do not create a backup history.

[root@testvm1 ~]#

Other than the help function, you will primarily use three of the options listed on the help page, -b, -c, and -u. The -b option tells the rsbu backup program to actually perform the backups. The -c option provides a very quick and superficial check of the backup medium so that you can verify that backups at least appear to be made.

I always use the -u option whether performing backups or just checking so that the backup device will be unmounted at the end of the task. This ensures that data is not lost when someone disconnects the backup device in order to remove it from the premises and take it to a safe, geographically separate location for offline storage.

Make Your First Backup

Performing the backup is the easy part. Enter the **rsbu -b** command to perform your first backup. I used the **time** command as a prefix to the main command, so I could determine the amount of time the command took on its first run. You don't need to use the time command.

```
[root@testvm1 ~]# time rsbu -b <Press Enter>
#################################################################################
#                       Backup partition space usage data                       #
#################################################################################
# Device index = 1
# Device Name = External USB hard drive
# Device Label =
# Mount Point = /media/MyBackups
# Maximum age of retained files = 60
Filesystem      Size   Used Avail Use% Mounted on
/dev/sdb1       457G    73M   434G    1% /media/MyBackups
Filesystem      1K-blocks   Used Available Use% Mounted on
/dev/sdb1        478996184 73756 454521072    1% /media/MyBackups
/dev/sdb1 on /media/MyBackups type ext4 (rw,nosuid,nodev,noexec,relatime,
seclabel,user)
#################################################################################
#################################################################################
PING testvm1.both.org (192.168.0.101) 56(84) bytes of data.
64 bytes from testvm1.both.org (192.168.0.101): icmp_seq=1 ttl=64 time=0.073 ms

--- testvm1.both.org ping statistics ---
1 packets transmitted, 1 received, 0% packet loss, time 0ms
rtt min/avg/max/mdev = 0.073/0.073/0.073/0.000 ms
Doing a date series backup.
```

```
/usr/local/bin/rsbu: line 360: cd: /media/MyBackups/Backups/testvm1/: No
such file or directory
/usr/local/bin/rsbu: line 363: cd: OLDPWD not set
################################################################################
################################################################################
#                      Backup partition space usage data                      #
################################################################################
# Device index = 1
# Device Name = External USB hard drive
# Device Label =
# Mount Point = /media/MyBackups
# Maximum age of retained files = 60
Filesystem       Size   Used Avail Use% Mounted on
/dev/sdb1        457G    73M  434G   1% /media/MyBackups
Filesystem       1K-blocks   Used Available Use% Mounted on
/dev/sdb1        478996184 73768 454521060   1% /media/MyBackups
/dev/sdb1 on /media/MyBackups type ext4 (rw,nosuid,nodev,noexec,relatime,
seclabel,user)
################################################################################
/dev/sdb1 /media/MyBackups ext4 rw,seclabel,nosuid,nodev,noexec,
relatime 0 0
Unmounting /media/MyBackups

real    0m0.743s
user    0m0.034s
sys     0m0.063s
[root@testvm1 ~]#
```

Results

As you can see, the program finished very quickly, in less than one second. This is primarily due to the fact that I have no data files in my home directory. There are some configuration files in /home/dboth and /root and the files for rsbu in /usr/local.

I had some interesting results as I researched and tested for this book using my primary workstation which has plenty of data to back up. Your results will be different from mine because the speed of your computer and the amount of your data will be different from mine. But I want to give you an idea what to expect when performing backups in the real world.

The first backup I made on my primary workstation after performing the setup took 34 minutes for almost 57GB of data from /home and /root. A second backup took a total of 53 seconds. This second backup was run on the same day as the first, so a new directory was not required and only a couple files had changed.

The third backup was performed two days later and took two minutes. In this case, a new directory structure was needed for this new day, and several files had changed.

Run the command **rsbu -cvu** in which -c is simply a check of the data on the backup device. It lists each daily backup directory for the computer.

```
[root@david Chapter-16]# rsbu -cvu <Press Enter>
Checking to ensure that Backup media is mounted at /media/MyBackups
/media/MyBackups not mounted. Mounting...
Media mounted OK

##########################################################################
# This Host = david
# rsbu Version = 2.4.0
# Config file = /root/development/Chapter-16/rsbu.conf
# Device index = 1
# Device Name = External USB hard drive
# Device ID =
# Mount Point = /media/MyBackups
# Maximum age of retained files = 60
# Base path = /media/MyBackups/Backups
# StartDate = 2021-12-08
# YesterdaysDate = 2021-12-07
##########################################################################

##########################################################################
Contents of /media/MyBackups/Backups/david/ for david
total 8
drwxr-xr-x 4 root root 4096 Dec  6 16:00 2021-12-06-RSBackup
drwxr-xr-x 4 root root 4096 Dec  8 07:43 2021-12-08-RSBackup
##########################################################################
```

```
#####################################################################
#                 Backup partition space usage data                 #
#####################################################################
# Device index = 1
# Device Name = External USB hard drive
# Device Label =
# Mount Point = /media/MyBackups
# Maximum age of retained files = 60
Filesystem      Size  Used Avail Use% Mounted on
/dev/sdf1       457G   58G  377G  14% /media/MyBackups
Filesystem      1K-blocks      Used Available Use% Mounted on
/dev/sdf1       478922436 59919952 394601132  14% /media/MyBackups
/dev/sdf1 on /media/MyBackups type ext4 (rw,nosuid,nodev,noexec,relatime,
user)
#####################################################################
/dev/sdf1 /media/MyBackups ext4 rw,nosuid,nodev,noexec,relatime 0 0
Unmounting /media/MyBackups
Program terminated normally
```

There are two days worth of backups in this example. I have highlighted the section that shows that in the preceding output. The directory for each day is a complete backup of that day. After running this backup program on a daily basis for 2 months, there will be 60 days of backups available. You will have 60 complete backups, one for each day for which there is a directory.

The rsbu program can easily deal with it if you skip daily backups, but I strongly recommend that you do not skip a day unless it is absolutely unavoidable.

Recovery Testing

No backup regimen would be complete without testing. You should regularly test recovery of random files or entire directory structures to ensure not only that the backups are working but that the data in the backups can be recovered for use after a disaster. I have seen too many instances where a backup could not be restored for one reason or another, and valuable data was lost because the lack of testing prevented discovery of the problem – until a backup was actually needed.

Restoring files from a backup made using the previous rsync commands is simply a matter of finding the file you want to restore from the backup device and then copying it to the location you want to restore it to. You can use the Thunar file manager that we covered in Chapter 11 to locate the desired files and restore them.

1. Connect the backup device to a USB port if it is not already. After a few seconds, an icon of the backup device will appear on the desktop. It will have the "MyBackups" label.

2. Click the backup device icon. This automatically mounts the device and opens the Thunar file manager with that device as the PWD.

3. Using the Thunar file manager, navigate through the backup of your home directory and locate a document. In this case, it can be any document since we are only testing the recovery of a file. Figure 14-2 shows the Documents/Linux-and-Computers directory of my test backup. It is difficult to see, but the location bar shows the entire path to this backup location.

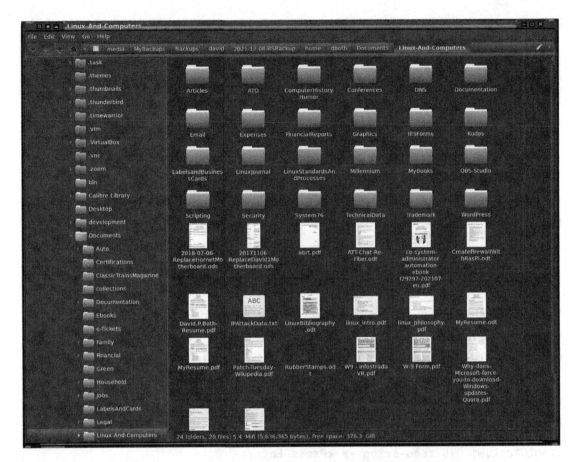

Figure 14-2. *You can use the file manager to locate files to restore from your backups*

4. Select one or more of the files in the directory you have chosen.
    Be sure to use a document or spreadsheet file that can be opened
    with LibreOffice.

5. Copy the file(s) to /tmp for now. We don't want to overwrite an
    existing file that has possibly been modified. Files being restored
    can be copied to any directory to which you have write access.
    They do not need to be restored to the directory from which they
    originated.

6. After copying the file(s) to /tmp, be sure to open it/them using the
    appropriate application to verify that it has not been corrupted
    during the entire backup and restore process. It happens though
    extremely rarely.

7. After testing the restore process, you can delete the test file(s) from /tmp.

8. Close the file manager.

9. Right-click the MyBackups desktop icon, and select the Unmount menu item. The icon will be grayed out when it is unmounted.

After being unmounted, the backup device can be disconnected from the computer. When you do that, the icon will disappear from the desktop.

If this test worked as it should, you now know that both the backup and restore functions are working properly.

Preparing Additional Backup Devices

I recommend that you perform regular backups and rotate the most recent one to an offsite, geographically separated location such as a bank safe deposit box. Implementation of a procedure like this requires multiple external USB backup storage drives.

You will need to prepare each storage device before it can be used for backups. The rsbu backup program will not recognize those devices unless they are prepared using the rsbu-setup program with the -p option.

```
[root@testvm1 ~]# rsbu-setup -p <Press Enter>


#####################################################################
#                         ATTENTION!!!                              #
#                                                                   #
#  Plug in the external USB hard drive you will be using for your backups.  #
#                                                                   #
#####################################################################

Have you plugged in the external USB hard drive? (ynq) y <Press Enter>


#####################################################################
#                                                                   #
#    Please be patient while we identify this new USB hard drive.   #
#                                                                   #
#####################################################################
```

```
###############################################################################
#                                                                             #
#                 A new device has been plugged in.                           #
#                                                                             #
###############################################################################
###############################################################################
#                                                                             #
# Verify that the information on the external storage device, especially      #
# that the device serial number matches that printed below.                   #
#                                                                             #
###############################################################################
###############################################################################

###############################################################################
#                                                                             #
#    WARNING!!   Be sure that this information is correct!   WARNINIG!!        #
#                                                                             #
#-----------------------------------------------------------------------------#
#                                                                             #
# The new storage device is:                                                  #
#                                                                             #
#    Model Family:     Western Digital Elements / My Passport (USB)
#    Device Model:     WDC WD5000BMVV-11GNWS0
#    Serial Number:    WD-WX71A30P3470
#                                                                             #
#-----------------------------------------------------------------------------#
#                                                                             #
# WARNING!!!    If the serial number printed above does not match that        #
#               printed on the physical label on the storage device, DO NOT   #
#               CONTINUE this procedure. Enter n or q below.                   #
#                                                                             #
#                                                                             #
#                                                                             #
###############################################################################
Are you POSITIVE that the device shown above is the correct one for your
backups? (ynq) y <Press Enter>
```

```
<SNIP>

Allocating group tables: done
Writing inode tables: done
Creating journal (262144 blocks): done
Writing superblocks and filesystem accounting information: done

#####################################################################
#                                                                   #
# Your new backup device has been prepared for use with the rsbu program.   #
#                                                                   #
#####################################################################
[root@testvm1 ~]#
```

External USB storage devices that have been prepared in this manner can now be
used in your backup rotation.

Automating Your Backups

It is a good idea to make backups by starting them manually each day for a week or so to
ensure that everything is working as it should. You can enable the timer I have created
and that was installed along with the **rsbu** program.

```
[root@testvm1 ~]# systemctl enable backup.timer <Press Enter>
```

This system timer runs the rsbu backup program each morning at about 15 minutes
after midnight. All you will need to remember is to rotate your backup media.

The Last Step

However, simply creating the backups will not save your business in the event of a
disaster. You need to make regular backups and keep the most recent copies at a remote
location, one that is not in the same building or even within a few miles of your business
location, if at all possible. This helps to ensure that a large-scale disaster does not destroy
all of your backups.

A reasonable option for most small businesses is to make daily backups on removable media and take the latest copy home at night. The next morning, take an older backup back to the office. You should have several rotating copies of your backups.

An even better solution would be to take the latest backup to the bank and place it in your safe deposit box and then return with the backup from the day before.

Chapter Summary

Making and managing backups of the data on your computer is one of the most important tasks you will perform. You should make regular backups, and you will appreciate it when you have your first disaster. Whether you deleted a single critical file or everything in your home directory, or your storage device just stopped working, having backups will be needed at some point in time. It will happen.

This chapter covered the use of the **rsbu** backup program and the **rsbu-setup** program in detail. You have installed and learned to use one set of tools to ensure that your personal and business data is backed up and stored safely. Putting these tools and procedures in place will allow you to recover your business and personal data from an inadvertently deleted file or a major disaster.

CHAPTER 15

Upgrades

Objectives

After reading this chapter, you will be able to

- Describe the difference between updates and upgrades

- Understand the reasons why upgrades are another important task required to maintain your Fedora hosts

- Prepare for the upgrade

- Perform the upgrade from one release of Fedora to the next

- Perform required post-upgrade tasks

- Automate upgrades

Introduction

Let's dive into how to upgrade from one release of Fedora to the next. Updates install fixes and enhancements to the installed software, but Fedora remains at the current Fedora release level such as Fedora 35. Upgrades install a complete version upgrade, for example, from Fedora 35 to Fedora 36.

Like updates, performing timely upgrades to keep your Linux hosts at the most recent Fedora releases is critically important to keep them secure and supportable. Using the procedures in this chapter, you can ensure that your Fedora systems can be maintained to the most current security and functional levels.

Updates as discussed in Chapter 13 are used to install security and functional fixes to software contained in a current release of Fedora. Sometimes, minor functional enhancements are included, but major new features are not.

257

© David Both, Cyndi Bulka 2022
D. Both and C. Bulka, *Linux for Small Business Owners*, https://doi.org/10.1007/978-1-4842-8264-9_15

Upgrades combine all of the security and functional fixes to Fedora at a given point in time, along with major new features that require significant changes to the operating system or user software. In this chapter, you will learn to perform a version upgrade, moving from one version of Fedora to the next. Each step is explained as you first prepare the computer for the upgrade, perform the upgrade, and finally perform a couple post-upgrade steps.

These upgrades are free of charge and do not require you to enter a product license key, your name, your phone number, or any personal information. You do not need an account or registration of any kind. The upgrade files are downloaded from the Internet, so you do need a good Internet connection.

Fedora Upgrades

Fedora has a rapid release schedule of a new version every six months or so. Despite occasional schedule slips, this six-month schedule has been mostly adhered to.

The best thing about open source software is that there is no marketing department complaining to development that they need the next release in order to maintain or increase the revenue stream. There is no pressure to release open source software like Linux before it is truly ready.

Whichever release of Fedora you start at, there will be a new release sooner than later. In order to continue receiving functional and especially security updates for more than 18 months after a version release, you will need to upgrade to newer releases on a regular basis.

First Things First

First, you need to know – and verify – your current release of Fedora. This is an easy one using the **hostnamectl** command.

```
[root@testvm1 ~]# hostnamectl
 Static hostname: testvm1.both.org
       Icon name: computer-vm
         Chassis: vm
      Machine ID: 5e0620101d8b44e3bb5b361895aeaa74
         Boot ID: ad26ac75276b40eeb929b0ac12fc0fc7
```

```
      Virtualization: oracle
    Operating System: Fedora 34 (Xfce)
        CPE OS Name: cpe:/o:fedoraproject:fedora:34
              Kernel: Linux 5.15.8-100.fc34.x86_64
        Architecture: x86-64
     Hardware Vendor: innotek GmbH
      Hardware Model: VirtualBox
[root@testvm1 ~]#
```

You can see definitively that this host is running Fedora 34. My primary workstation returns the following results:

```
[root@david ~]# hostnamectl
   Static hostname: david.both.org
         Icon name: computer-desktop
           Chassis: desktop
        Machine ID: 0b07292c495a42ee9f5867ebff1ccee2
           Boot ID: 02272134c9cd4a8397e33f3f1229bf04
  Operating System: Fedora Linux 35 (Thirty Five)
       CPE OS Name: cpe:/o:fedoraproject:fedora:35
            Kernel: Linux 5.15.10-200.fc35.x86_64
      Architecture: x86-64
   Hardware Vendor: System manufacturer
    Hardware Model: System Product Name
[root@david ~]#
```

The next thing you need is to know when a new version release of Fedora is available. There are a couple ways to do this.

The online publication, *Fedora Magazine*,[1] is an excellent source of news about Fedora including announcements of availability of new releases. *Fedora Magazine* also has an amazing variety of articles about Fedora, how to install, upgrade, and use it, and the huge number of applications that run on it. You can find articles on anything related to Fedora.

---

[1] https://fedoramagazine.org/

The announcement of the availability of Fedora 35 is there[2] as will be all future release announcements.

You can also subscribe to *Fedora Magazine* on any page of the *Fedora Magazine* website. You will get notifications of new articles as well as new release announcements. This is my primary method for keeping track of new Fedora releases.

Six Easy Steps

Once you are aware of the availability of a new release of Fedora, the upgrade is performed in six easy steps:

- Backup your data.

- Install the latest updates.

- Install the DNF system upgrade plug-in.

- Download the files required to upgrade your system.

- Reboot and perform the upgrade.

- Post upgrade cleanup.

All of these steps must be performed as the root user. Open a terminal session and switch user (su -) to root.

Backups

We just covered this in Chapter 14. No excuses. Even if you did backups a few minutes ago, do it again. If you do backups and the upgrade fails catastrophically, you can fall back to a complete reinstall of Fedora and restore your data.

Only once has an upgrade failed, and it was really more my fault than that of the upgrade procedure itself. It worked fine on all 17 other computers that were in my care at that time. Take no chances. Before proceeding any further, back up one more time.

---

[2] Miller, Matthew, "Worth the wait: Fedora Linux 35 is here!," *Fedora Magazine*, https://fedoramagazine.org/announcing-fedora-35/, November 2, 2021

Install Updates

There is a special method for installing updates prior to a version upgrade that helps prevent problems that might otherwise occur during the upgrade. Use this command to ensure proper preparation for the upgrade:

```
[root@testvm1 ~]# dnf -y upgrade --refresh
```

Although this will look like a normal update on the surface, it does perform some additional tasks that help to prepare for the upgrade to the next release of Fedora.

Install the Plug-in

There is a special plug-in to the DNF system that is needed to actually perform the upgrades. Plug-ins are add-ons that extend or add to the functionality of existing software, in this case, the DNF software management system.

```
[root@testvm1 ~]# dnf install -y  dnf-plugin-system-upgrade
```

Download the Files

In this step, the system upgrade plug-in downloads all of the files for the designated release and stores them for the next step. Only files that are already installed on your computer are downloaded. This step does not download files that are not already installed. First, there is no need, and second, it saves a great deal of time.

Be sure to specify the correct new release version in the command:

```
[root@testvm1 ~]# dnf -y system-upgrade download --refresh --relea
sever=35 --allowerasing
```

This procedure supports upgrading only one or two releases at a time. For example, you could upgrade from release 35 to release 36 or 37 but not to release 38. I usually upgrade by a single release, but I have successfully upgraded by two releases on a few occasions.

Reboot and Do the Upgrade

Everything up to this point has been preparation. This special DNF command initiates a reboot into a special state that installs all of the packages that were downloaded in the previous step.

```
[root@testvm1 ~]# dnf system-upgrade reboot
```

Your computer will reboot immediately, and the display will look like Figure 15-1 until the upgrade is complete.

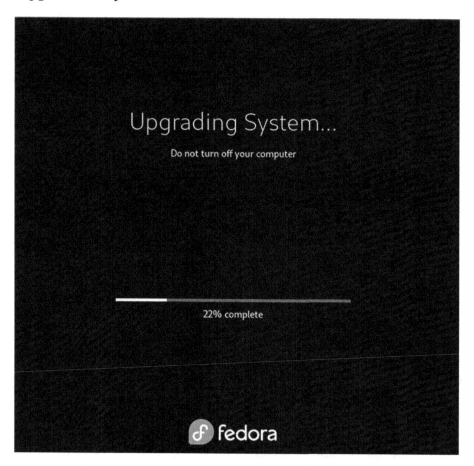

Figure 15-1. *Fedora during an upgrade from one release to the next. In this case from Fedora 34 to Fedora 35*

When complete, the upgrade procedure reboots the computer into the new release of Fedora.

Optional Post-Upgrade Tasks

The Fedora Project web page mentioned in footnote 3 contains a list of optional post-upgrade tasks. I typically skip over those because the results of two or three tries in the past left my test computer in a somewhat less than fully operational state.

You should only do these post-install tasks if you suspect that there was a problem with the upgrade. You should be sure to follow the directions exactly.

Chapter Summary

Performing upgrades is just as important as it is to do updates on a regular basis. This keeps your Linux system up to date and ensures that it can be secure and supportable.

It does take some time for the upgrade to process but not more than a few minutes of your time to enter the commands.

CHAPTER 16

Printing

Objectives

After reading this chapter, you will be able to

- Define the capabilities needed in a printer to meet the needs of your business

- Determine which printers work well with Linux and which to avoid

- Add a new printer when it really is plug and play

- Add a new printer when it is not plug and play

- Print a test page

- Perform printer setup in common applications such as LibreOffice

- Print from common applications like LibreOffice

- Configure and use multiple printers

- Manage the print queue

Introduction

Regardless of past attempts to create the "paperless office," paper documents are still required for many purposes. Our Linux computers still need to print.

We won't mislead you about printing. While Linux provides complete support for many printer brands and models, others are not well supported, and still others are not supported at all. Finding the right printer can be challenging. Trying to force an unsupported printer to work can be frustrating.

© David Both, Cyndi Bulka 2022
D. Both and C. Bulka, *Linux for Small Business Owners*, https://doi.org/10.1007/978-1-4842-8264-9_16

We provide some guidance to help you select the right printer or printers for you. If you have a printer that is not supported, you will need to purchase one that is.

Although adding a supported printer to Linux should be easy – and it usually is – there are always exceptions and your experience may be less than easy. This chapter covers the easy stuff and the steps required when printer configuration goes beyond the easy plug and play.

We start by exploring how to choose a printer.

Choosing a Printer

Choosing a supported printer is not difficult. You need to determine the purposes for which you will use the printer and then determine which printers that are supported by Linux meet those needs. There are a number of factors to consider, and some important resources are available.

Determine Your Needs

Most of us need to do simple document printing to standard paper sizes.[1] To complicate things, the United States, Canada, the Philippines, and parts of Mexico use the North American ANSI standards, while the rest of the world uses the ISO standards.

The most common commercial paper size in the United States is 8.5"x11" letter size, which can also be referred to as "A." The second most common size is 8.5"x14" legal paper. Less common is the 11"x17" ledger/tabloid or "B" size. Of course, the US government also has its own standards for letter and legal paper sizes which are just slightly different from the commercial sizes.

I have a Brother printer that supports legal, letter, and tabloid, plus A4, A5, B6, and A6. The paper trays in most modern printers are embossed with the paper sizes that they support to help users configure the tray for those common sizes. Most printers also support some standard envelope sizes.

I use 8.5x11 for printing and never anything else, so paper size is not an issue for me. My church uses tabloid size paper for printing the weekly bulletins, and only the more expensive printers support that size. Choose the specifications that will best serve your needs.

---

[1] "Paper Sizes," www.papersizes.org/

There are other technical factors to consider in addition to paper size. How much printing will you do? Do you need a heavy-duty printer that can do thousands of pages per month, or do you print just a few pages? Do you need color or will monochrome do? I print very few pages per month and use color but plain monochrome work for most things.

Do you need functions such as scanning, copying, or faxing? I make copies on my printer but haven't used faxes in years. Faxes have become somewhat obsolete. It is far easier to scan a document and email the result. Linux has multiple tools for scanning. My favorite scanning software is Xsane.

Do you need to connect your printer to the network to share with many computers, or will a USB connection be sufficient? Although a USB-connected printer can be shared on the network, it is only available to other devices as long as the computer to which it is connected is present, connected to the network, and turned on. When connected directly to the network, it does not depend on the presence of a specific computer on the network in order to work.

Automatic multiplex printing is a good feature to look for because it saves paper which saves money and is good for the environment.

Many modern printers have wireless (Bluetooth) capabilities and can be used to print from your mobile devices. I prefer not to use this feature, but it can be difficult to find a printer with the other features that I want that does not also have wireless connectivity.

Printers That Meet Your Requirements

Knowing your requirements, you can search online for printers that provide the features and functions you need.

I like to start by using a search engine to locate printers with the requisite features. I also use Amazon, big box store websites such as Best Buy, and office products stores like Staples and Office Depot/Office Max.

Find Compatible Printers

Now that you have a list of printers that meet your production requirements, you can determine their degree of compatibility with Linux.

Some vendors list Linux compatibility in their marketing but not many. In most cases, I find that the printers I really want don't state that in their marketing materials. You can go online to the vendors' websites and look at the detailed specifications for the printers in which you are interested; however, there is no consistency between manufacturers or even the different models of any given manufacturer.

We need a place to go that maintains lists of printers and their level of compatibility. The Linux Foundation[2] has a large database of printers[3] listed by manufacturer and collected into four categories based on their degree of compatibility with Linux. The Linux Foundation defines these categories as

- **Perfectly** – Perfect printers work perfectly; everything the printer can do works with Linux and Unix. For multifunction devices, this must include scanning/faxing/etc.

- **Mostly** – These printers work almost perfectly - funny enhanced resolution modes may be missing, or the color is a bit off, but nothing that would make the printouts not useful.

- **Partially** – These printers mostly don't work; you may be able to print only in monochrome on a color printer, or the printouts look horrible.

- **Paperweight** – These printers don't work at all. They may work in the future, but don't count on it.

We strongly suggest that you check this database for any current printers you already have and would like to use when you convert to Linux. This database will be invaluable in helping you to choose a new printer.

In addition, here are some general considerations that I think are important for choosing a printer whether for use with Linux or not:

1. Choose USB connectivity over a network connection. Most printers today support USB and many also support a network connection. Stick with USB for the primary connection unless you need that network connection for sharing the printer. USB printers

---

[2] The Linux Foundation, `www.linuxfoundation.org/`

[3] Linux Foundation, Open Printing Database, `https://wiki.linuxfoundation.org/openprinting/database/databaseintro`

are much easier to set up, and many times Linux can do it without any intervention from you.

2. Always choose a laser printer rather than an inkjet printer. Ink is extremely expensive for the amount of print it produces, and the ink can dry and clog the print heads.

3. Prefer name brands over less well-known ones. This can make a big difference when it becomes necessary to choose between fixing a broken printer and purchasing a new one. I recently had a problem with my expensive Brother all-in-one printer. The parts were readily available, and it was much less expensive to have it repaired than it would have been to replace it. This can also mean the difference in finding supplies like toner which may be difficult for off brands.

How to Install a Printer

I use common, name brand printers that are well supported by Linux. At home, I use a Brother multifunction MFC-9340CDW.[4] I also support my church which uses two printers. One is a high-volume multifunction Xerox VersaLink C7020,[5] and the second is a Brother HL-L2370DW.[6]

Cyndi has a HP Officejet Pro 8610. Unfortunately, this printer is listed in the "Paperweight" section of the Linux Foundation Open Printing Database.

This section outlines the installation procedures used for each of the supported printers. They were all different and the difficulty level ranged from totally easy plug and play to complex.

Plug and Play

The Brother HL-L2370DW monochrome laser printer used by my church is the definition of plug and play. I plugged it into a USB port and Linux detected it; located a

---

[4] Brother, www.brother-usa.com/products/mfc9340cdw

[5] Xerox, www.office.xerox.com/en-sa/multifunction-printers/versalink-c7020-c7025-c7030

[6] Brother, www.brother-usa.com/products/hll2370dw

Postscript Printer Definition (PPD) file, which acts as a device driver; installed the PPD file; and added an icon to the Print Settings dialog window.

After printing a test page at the urging of the installation procedure, this printer was ready to work.

Over the last dozen years or so, I have had three of the Brother printers in this line. All worked well with Linux, installed just this easily, and were inexpensive. After purchasing my multifunction printer, I recycled the last one of these I had when it broke.

Guided

My Brother MFC-9340CDW can print, copy, scan, and can send and receive faxes. Although this printer was not quite plug and play, it was still easy to install. The procedure is easy because all of the choices were made for me by Fedora and all I did was to accept each choice.

After I plugged in this printer, Fedora mostly ignored it. It was found and registered on the USB bus by Fedora, but there was no automated installation for it. As a result, I needed to perform a simple installation myself. These are the steps it takes to do that.

Start by opening the Print Settings dialog. If you have not added it to the lower panel, you can find it in **Applications ➤ Settings ➤ Print Settings**. Figure 16-1 shows the Print Settings dialog with no printers configured.

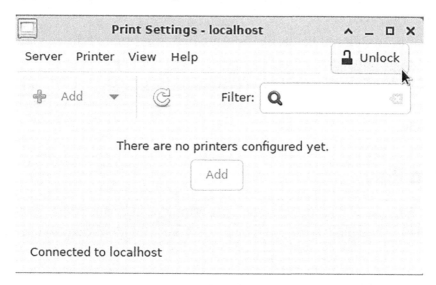

Figure 16-1. *The Print Settings dialog before configuring any printers*

The mouse pointer in Figure 16-1 is over the **Unlock** button. Click the Unlock button. Then type in the root password for your host as shown in Figure 16-2. Then press the **Enter** key. This opens the **New Printer** dialog.

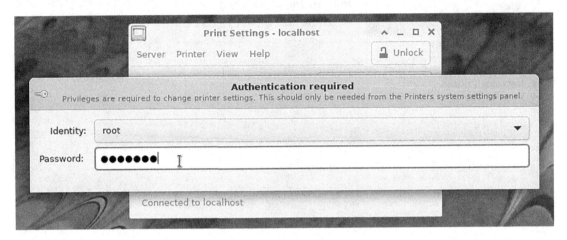

Figure 16-2. *Enter the root password in this dialog to access printer configuration tasks*

Figure 16-3 shows the **New Printer** dialog in which you can see that Fedora has identified the newly plugged in printer on the USB port. There are also options that can be used to add a network printer and to add printers that have not been explicitly identified such as ones shared by a host on the local network.

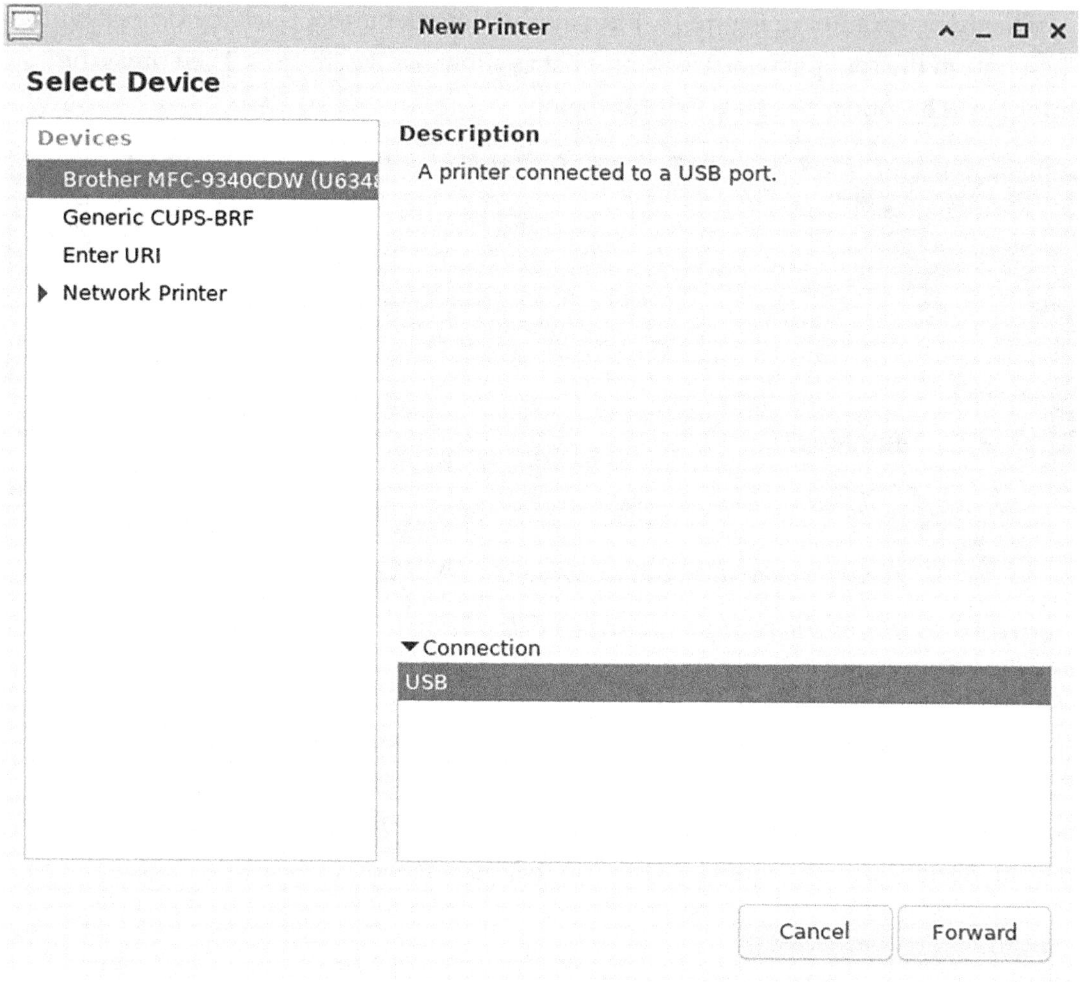

Figure 16-3. *The New Printer dialog shows the printer just plugged into the USB port*

If your Fedora system does not recognize the device plugged into the USB port or some other port like a serial or parallel printer port, you could use some command-line tools to determine its Universal Resource Locator and enter that directly into the URL item in the New Printer dialog. This more complex situation is covered in the next section of this chapter.

Since the **New Printer** dialog displays the printer I just connected, I ensure that it is still highlighted and click the **Forward** button. This brings us to the dialog in Figure 16-4.

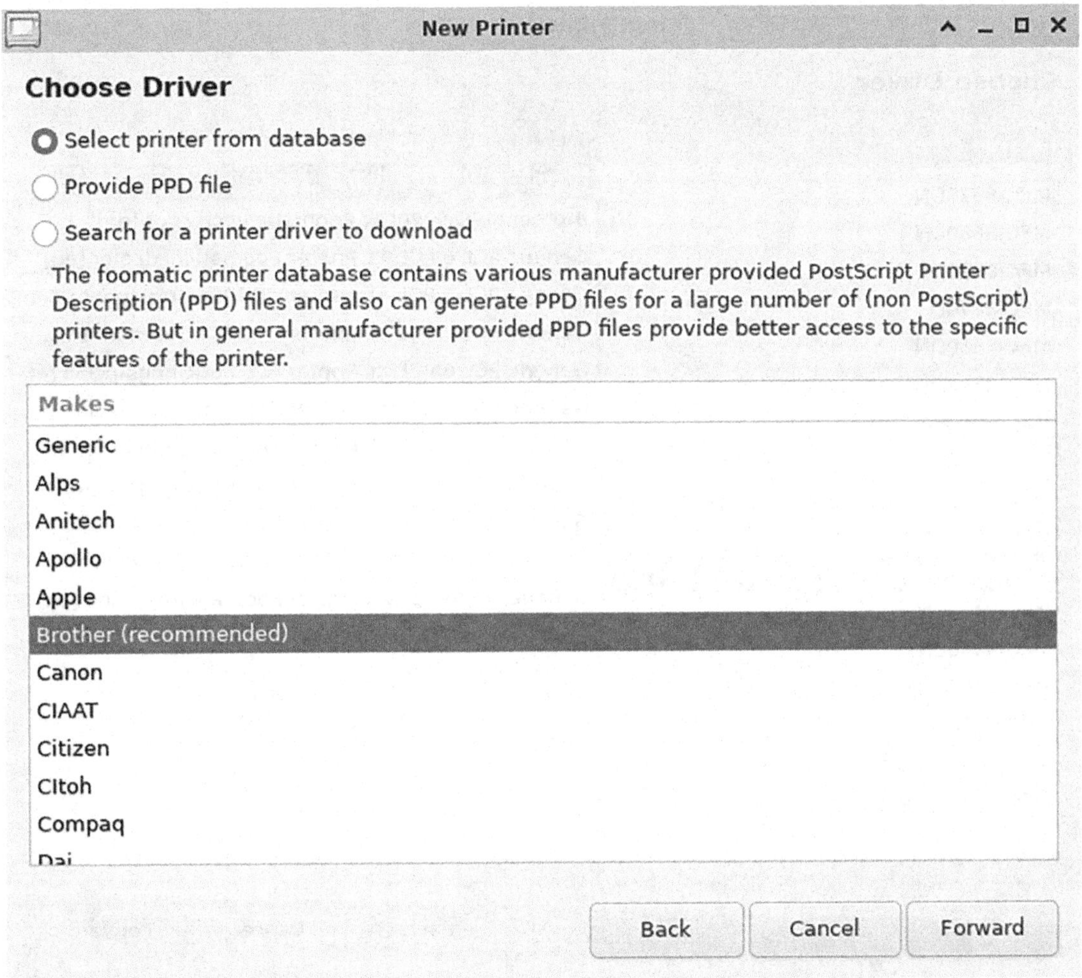

Figure 16-4. *The New Printer dialog has already highlighted the recommended printer manufacturer*

The **New Printer** dialog has highlighted the printer manufacturer for me, so all I needed to do was to click the **Forward** button again.

In Figure 16-5, the dialog now shows the recommended driver/PPD file for this printer. Notice that it is not the exact model that I have, which is the MFC-9340CDW. The New Printer dialog has listed all of the PPD files that will work for this printer with decreasing levels of compatibility. Since the most compatible – and hence recommended – PPD file is at the top and already highlighted, all I needed to do was to click the **Forward** button.

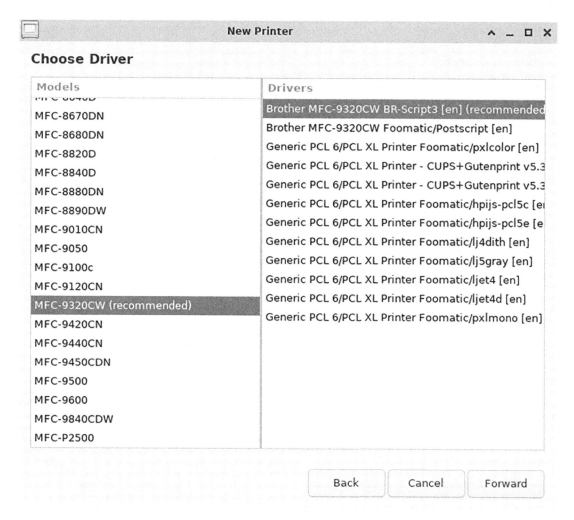

Figure 16-5. *The New Printer dialog automatically highlights the recommended PPD file for the printer it has detected*

Figure 16-6 shows the next dialog which is the place to change the data which identifies the printer to us humans. Some of this data will be placed in the fields by the New Printer application. You can keep or change any of it. I used the data provided by the configuration procedure for this printer.

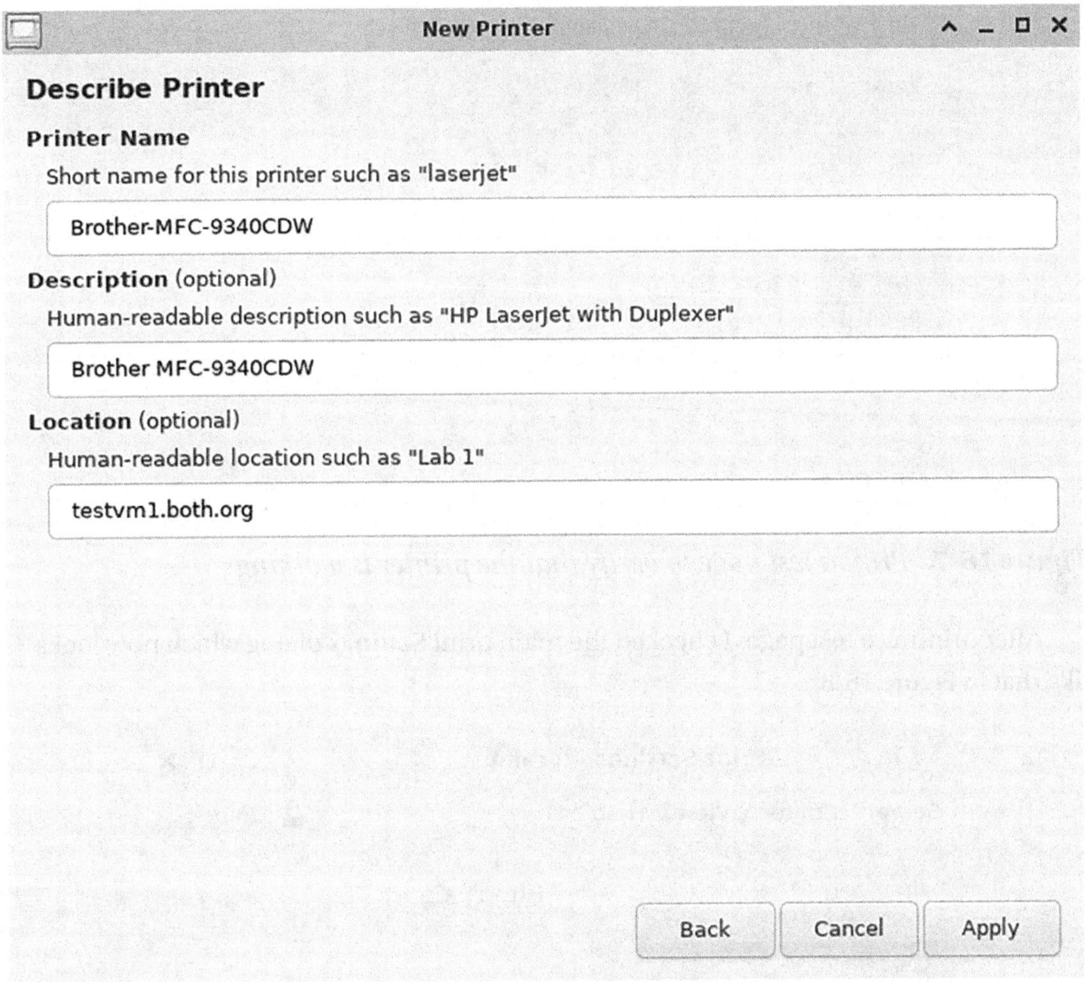

New Printer

Describe Printer

Printer Name

Short name for this printer such as "laserjet"

> Brother-MFC-9340CDW

Description (optional)

Human-readable description such as "HP LaserJet with Duplexer"

> Brother MFC-9340CDW

Location (optional)

Human-readable location such as "Lab 1"

> testvm1.both.org

Back   Cancel   Apply

Figure 16-6. *Identifying the printer and its location*

The first field, the Printer Name, is used to identify the printer to the computer. This name can be used from the command line if needed to send commands to the printer.

I then clicked the **Apply** button to create the printer configuration.

After I clicked Apply, I was given the option of printing a test page as shown in Figure 16-7. Do this. It helps to ensure that the configuration works.

Figure 16-7. *Print a test page to verify that the printer is working*

After printing a test page, I checked the main print Settings dialog which now looks like that in Figure 16-8.

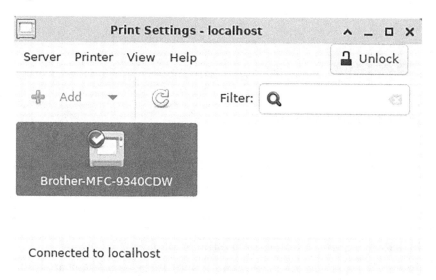

Figure 16-8. *The Print Settings dialog with the newly configured printer*

The icon for my Brother multifunction printer shows a green check mark which indicates that this is the default printer. Adding more printers does not change the default printer automatically. If you install another printer that you want to be the default, you can right-click the icon for that printer and choose the appropriate item from the context menu.

Complex

A couple years ago, my church leased a high-volume multifunction Xerox VersaLink C7020.[7] This printer was the most difficult of all these to configure. Fedora could not locate the PPD file for this printer on the Internet. Xerox does provide Linux support for many of its printers on its support website.

At the time, I downloaded a file from Xerox support for use with this printer under Linux and followed the directions to install the PPD and other supporting files. This was one of the more complex printer configurations I have had to perform, but the printer works as expected and all of its features work.

Unless your business absolutely requires a feature of a large printer such as this one, you should use a fully or mostly supported printer that does not require extraordinary installation procedures.

Alternatives

Suppose that your existing printer does not work with Linux or you just don't do enough printing to justify purchase of a new printer if you don't already have one. Or your printer may be broken. There are some alternatives available.

Many times it is not necessary to print a document onto physical paper. Even though I have a printer, I try to print as little as possible in order to save trees, toner, and electricity. I print to PDF documents and send those via email or copy them to a cloud drive where the other party can access them. I keep a graphic file of my signature that I can "paste" onto any documents that need to be signed, save that, and then email it.

Another option can be services like DocuSign which also provide a verifiable "paper trail." Even lawyers use these services, so they must be OK, right? Such services are not free to the document originator.

---

[7] Xerox, `www.office.xerox.com/en-sa/multifunction-printers/versalink-c7020-c7025-c7030`

There are some alternative ways to print those few documents that need to be on physical paper. Many office supply chains provide printing services for a fee. Even when I had a working printer, some print jobs just needed to be printed and bound, so I sent the files to the local office supply store and picked them up when they were ready.

Chapter Summary

Many printers are well supported by Linux and can be easily configured by plug and play or a simple guided configuration. These are the best printers for small businesses, and there is a good database at the Linux Foundation website to help you determine which ones fall into these categories.

Other printers require more effort to configure but can be well supported by their manufacturers. These are not the best printers for a small business.

There are also alternatives to printing on paper. PDF documents are a good way to go, and you can print documents at most office supply stores.

CHAPTER 17

Security

Objectives

In this chapter, you will learn to

- Identify typical security issues

- State the difference between "hacker" and "cracker"

- List typical attack vectors against computers

- Implement additional aspects of password security

- Take some basic steps to improve security of any Linux host

Introduction

Linux is a very secure operating system. It provides a secure environment in which to work and store files. However, good security, by its very nature, can be a bit obtrusive. Security must not be an afterthought; it must be an integral component of our computer systems.

Any device connected to the Internet is subject to attack and no operating system, even Linux, is completely free of exploitable flaws. Linux just happens to be more secure than other operating systems and, when it is breached, is much less vulnerable to widespread damage.

There are only four rules required to achieve complete and unbreakable security:

1. The computer must be locked in a blast-proof room to prevent both unauthorized access and destruction of the computer and its contents.

© David Both, Cyndi Bulka 2022
D. Both and C. Bulka, *Linux for Small Business Owners*, https://doi.org/10.1007/978-1-4842-8264-9_17

2. It must be inside a Faraday cage[1] to prevent its own radio frequency emissions from escaping to be captured by "the bad people." This would also protect the host against an EMP blast but assumes a power source completely within the confines of the cage.

3. It must have a 100% air gap – that is, it must not be connected to any network and especially not to the Internet. This includes all hard-wired and wireless connections such as Wi-Fi, Bluetooth, infrared, and anything else that transmits data outside of the computer.

4. It must be turned off and the rest of the rules don't count.

Unfortunately, these rules mean the computer is unusable even for its intended purpose. That, in turn, means that any computer that is turned on is vulnerable to cracking. A cracker is the correct name for a hacker with evil intent. Hackers – the good people who hack, that is, work on, hardware and code – are the ones who gave us things like free and open source tools like Linux and the many applications that run on it. Unfortunately, we must use our computers in an imperfect and unsafe environment at all times.

I want to reiterate: security is *not* an afterthought – it is something that must be considered as part of all we do as SysAdmins. Let's look at some important security considerations.

Security by Obscurity

"Security by obscurity" cannot be counted on to protect your computer. In fact, the worst assumption you can make is that some level of obscurity can protect your computers. Some small businesses I have worked with, including my own systems, are constantly subjected to attempts to crack into their firewall servers, hundreds of attempts per day and thousands per month. And that is *after* I have instituted measures to reduce the total number of attacks. Every computer that is connected to the Internet is a target.

---

[1] Wikipedia, "Faraday cage," `https://en.wikipedia.org/wiki/Faraday_cage`

Although there are a number of measures that can be instituted to protect your computer, it will never be impervious. Exercise care in the way you use the Web and deal with spam email.

There are a number of good websites with information on how to protect yourself online. Although I cannot verify all of the information on them, there is one I especially like, Get Safe Online.[2] It even has a section on safe Linux use.

What Is Security?

Security is about far more than simply preventing unwanted people from logging in to our Linux computers. Although good passwords and other security measures are helpful and can help to prevent that type of security vulnerability, they are the response to only one part of the security problem. There are many aspects to security. It is important to understand that fact as well as to know the things that we are using various security protocols to protect.

What are we trying to protect? Not surprisingly, a large part of security is designed to protect our data, but perhaps in ways and for reasons you have not previously considered.

Data Protection

There are three major considerations to data protection and different tools and strategies apply to each.

First, we want to protect our data from loss so that it will be available to us. This ensures the data will not be destroyed or lost and hence no longer available for access. As a business owner, loss of my financial records in a fire or natural disaster would be a disaster that might be impossible to recover from. The accessibility of our data ensures the continuity of our business.

Second, we want to protect our data from unauthorized access. We need to ensure that company and personal data is not available to someone who might use it for nefarious purposes. In many organizations that data contains information that a competitor might use to gain advantage over us or personal information about ourselves, our employees, and our financial data. The confidentiality of our data is essential.

---

[2] Get Safe Online, www.getsafeonline.org/protecting-yourself/

Third, we need to ensure that our data is safe from unauthorized changes or corruption, perhaps by malware, a disgruntled employee, or one who is simply a thief. We need to make sure that we are not blocked from access to our own data by ransomware which would encrypt the data and keep us from accessing it until the ransom is paid. This protects the integrity of our data.

It's not just about keeping data safe, but being confident that the data is kept safe from espionage, destruction, and corruption.

Attack Vectors

Attack vectors are many and varied. These vectors are all classifiable into five major categories: self-inflicted, environmental, physical, network, and software vulnerabilities. There are some things that can be done, in addition to some of the obvious ones hinted at in this section, and we'll explore those later in this chapter.

This is where I try to scare you enough to apply some common sense and freely available open source tools to improving the security of your Linux systems.

Self-Inflicted Problems

Self-inflicted data loss comes in many forms. The most common form being the semi-intentional erasure of important files or directories.

Sometimes, erasing needed files is accidental. For example, I might have erased a large number of old files in a directory, and it turns out that one or two are still needed. On other occasions, I have been working on the back side of a computer rack and accidentally pulled the power plug from the wrong computer. Although hard drives and modern journaling filesystems can generally withstand a power loss, it still happens.

This category also includes things like using poor passwords that can be easily cracked and leaving a USB drive with critical data stored on it in an accessible location. Leaving a laptop unattended in a public place like a coffee shop and using unencrypted wireless links are also common points of data loss.

System Problems

System issues that can affect the security of computer systems are misunderstood by most people. When we use the word environmental, we tend to think in terms of electrical power backup units, cooling the data center, and so on. There is so much more that many of us don't think about.

Power failures can occur for many reasons. Regardless of the reason, there is the danger of losing data, especially from documents that have not been saved. Modern hard drives and filesystems employ strategies that help to minimize the probabilities of data loss, but failures still happen.

Hard drive failures also cause data loss. The most common failures in today's computers are devices that have moving mechanical components. Leading the frequency list are cooling fans with hard disk drives a close second.

Modern computers are well protected against many of these problems. All we need to do is ensure that we use battery backup units, which are also known as uninterruptible power supplies (UPS) and that they are plugged into properly grounded outlets. This will minimize the possibilities.

Physical Attacks

Physical security is about protecting the hardware from various types of harm. Although we tend to think in terms of keeping bad people away from the hardware on which we run our systems, we also need to consider disaster scenarios as a major part of our planning.

Disgruntled employees, common theft, and natural disasters – fire, flood, hurricanes, tornadoes, mud slides, tsunamis, and so many more kinds of disasters can destroy computers and locally stored backups as well. I can guarantee that even if I have a good backup, I will never take the time during a fire, tornado, or natural disaster that places me in imminent danger to save the backups.

Network Attacks

Attacks via networks, both local and the Internet, are common and can be extremely dangerous. These attacks can take many forms ranging from direct attacks from the Internet against firewalls and servers to indirect attacks in which malware is introduced into a host by some stealthy means such as hiding in a downloaded file, an email, or a click-bait link on a website.

This type of attack does not require direct physical access to your computers. Rather, they come through your connections to the outside world.

Scripted attacks are generally used by so-called script kiddies. This derogatory term is used because they are not usually smart or determined enough to create the attack scripts themselves, so they purchase them from those who are – it's actually a lucrative business. The scripts they use are simple brute-force remote login attempts. Their malicious attacks are useless against today's well-protected Linux hosts.

These attacks typically consist of automated dictionary probes against a large number of remote hosts, usually those on a specific network address range, rather than against a specific single host or organization.

Malware is a very generic term for software that can be used for various malicious purposes including destroying or deleting your data.

Drive-by malware is a malicious link in an apparently innocuous advertisement on an otherwise legitimate web page. You do not even need to click this link for your computer to be affected.

Targeted login attempts are aimed directly at you or your organization. These attacks are usually carried out by someone or some group with a specific reason to target you. If someone targets you specifically and really wants to crack into your system, they will be able to do so, given enough time and even just a little bit of carelessness on your part.

Ransomware is a specific form of malware that encrypts your data and holds it for ransom. If you pay the ransom, you may get the key that will allow you to decrypt your data – if you are lucky.

Scareware is similar to ransomware except that your data is not really encrypted. In this case, the crackers are trying to scare you into calling their fake "support" number where they will con you out of your credit card information so that you can "pay" for their services. Some of these scams may try to get enough information to steal your identity as well. Scareware works through your browser which means that it also works on Linux.

Example: Scareware

There is a "tech support" scam that can be loaded to your browser when you attempt to go to a legitimate website. Your attempt to link to the valid website is intercepted and redirected to a website that downloads the malicious code onto your computer. There are a number of methods that the scammers can use to intercept your link to the valid website, but those details are beyond the scope of this book.

The malicious website is not intended to actually damage your computer or the data on it. It is intended to scare you into calling the scammers alleged "tech support" phone line where they will attempt to get your credit card information. The scary mess on your computer screen is basically social engineering intended to scare you into calling the phone number where the scammers will go on a phishing expedition to steal your credit card info and possibly your identity.

Ironically, Cyndi encountered this just as she finished editing this chapter on security and used her browser (she runs Firefox in Linux, of course) to go to pay a credit card bill. That is when the pop-up windows shown in Figure 17-1 appeared along with a very loud audio message with very nerve-wracking loud music intended to intensify your sense of urgency and to raise your anxiety level.

Notice that one of the pop-ups says, "Windows Firewall," and another, "Windows Defender." You know that since you are on Linux, you cannot be using anything with "Windows" in the name. Also, note the spelling errors and other references to Windows.

Figure 17-1 also shows the very random URL name of `https://hfrrrsijds.buzz` which should also give you a clue that this is not legitimate for Linux or Windows.

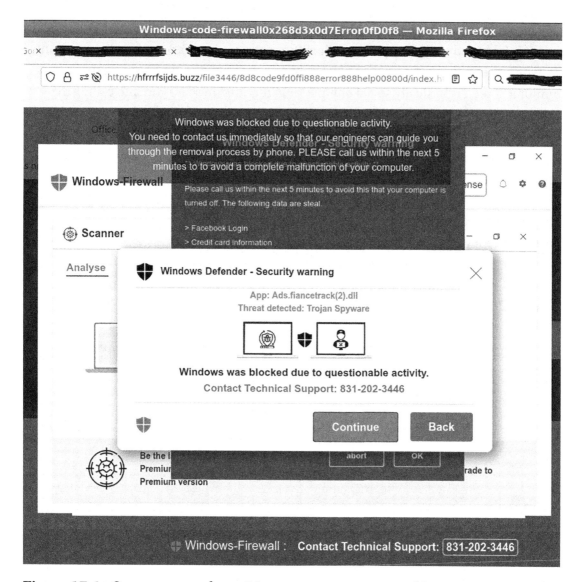

Figure 17-1. *Scareware works on Linux computers, too, and it can give you quite the scare*

If and when this or anything else like it happens to you, first, ***don't panic!*** Second, ***do not call the number on the screen!*** The attack is harmless – except to your nerves. It is intended to cause you to panic.

It is easy to get out of. Just exit from your browser. The *browser* – not the individual pop-ups. The pop-ups will just keep reappearing.

If this happens to you, do not panic! Just steel yourself, turn the sound off so you aren't being subjected to the frantic exhortations to call the support center, and work to close your browser. You can use the "X" button on the top right of the browser window, or you can locate the browser button on the top Xfce panel, right-click to raise the context menu, and choose the **Close** menu item.

Whatever you do, do not call the number on the screen. If nothing else works, hold down the power button on your computer for at least five seconds until the computer powers off. When you power back on, all should be well unless you have your browser set to launch when you log in.

The thing to realize is that the crackers who are trying to steal data from your computer will do it quietly. If they succeed, you will never know they have been there until your bank warns you of the attempted credit fraud.

The loud and obnoxious displays used with scareware are an indicator that the scammers can't or won't steal the data from your computer – they want to steal your credit card info or your identity by frightening you into revealing it to them. Since they need your help to do that, you can safely ignore the noise and onscreen fright show while figuring out how to get rid of it.

Software Vulnerabilities

Many attacks on connected computers are aided and abetted by vulnerabilities in the host's software. These vulnerabilities are exploited by the attackers and can be leveraged to install malware of various types. However, just because a vulnerability exists does not mean that an exploit is available to take advantage of it.

Always keep systems up to date so that the latest security patches are installed. Ensure that good firewalls are in place and properly configured. And check frequently for evidence of break-ins.

Linux and Security

So, did that scare you? It should have.

The good news is that Linux is very secure. Linux is very secure immediately upon installation. Fedora has an excellent firewall in place to protect against unwanted intrusions. Some things are unavoidable like the scareware that rides in on a hijacked browser connection. But those attacks are very limited in what they can do because of the intrinsically secure nature of Linux.

Login Security

Login security – making sure that only authorized users have access to log in and use the system's resources is the first line of defense. Generating and using secure passwords is the main tool we have to provide this security, whether a local or remote login. But it seems a bit silly for me to write an entire section on password security when the passwd man page already has an excellent section on just that. So here it is, directly from the passwd man page:

Remember the following two principles

Protect your password.

Don't write down your password - memorize it. In particular, don't write it down and leave it anywhere, and don't place it in an unencrypted file! Use unrelated passwords for systems controlled by different organizations. Don't give or share your password, in particular to someone claiming to be from computer support or a vendor. Don't let anyone watch you enter your password. Don't enter your password to a computer you don't trust or if things "look funny"; someone may be trying to hijack your password. Use the password for a limited time and change it periodically.

Choose a hard-to-guess password.

passwd, through the calls to the pam_cracklib PAM module, will try to prevent you from choosing a really bad password, but it isn't foolproof; create your password wisely. Don't use something you'd find in a dictionary (in any language or jargon). Don't use a name (including that of a spouse, parent, child, pet, fantasy character, famous person, and location) or any variation of your personal or account name. Don't use accessible information about you (such as your phone number, license plate, or social security number) or your environment. Don't use a birthday or a simple pattern (such as "qwerty", "abc", or "aaa"). Don't use any of those backwards, followed by a digit, or preceded by a digit. Instead, use a mixture of upper and lower case letters, as well as digits or punctuation. When choosing a new password, make sure it's unrelated to any previous password. Use long passwords (say at least 8 characters long). You might use a word pair with punctuation inserted, a passphrase (an understandable sequence of words), or the first letter of each word in a passphrase.

You can access this same man(ual) page with the command **man passwd**.

Password Security

It is advisable as a good security precaution to change your password about once a month. This prevents other people from using your password for very long even if they happen to discover it. Once you have changed it, they can no longer use your previous password to access the system. You never know when or how someone might obtain or guess your password, so even if you do not think it has been compromised, you should change your password regularly. Of course, a password should be changed immediately if you suspect that it has been compromised.

Passwords should be protected and never written down. If a password is stolen, it can be used to access your computer and the network if your computer is so connected and thus compromise your data.

Linux requires passwords to be a specified minimum length. The default is five characters, but that can be changed. I recommend that you use a longer password to increase the difficulty of someone guessing your password. Passwords should never be dates, initials, acronyms, words, or easy-to-remember sequences such as "ASDFG" from the left of the middle row of the keyboard. Passwords should be composed of upper- and lowercase alphabetic characters as well as numbers and special characters.

My personal calculations show that an automated attack of 500 access attempts per second on a host with a 5-character password can be cracked in anywhere from 6 hours to 21 days depending upon whether the password contains only lowercase alpha or upper- and lowercase as well as numbers. The time to crack a really good randomly generated password that includes special characters (#$%^, etc.) rises to 152 days. This should be set to a minimum of eight to ensure a reasonable amount of security. The time to crack an 8-character password rises to 13 years to over 325,000 years, once again depending upon using upper- and lowercase, numbers, and special characters.

The crackers – the malicious hackers who want to get into your computer – have dictionaries of words, common acronyms, and key sequences that they can try to attempt to crack into your system. They also try easy-to-guess sequences that are available to anyone with a little persistence such as birthdays; anniversaries; the names of spouses, children, pets, or significant others; as well as social security numbers and other possible passwords of this type. The point is that when you change your password, you should choose one that is not based on a dictionary word or one that will be easy to guess or deduce from your personal information. Passwords based on any of these nonrandom sources will likely be cracked in seconds.

There is a significant downside to changing passwords frequently and setting strict policies that require them to be excessively long and not easily memorized. Such policies will almost certainly result in users who write their passwords on post-it notes and stick them on the display or under the keyboard. There is a fine line between workable security and self-defeating security.

Password Encryption

Passwords cannot be safely stored on the hard drive in plain text format as this would leave them open to incredibly easy hacking. In order to ensure that the user passwords are secure, passwords are encrypted using the well-tested OpenSSL encryption libraries.

Theoretically, the well-known algorithms used to generate password hashes[3] do so in such a way that there is no known algorithm that can reverse the process and generate the plain text password from the password hash. However, if a cracker has access to the hash, a brute-force attack could conceivably find the plain text that generated the hash. This would not take long if the password was based on dictionary words, but could take years if good passwords were used.

Generating Good Passwords

Creating good passwords is a challenge. It can take some thought and effort. Linux has at least one command-line tool that provides us with suggestions for good passwords.

The **pwgen** (password generator) utility gives us the ability to specify the number and length of passwords we want to generate as well as to make them relatively easy or impossible to remember. By default, when used without the -s (secure) and -y (use special characters) options, the resulting passwords are alleged to be easy for humans to memorize. My experience is that some are and others not so much.

---

[3] A hash is your encrypted password that is stored on the computer.

Let's explore the **pwgen** utility to learn how it can help us create reasonably secure passwords. Start by using **pwgen** with no options which generates a list of 160 random 8-character passwords using uppercase, lowercase, and numeric characters. I can choose one of the passwords from the list to use.

```
[dboth@testvm1 ~]$ pwgen
Iiqu4ahY Eeshu1ei raeZoo8o ahj6Sei3 Moo5ohTu ieGh6eit IsoEisae eiVo5Ohv
Gooqu5ji ieX9VoN5 aiy3kiSo Iphaex4e Vait1thu oi5ruaPh eL7Mohch iel2Aih6
Elu5Fiqu eeZ4aeje Ienooj6v iFie2aiN ruu7ohSh foo4Chie Wai5Ap1N ohRae1lu
<SNIP>
Gae5ahsh Eech1re7 feeDah4v wou7Oek4 iefoo9AJ zei4ahVi uMiel7sh jae3eiVo
zahC3Tue Eiphei6E ke6GiaJ8 oquieBaO chi8Ohba ooZ9OC3e deiV7pae sieCho6W
nu1oba1D aiYoh2oo OoluaZ7u Ahg5pee7 Teepha6E oochOMod ThaiPui5 Ehui9ioF
ekuina3Z Oafaivi1 Pusuef9g aChoh2Eb Cio7aebe eoPOiepu seGh2kie fiax4Cha
```

The pwgen program recognizes two arguments in the syntax, **pwgen password_length number_of_passwds**. Try this for more control over the number and length of the passwords.

```
[dboth@testvm1 ~]$ pwgen 25 10
EetahchOhiuvaedodu1iPh5Oh Ahvoosoh5Eifei8eiyahWee1s
Hout4ichoh9eiBeip5ChaiRe2
aGuuquaexiet8epao1phiOthu yuwoo3pei5nooQua7koo9kube
wa6ahcho8Aey1ahthaegaeB9w
ahg5oo8xeivo6fahw6shila1C een9eeGOquoov3Iegheixahde
hae6IeBe1eiZoh2laa9phivae
naengeiHohshaikahghie4aer
```

Keeping Track of All Those Passwords

We all have many places that we use passwords, and the very best practice is to use a different login ID and password for each and every one of those. The problem with that is remembering all of those many IDs and their corresponding passwords.

I used to keep all of my passwords in a LibreOffice Writer document that I had password protected. That works but was not nearly as efficient as using a good password manager.

A password manager is software that provides a secure and consistent way to keep and protect all of your passwords, even those that are not related to your Linux computer. There are many password managers available, some of which store your passwords locally and others that store your passwords in the "cloud."

A quick Internet search for "password manager for Linux" results in a huge number of hits. I used "Best Linux Password Managers of 2022" which listed 15 password manager along with a brief review of each.

I looked for an open source, free of charge password manager that keeps my data locally and not in the cloud. See the section "The Cloud" for why.

KeePassXC

The password manager I chose was KeePassXC[4] because it meets my requirements and is also available directly from the Fedora repository which makes it simple to install. KeePassXC can store an unlimited number of user IDs and passwords along with other related data. It uses an encrypted database to ensure the security of your data. It is being currently maintained and supported which are important considerations.

The other choices are all fine depending upon your needs. Seth Kenlon, our technical reviewer, uses Bitwarden which has both free and inexpensive paid plans.

This password manager can be a single password management solution because it – like many open source tools – supports Linux, Windows, and MacOS. It has a good set of documentation on its website including a getting started section.

Installing KeePassXC

Install KeePassXC with the following simple command:

```
[root@david ~]# dnf install -y keepassxc
```

The KeePassXC launch icon appears in the **Applications ➤ Accessories** menu, so launch it from there. I found the interface friendlier than the other password managers I tried, including those related to the original KeePass and KeePassX. Figure 17-2 shows the interface which has some helpfully named buttons to make it easy to get started.

---

[4] KeePassXC website, `www.keepassxc.org/`

Figure 17-2. *The KeePassXC interface has a number of options displayed to help you get started*

The KeePassXC password generator can also be accessed while it is running so that you can generate new passwords at any time and not just during creation of the database. One of the key features of KeePassXC is its ability to integrate with your browser and your online accounts. Passwords generated in KeePassXC can be automatically applied to your online accounts when you create them or change passwords.

KeePassXC has excellent documentation, so I won't attempt to duplicate it here. You can find it at the URL `https://keepassxc.org/docs/`.

Firewalls

Firewalls are a very important part of computer and network security. Firewalls can block any and all attempts to access our Linux hosts by way of the networks to which we are connected.

A tool called firewalld is the default firewall management tool used by current releases of Fedora. It is turned on by default, and its default state blocks all connection attempts to your computer. This is a good thing and can prevent many attacks.

This does not mean that your computer is completely immune from Internet threats. Downloading a file from the Internet, especially from an untrusted source, can open your computer up to an infection.

Dynamic Firewall

A dynamic firewall is one that can adapt as the threats change. I needed something like this to stem the large number of attacks via SSH and my web server that I had been experiencing a few years ago. In response to these attacks, I would identify the IP addresses of the worst offenders each day and manually add them to the block list on my firewall. That was very time consuming.

After some research, I found fail2ban, an open source software which automates what I was previously doing manually.

The Fail2Ban tool is not useful if you only have a single computer and you are not running any servers such as your own web server, email server, and more. Linux allows you to easily and freely do that, but most small business owners find it more productive to hire someone else to host and manage those tools. Cyndi has certainly found this to be true.

Public Wi-Fi

Never use public Wi-Fi. Your favorite Wi-Fi connection can be easily hacked by scammers or spoofed so that you are not even using the real Wi-Fi for that coffee shop.

OK, only use public Wi-Fi if it requires a password. This is not sufficient by itself but is a start to public Internet safety.

You should always verify that the Wi-Fi link you intend to use is the correct one for the location you are in. Be sure to double check this. The SSID (the network name) can be made to look very close to the real one by the scammers. They sit in locations with Wi-Fi and use a portable Wi-Fi connection with a name so similar to the real one for that location that it is easy to assume it is the correct one. This is the "evil twin" scam. It is OK to ask the staff for the exact name of its Wi-Fi network to make sure that's the one you plan to use.

You are much better off in most public places using your cell phone in "tethered" mode in which it becomes a Wi-Fi hotspot. You need to activate this service with some providers. Be sure to set up a strong password for your mobile phone, or the scammers could hack into it as well.

The Cloud

The "cloud" offers some really cool tools for collaboration and sharing documents. But don't use the cloud as a long-term solution for data storage. "Cloud" is just another name for someone else's computer, and you have no control over the security precautions implemented on that computer. You don't know whether that computer is running Linux, Windows, or something else.

Always keep your files on your own computer. But it is OK to copy a file to a place like Google Drive or Dropbox and then delete it when the other person downloads it for themselves.

If you use something like Google Docs for collaboration, always save a copy on your own computer and delete the shared copy when you are finished.

Steps to Improve Your Security

There are some steps that can be taken for any Linux host to harden it against attacks of many different types. Other common sense steps can be taken to ensure the security of your devices and various Internet accessible accounts.

These steps range from easy to difficult, and the ones you choose to put in place depend upon the amount of pain you would be in should the defenses of your systems be breached. The cost trade-off is a judgment that must be made by you as a small business owner. I recommend taking as many of these steps as possible.

1. Back up everything – frequently.

2. Keep your operating system and applications updated at all times.

3. Use strong passwords. They are a simple security measure and make brute-force cracking of passwords much more difficult.

4. Change passwords frequently to ensure that any that are cracked are not usable for more than a short period of time. Password aging can be used to enforce this.

5. Don't use the same passwords for multiple accounts. Try to make your passwords unpredictable and avoid using names, dates, or common words. Never share your passwords with anyone you don't trust.

6. Use two-factor authentication. This is when you begin to log in to a website and provide your ID and password; they send a one-time code that you need to enter in order to complete the login. Many financial and health-related websites use two-factor authentication.

7. Use biometric authentication such as facial recognition or fingerprint scans on all devices that support it.

8. Do not share user accounts. When multiple users have access to a common account, it becomes more difficult to determine the user responsible for security problems. If users must collaborate on shared documents, create a shared directory separate from their own home directories and use a separate group to allow access to only the people who need it.

9. Delete old user accounts to help keep a system secure. Old, unused accounts can be used to gain access to a system.

10. Strong firewalls are always an important part of any security regimen. Fedora already implements this.

11. Don't store your data in the "cloud."

12. Don't send anything in an email that you want to keep confidential or private. Email is not secure.

13. Don't click links in emails that you were not expecting.

14. Don't click links that appear to have come from someone you do know but that don't make sense in any context related to that person or business.

15. Don't give out personal information over unencrypted websites. Only trust encrypted sites that begin with "https" (the "s" means they're secure). They convert your information into a code that prevents exposure to potential scammers.

16. Keep your computer software updated at all times. Install fixes, patches, and security updates on a regular basis. I suggest weekly or immediately upon release of a security update.

17. Always upgrade to the latest versions of your operating system, web browsers, and apps. Do this as soon as a new release of Fedora is available.

18. Don't use public computers such as those you would find in a public library or so-called Internet café.

19. When using your own computer in public, ensure that no one is looking over your shoulder – including "security" cameras.

20. Never use a public Wi-Fi link. This would be the best case, but if you must, the next few items are intended to mitigate your risk.

21. Use your mobile phone as a Wi-Fi hotspot instead of public Wi-Fi.

22. Never sign into a public Wi-Fi link unless it requires a password and you already know and trust the link.

23. Verify the SSID of any public Wi-Fi link you use with the store staff to ensure it is the correct one and not a similar one used by scammers.

24. Turn off both Wi-Fi and Bluetooth if you are not using them.

25. Learn how to spot common scams and fraud. Learn the warning signs of Internet fraud,[5] phishing,[6] and other online scams.[7]

---

[5] www.usa.gov/online-safety#item-37232

[6] www.consumer.ftc.gov/articles/how-recognize-and-avoid-phishing-scams

[7] www.fbi.gov/scams-and-safety/common-scams-and-crimes/internet-fraud

26.   Learn the basics of cyber security.[8] Find out what to do during and after cyber attacks and what you can do beforehand to prevent them.

27.   Use the links in the footnotes of this list to learn more about cyber security.

28.   Back up everything – frequently.

29.   Keep your operating system and applications updated at all times.

We know that seems like a lot of work, and there is much to be aware of. You are correct; it is a lot of work. Unfortunately, there are a lot of ways to get hacked. It takes some awareness and effort to protect your data assets and your identity.

Chapter Summary

Security is a big part of our job as small business owners who are also SysAdmins.

Realistic security is a cost/benefit trade-off between the owner of the computer network and the cracker. The question is how much is our data worth? Good security should be a pain for users and they will likely complain, but it should not be enough to engender bad behavior such as writing down passwords and sticking them under the keyboard.

Linux is already configured to a very high level of security. Using good passwords, the already enabled firewall, following basic security precautions when working on public Wi-Fi, and following the list of security steps create a very secure environment with little trouble and no additional cost.

Remember that the "cloud" is just someone else's computer – one over which you have no control.

Security takes work. The cost of losing your data or having it stolen is far greater than implementing realistic and effective security precautions.

---

[8]www.ready.gov/cybersecurity

## CHAPTER 18

Automation

Objectives

After reading this chapter, you will be able to

- Define automation in the context of computers in small business
- State why "automate everything" is an important part of computer maintenance and management
- Use simple automation tools like scripts and programs that are already available

Introduction

In this chapter, we introduce you to the concept of automation as one of the tools already in use by the business owner to reduce their direct involvement in common and frequently performed tasks. You are probably not aware of the amount of automation you already use. We have already covered things like installing new software, backups, and keeping your system up to date with updates and version upgrades.

We define the term automation and look at some of the ways in which you have already used it. This short chapter does not provide a detailed guide to creating and implementing your own automation. You should instead be using automation already created by others such as the backup program we covered in an earlier chapter.

© David Both, Cyndi Bulka 2022
D. Both and C. Bulka, *Linux for Small Business Owners*, https://doi.org/10.1007/978-1-4842-8264-9_18

What Is Automation?

Most of the time we think of computers as a means to automate the business-related tasks performed by ourselves or others. We typically think in terms of word processing, creating and modifying documents, managing a budget, bookkeeping, creating reports, managing email, and customer-related tools that enable you to perform the specific tasks that you went into business for – the primary purpose of the computer as a business tool.

For us, when we assume our role as system administrators, automation is different. Automation is a tool for system administrators to manage one or more computers. Automation for SysAdmins can take a number of forms, some of which you have already experienced. Let's look at some that should be obvious and some that are not.

First, in Chapter 9, the live USB thumb drive is an automated tool that prompts and enables you to enter information about how you want your computer to be configured as it installs Fedora. It performs all of the tasks required to do that based on the information you provided and leaves you with a working, if somewhat basic, Fedora installation.

In Chapter 13, you used the DNF tool to install new software and updates. That is another form of automation. You just entered the commands to tell DNF to perform updates or to install new software, and it performs all of those tasks necessary to download and install the needed updates.

The rsbu program and the rsbu-setup program that I wrote to configure rsbu are both Bash shell programs – commonly called scripts – that help you deal with backups. You could issue all of the individual commands yourself from the command line, but it is much easier to just run the script that contains all of those same commands.

More advanced forms of automation include tools like Ansible[1] which can be used to perform maintenance tasks on any number of Linux computers from one to thousands.

Anything Can Be Automated

Any task that can be performed on a computer that is related to system maintenance, software management, cleanup, and even system monitoring can be automated to at least some extent. Automation, in the form of various types of programs including scripts, as well as significantly more advanced – and correspondingly complex – tools can be used to provide any level of automation needed for your business.

---

[1] Opensource.com, "What is Ansible?", `https://opensource.com/resources/what-ansible`

Should I Automate Things Myself?

No. Definitely not.

If you feel the need to automate your computer administrative operations more than they already are, you will be spending too much time on tasks that don't contribute directly to revenue generation for your business.

Our purpose in this chapter is only to introduce you to the concept of using automation for the purpose of systems management. Most small business owners, those who have only a single computer, will not need automation beyond what is already installed with Fedora and the backup and update scripts that you have hopefully downloaded and use regularly.

The time to consider additional automation is when you have one or more additional computers on your premises with Fedora installed and connected together into a local area network (LAN). At that time, some additional documentation will significantly reduce the amount of time you or your staff will spend on system maintenance.

When you start thinking about automating more system maintenance tasks, it might be time to consider hiring a system administrator for your business or to look for a consulting company that can provide professional help for businesses using Linux.

We look at how to get help, including hiring consultants in Chapter 19, "Finding Help."

Chapter Summary

No. Do not try to automate your computer any more than it is already. You do not need it – yet. When you need or have a network with multiple computers, hire an employee or a consultant to perform that work.

CHAPTER 19

Finding Help

Objectives

After reading this chapter, you will be able to

- Locate Linux User Groups that can provide support and help
- Find and use the help resources for GUI desktop software
- Locate help resources on the World Wide Web
- Find and hire consultants for Linux and open source software

Introduction

There are many options for obtaining help and guidance for Linux and open source software. This chapter provides explicit directions for obtaining help with some open source software. Concentrating on Fedora and the many sources of information available to its users, we explore help options, books, websites, and local Linux User Groups as sources for information and assistance.

We also look ahead to the time when your business begins to grow and you need someone like a consultant to help manage your Linux systems.

Getting Help

We have all been working on a project and needed some help with the intricacies of the program we were using. I have been in the computer and technology space for over 50 years, and I have never been able to remember everything – especially stuff that I only do infrequently or have never done before.

303

© David Both, Cyndi Bulka 2022
D. Both and C. Bulka, *Linux for Small Business Owners*, https://doi.org/10.1007/978-1-4842-8264-9_19

All of the open source programs I use regularly, including LibreOffice which I am using to write this book, have excellent options for obtaining the help I need. Since LibreOffice is an application that most small businesses will use and it has some of the best tools for obtaining help of any software I have ever used, I will use it as the prime example of what various forms of help should be.

Built-In Help

Like most GUI-based application programs, the LibreOffice Menu bar has a Help menu. Open LibreOffice Writer and click the Help menu item. This opens the sub-menu shown in Figure 19-1 which contains multiple selections to enable you to find the appropriate level of help.

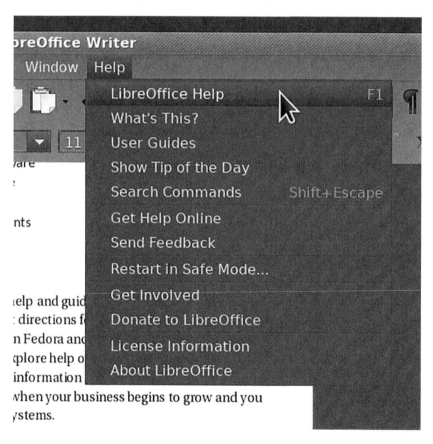

Figure 19-1. *The LibreOffice Help menu has multiple options to obtain help*

Let's start with the LibreOffice Help which is a complete set of documentation, for Writer in this case.

Tip   The F1 key is the typically used keyboard shortcut to access Help for most GUI applications.

Take the menu sequence **Menu bar ➤ Help ➤ LibreOffice Help** to open the LibreOffice built-in Help. This opens the new window in Figure 19-2.

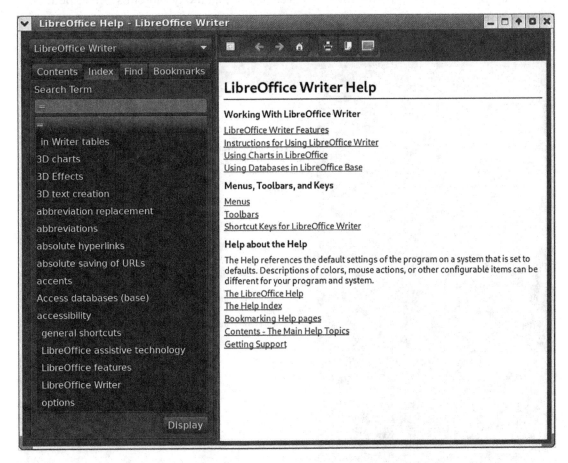

Figure 19-2.   *The LibreOffice built-in Help has a number of methods for finding help*

The right Side Pane of the Help dialog window in Figure 19-2 shows a list of high-level topics you can use to get started. The bottom portion of this pane covers help about getting help, including how to get additional support and how to use the Navigation Pane on the left side including the Index and Contents. You can always return to this "Help for the Help" page by clicking the little Home icon in the icon bar.

The Index and Contents views of the Help Navigation Pane work like those same tools in a print book. There is also a search tool for the Index and Find tabs that can help you find entries that contain a particular word or phrase.

Try it. Click the Search tab in the Navigation Pane. Then enter the search term "insert graphic" (without the quotes), and press **Enter** or click the **Find** button. Figure 19-3 shows that you can get many hits from a search. The most likely matches will appear starting at the top of the list.

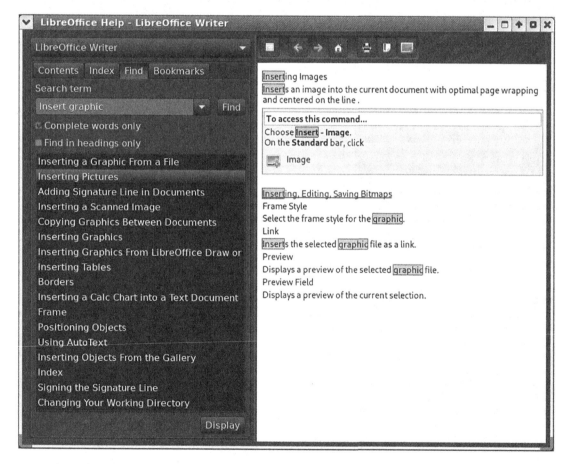

Figure 19-3. *The results of a search show the matched terms highlighted in the text of the Help page*

Double-click the **Inserting Pictures** entry to view the help page for that topic. Take a bit of time to check out the other items in the results list. See why they were included in the list.

I find that using the Search tab gives me better results for the way I like to search than does searching in the Index tab. You may find the opposite to be true, but that's why I find the LibreOffice Help so good; there are multiple methods of finding what you want and some users prefer one way while others prefer a different way.

Command Help

All Linux commands have a man(ual) page which can be accessed directly from the command line. You have learned a few Linux commands as you progressed through this book, and I have explained as much as was necessary to carry out the tasks we covered such as performing upgrades and installing new software. But at some time, you may need to know a little more.

Getting more information about Linux commands like you have used in this book is easy. Just use the command structure **man <command name>**. For example, to get more information about the dnf command, enter the following on the command line:

```
[dboth@testvm5 ~]$ man dnf
DNF(8)                          DNF                          DNF(8)

NAME
       dnf - DNF Command Reference

SYNOPSIS
       dnf [options] <command> [<args>...]

DESCRIPTION
       DNF is the next upcoming major version of YUM, a package man-
       ager for RPM-based Linux distributions. It roughly  maintains
       CLI  compatibility  with YUM and defines a strict API for ex-
       tensions and plugins.

       Plugins can modify or extend features of DNF or provide addi-
       tional  CLI  commands on top of those mentioned below. If you
       know the name of such a command (including commands mentioned
```

below), you may find/install the package which provides it using the appropriate virtual provide in the form of dnf-command(<alias>), where <alias> is the name of the command; e.g.``dnf install 'dnf-command(versionlock)'`` installs a versionlock plugin. This approach also applies to specifying dependencies of packages that require a particular DNF command.

<SNIP>

Page through a few pages of this man page. Press "q" to exit from the **less** pager that is automatically launched when using the **man** command.

Look at the man page for the **ls** and **less** commands to see some of the many options that these seemingly simple commands have available.

Online Help

All of the popular and important Linux distributions and open source applications have some form of online website to provide help when it is needed. Fedora is no exception to this.

Some applications, like LibreOffice, have both built-in and online help. Other applications, like the Thunar file manager, do not have built-in help at all. Instead, they opt for online help.

Online help for most open source software typically consists of websites that contain documentation such as you would find in a user's manual, guidance for installation on Linux and other operating systems, News about latest releases and features, and Frequently Asked Questions (FAQs). You may also find links to a Wiki, an IRC chat where you can discuss problems live with other users and developers, bug reports, and mailing lists to which you can subscribe. Mailing lists also allow you to interact directly with both users and developers.

LibreOffice provides easy access to multiple types of online help. LibreOffice maintains a **Get Help** web page. You can access this page from the LibreOffice home page at www.libreoffice.org/, then click the **Get Help** menu option at the top of the page, and select the **Community Assistance** menu choice. You could also go directly to www.libreoffice.org/get-help/community-support/.

You can check out the LibreOffice online help options yourself for more details.

GnuCash has online documentation on its website at www.gnucash.org/.

The GnuCash and LibreOffice websites both have links for developers and even a link directly to the source code so that you can view it if you want.

The Fedora Project keeps documentation for Fedora at https://docs. fedoraproject.org/en-US/docs/. These online-only documents are aimed at Fedora installation and administration. As a small business user, you can use these documents to reference subjects such as using graphical applications, some basic configuration, managing users, and package management. This documentation is useful, but this book already covers most of the basic operations you will find in the Fedora documentation.

Red Hat, which is a strong supporter of and contributor to Fedora, provides and supports two excellent websites. Opensource.com[1] and Enable Sysadmin[2] are amazing repositories of articles on nearly every aspect of Linux in general, as well as Red Hat Enterprise Linux (RHEL), and Fedora in particular. I write for both of these sites and have well over 125 articles in both combined. Some of the smartest people I know from around the globe write prolifically for these sites. The content ranges from introductory to highly technical.

Books

Books in hard copy or PDF format are also great sources of information. The full set of guides for LibreOffice are located at https://documentation.libreoffice.org/en/english-documentation/. These are available as web documents which you can read on your web browser, PDF documents which you can download, and in printed hard copy formats. The hard copy versions of these books are sold for a nominal fee to cover printing costs.

Many books can be purchased online, but some are quickly outdated due to the rapid rate of change for software of all kinds. If you purchase a book, be sure that it is for the current or recent version of the software.

Yes, this book is based on Fedora 34 using the Xfce GUI desktop. In my estimation, the information in this book should be good for several years because the things we discuss here with any specificity are among those features, functions, and administrative tasks that have a slow rate of change. Many aspects of choosing and using Linux are not affected by the changes that take place in the software itself.

---

[1] OpenSource.com, Red Hat, https://opensource.com/
[2] Enable Sysadmin, Red Hat, www.redhat.com/sysadmin/

User Groups

Linux User Groups – also referred to as LUGs – are a rich source of information about Linux, the hardware it runs on, and many open source applications. The Triangle Linux User Group (TriLUG) here in North Carolina is an excellent resource for me.

The Fedora Project keeps a list of LUGs on their Wiki at `https://fedoraproject.org/wiki/LinuxUserGroups`. The information provided on this site is probably the most complete I have found. Be aware that because the information found here is provided voluntarily by a person associated with each LUG, some of it may be out of date.

If you don't have a local LUG, you can choose one of the others from the list to join. The TriLUG has Linux users from many far-flung locations.

Consultants

One thing that small business owners all need to do occasionally is to find and hire consultants to assist us with tasks for which we do not have the time, knowledge, skills, or the desire to do. Linux and open source software is no exception, and you can hire consultants to help with that, too.

I recently did some searches for Linux consultants, and there are a number of them, especially in and around high-tech centers. Even if there are none near you, Linux can be easily managed remotely. These consultants can not only help you automate tasks, they can also perform those other tasks that take away from time you need to spend earning income.

When it is time to look for help with your Linux systems, you can start with an online search. If you cannot find a local company, there are some national ones that support Linux. None of these companies will be cheap, but most have some form of hourly or per incident rate.

Cyndi has already told you how she connected with me through her yoga classes. Sometimes, it really is about who you know. Since most of you won't be friends with a Linux geek, you will go to where they are. Linux User Groups are a great place to start. Members of these groups may be consultants themselves, or they can help you search for a Linux consultant.

Chapter Summary

Although LibreOffice has the best help functions I have encountered, all of the application programs I use have very good help in one form or another. The best place to begin looking for help with desktop GUI applications is to use the F1 key or the Help item on the Menu bar. The **man** command provides extensive help for each Linux command.

Other forms of documentation vary from one application to another, but all I have used are very good. With some occasional online support from other users and even developers, I have found the documentation for Linux and the other open source software I use to be world class.

Books, online articles from trusted sources like Red Hat's Opensource.com and EnableSysAdmin, and user groups are all good options for help. And you still know enough to do the basics like backups, updates, and upgrades if need be.

## CHAPTER 20

Where Do I Go From Here?

Cyndi

Hey, I get it. Switching operating systems is a big deal. There's a lot to think about. Making such a change has a learning curve, and as a small business owner, you may be wondering where you'll find the time to learn it all. Nobody likes to have hairpulling tantrums trying to figure out new technology. Perhaps, you're even second guessing yourself, trying to convince your inner geek that the system you've been using is good enough, so why take this on.

Take a deep breath. It's easier than you may think!

You wouldn't be reading this if you didn't have very good reasons for making a switch. So congratulations! Dive right in. I hope sharing my experience having made the switch, and now using Linux for several years will help you make the switch with confidence. Remember, my business is yoga and wellness, not technology – and there are few small business owners who are more technophobic than I. I am living proof that Linux is user friendly!

Will you have moments of frustration or confusion? Maybe, but this book covers just about everything you'll need to know, and if you do get stuck, there's the open source community that is full of folks eager to help. I'm grateful for David who has been my go-to guy for troubleshooting all these years because there wasn't a book like this available then. Most often when I would encounter a problem, it wasn't because of Linux; it was because my computer itself had hiccups.

When I made the switch, I felt timid and unsure of myself at first. But as I moved through the process of learning Linux, I found time and time again that their programs actually behaved quite similarly to what I had been used to. Oftentimes, I was my own worst enemy because I was anticipating problems that weren't problems at all. I relished the cost savings, reliability, and security from the get-go. That still holds true.

D. Both and C. Bulka, *Linux for Small Business Owners*, https://doi.org/10.1007/978-1-4842-8264-9_20

I'll admit that I utilize only a fraction of the many tools available with Linux, primarily LibreOffice Writer and Impress. I develop yoga training, I write curriculum, and I write digital learning programs, so they have served me well. Until recently, my work hadn't required much more than that. Writer behaves just like Word, and Impress very similarly to PowerPoint. They're intuitive. The biggest challenge was to get used to the different Menu bars and finding where the things I needed were. I can honestly say that it took very little time to get used to Writer and Impress. My biggest problem with writer was remembering to save my documents in a format that can be universally read, like docx. Odt documents didn't always translate for other platforms, although I understand that has improved over the years. Writer has so many options for creating great documents! I've just scratched the surface.

Since the pandemic, the way I work has drastically changed, so I have been using new programs like Audacity, OBS, OpenShot, and Pragha. The interface on these programs, which can be downloaded on most operating systems, may look different on Linux, and that will just take just a bit of getting used to. This would be true for me with any audio visual platforms.

Once you get your operating system switched to Linux, don't fret if things may feel a bit foreign at first. The application interfaces on Linux may appear different from the applications you're accustomed to using, but the functionality is the same or oftentimes better. Spend some time toggling about and you will see that everything you need is right there. The more I dove in, the more I discovered that the Linux system is quite intuitive.

You may encounter some raised eyebrows when people ask you what operating system you're using, but that's inconsequential. Linux is still a relatively well-kept secret, and many people react with surprise just because they are unfamiliar with it and they've bought in to Microsoft or Apple operating systems for so long. When I was using Microsoft, I had become numb to all the glitches and corruption because it just seemed "normal," like something that had to be tolerated. Linux shed light on the fact that there's nothing normal about corrupted operating systems and software. It raises the bar. There's something really reassuring about having an operating system that, to date, has been invincible to corruption.

I switched to Linux for security, reliability, and cost savings, not so much because the software and applications I was using malfunctioned. My software in Linux has never malfunctioned. If you do the updates and backing up religiously, you too can have a seamless experience just as I have.

Being able to focus on my writing and creating curriculum is the real gift using Linux has given to me. It's the kind of platform that just quietly does its thing without distracting me or hanging me up. I used to have problems with Microsoft booting slowly. Never has been an issue with Linux. I lost documents while using Microsoft programs, and that's never happened with Linux. I had several episodes with malware and viruses with Microsoft, never with Linux. I can't count the hours that getting on board with Linux has saved me time I've used in much more constructive ways in my business.

I'm delighted that David has organized this comprehensive how-to guide for new Linux users. Let it be your bible. If you do get stuck and need help, David has compiled a great resource for you in Chapter 19. If it's software you're boggled by, check out Chapter 6.

My experience working with David, a dyed-in-the-wool Linux geek and guru, has been reassuring. As I understand from David, open source people are a different breed. There's a unique kind of pride taken in being able to offer access to so many quality applications to so many people without it costing you more moola every time you turn around. That's my kind of people!

APPENDIX 1

About Files

Objectives

After reading this appendix, you will be able to

- Describe how user accounts and file attributes are used to implement security

- State the three meanings of the term "filesystem"

- Describe the Linux hierarchical filesystem and the benefits it provides

Introduction

Tip This appendix covers advanced topics about files and filesystems. You do not need to read this to be able to use Fedora for your small business. It is included here in case you are curious or find some need for it.

Chapter 11 explored the use of the Thunar file manager but covered little about files themselves or how to manage files on the command line. This appendix discusses the relationship between file attributes, ownership, and security. The attributes of permissions and file ownership are the basis for the security provided by Linux.

This appendix also looks at the Linux directory structure which is defined in the Linux Filesystem Hierarchical Standard. The FSHS defines a consistent standard for the directory structure itself as well as the locations of files within that structure.

© David Both, Cyndi Bulka 2022
D. Both and C. Bulka, *Linux for Small Business Owners*, https://doi.org/10.1007/978-1-4842-8264-9

User Accounts and Security

User accounts are the first line of security on your Fedora computer. They are used in the Linux world to provide access to the computer, to keep out people who should not have access, and to keep authorized users from interfering with other user's data and usage of the computer.

The security of the computer and the data stored on it is dependent on the user accounts created by the Linux system administrator. A user cannot access any resources on a Linux system without logging on with an account ID and password. The administrator (yes, that is you!) creates an account for each authorized user and assigns an initial password. In many small businesses, only one user account is needed, but others may require more than one account on a given computer.

Files have attributes of ownership and permissions that are used to determine which user accounts have access to read or write files or to execute program files. Directories have permissions that determine which users can have access to them.

File Attributes

You do not need to create any files for this appendix. I used this command-line program to create some files on the VM I am using for testing so that there are files to look at here:

```
[dboth@mycomputer ~]$ for I in `seq -w 20` ; do echo "Hello world file$I >
testfile$I.txt ; done
```

A long listing of the contents of my home directory shows the ownership and file permissions for each file and subdirectory:

```
[dboth@mycomputer ~]$ ls -l
total 80
drwxr-xr-x. 1 dboth dboth  0 May 25 14:12 Desktop
drwxr-xr-x. 1 dboth dboth  0 May 25 14:12 Documents
drwxr-xr-x. 1 dboth dboth  0 May 25 14:12 Downloads
drwxr-xr-x. 1 dboth dboth  0 May 25 14:12 Music
drwxr-xr-x. 1 dboth dboth  0 May 25 14:12 Pictures
drwxr-xr-x. 1 dboth dboth  0 May 25 14:12 Public
drwxr-xr-x. 1 dboth dboth  0 May 25 14:12 Templates
-rw-r--r--. 1 dboth dboth 22 Oct 11 15:57 testfile01.txt
```

```
-rw-r--r--. 1 dboth dboth 22 Oct 11 15:57 testfile02.txt
-rw-r--r--. 1 dboth dboth 22 Oct 11 15:57 testfile03.txt
-rw-r--r--. 1 dboth dboth 22 Oct 11 15:57 testfile04.txt
-rw-r--r--. 1 dboth dboth 22 Oct 11 15:57 testfile05.txt
-rw-r--r--. 1 dboth dboth 22 Oct 11 15:57 testfile06.txt
-rw-r--r--. 1 dboth dboth 22 Oct 11 15:57 testfile07.txt
-rw-r--r--. 1 dboth dboth 22 Oct 11 15:57 testfile08.txt
-rw-r--r--. 1 dboth dboth 22 Oct 11 15:57 testfile09.txt
-rw-r--r--. 1 dboth dboth 22 Oct 11 15:57 testfile10.txt
-rw-r--r--. 1 dboth dboth 22 Oct 11 15:57 testfile11.txt
-rw-r--r--. 1 dboth dboth 22 Oct 11 15:57 testfile12.txt
-rw-r--r--. 1 dboth dboth 22 Oct 11 15:57 testfile13.txt
-rw-r--r--. 1 dboth dboth 22 Oct 11 15:57 testfile14.txt
-rw-r--r--. 1 dboth dboth 22 Oct 11 15:57 testfile15.txt
-rw-r--r--. 1 dboth dboth 22 Oct 11 15:57 testfile16.txt
-rw-r--r--. 1 dboth dboth 22 Oct 11 15:57 testfile17.txt
-rw-r--r--. 1 dboth dboth 22 Oct 11 15:57 testfile18.txt
-rw-r--r--. 1 dboth dboth 22 Oct 11 15:57 testfile19.txt
-rw-r--r--. 1 dboth dboth 22 Oct 11 15:57 testfile20.txt

[dboth@mycomputer ~]$
```

File Ownership

The file permissions **drwxr-xr-x** for some of the items in the listing – those with the leading "d" – indicate that they are directories. The rest have a dash (-) in that first position indicating that they are regular files. Regular files is the correct term.

Each file and directory has a set of permissions as shown in Figure A-1. These permissions are three triplets of (R)ead, (W)rite, and e(X)ecute. Each triplet represents User, – the owner of the file; Group, the group that owns the file; and Other, for all other users.

User	Group	Other
rwx	rwx	rwx

Figure A-1. *Linux file permissions*

These file attributes are sometimes referred to as the file mode. The file permissions, the number of hard links, the User ownership, Group ownership, the file size, the date and time it was last modified, and the file name itself are all shown in that order in the long listing.

Let's look at the details of a single file. We will use the file shown in Figure A-2 to explore the structure and attributes of a file.

```
-rw-r--r--. 1 dboth dboth 22 Oct 11 15:57 testfile01.txt
```

Figure A-2. *Permissions of a single file*

There are two owners associated with every file. In this case, the first is the User student. The second is Group ownership, which is also student. This is normal for the files in your home directory structure. The reasons for this are beyond the scope of this book.

The User permissions are the first triplet rw- which indicates that the student user can read and write this file. Because the last position in this triplet is a dash (-), this file cannot be executed. That is OK because it is not an executable file.

The Group permissions are the second triplet. This triplet r-- indicates that members of the group student, if there are any others, can only read the file. They cannot write to it – that is, they cannot change it – and it cannot be executed.

The final triplet is for all other user accounts on the system. In this case, the permissions of r-- means the file can only be read by those other accounts.

The user who created the file is always the owner of a file – at least until ownership is changed.

The root user can always change user and group ownership – or anything else. The User (owner) of a file can only change the Group ownership under certain circumstances.

Directory Permissions

Directory permissions are not all that different from file permissions. They are also part of the Linux security structure.

- The read permission on a directory allows access to list the content of the directory.

- Write allows the users with access to create, change, and delete files in the directory.

- Execute allows the users with access to make the directory the present working directory (PWD).

A group is an entity defined in the /etc/group file with a meaningful name, such as "development" or "dev" that lists the user IDs, like "student," of the members of the that group. So by making group ownership of a file to be "development," all members of the development group can access the file based on its Group permissions.

The bottom line is that there are many directories on a Linux system that regular users do not have access to. If a regular user cannot access a directory, it is because they do not have the proper permissions.

But regular users do have access to their entire home directory tree. All users also have access to create files and directories in the /tmp directory which is a place to store files temporarily. Duh! Thus, its name – which is short because... lazy Sysadmin.

It is unlikely that most small business owners will need to add users or users to groups. It is good to know this just in case.

Filesystems

Every computer needs to store data of various types on a storage device such as a hard disk drive (HDD), a solid state drive (SSD), or some equivalent such as a USB memory stick. There are a couple reasons for this. First, RAM loses its contents when the computer is switched off so that everything stored in RAM gets lost. There are nonvolatile types of RAM that can maintain the data stored there after power is removed, such as flash RAM that is used in USB memory sticks and solid state drives (SSD). But flash RAM is more expensive and slower than regular RAM.

The second reason that data needs to be stored on storage devices is that even standard RAM is still more expensive than disk space. Both RAM and disk costs have been dropping rapidly, but RAM still leads the way in terms of cost per byte. My calculations show that RAM is about 70 times more expensive per unit than the hard drive.

The term filesystem needs a bit of explanation because it can be used in either of two different contexts:

1. A specific type of data storage format for disk and solid state storage devices. Types of filesystems include EXT4, BTRFS, XFS, and others. Each filesystem type has its own metadata structure on the storage device that defines where the data is stored and how the operating system can access it. BTRFS is the default filesystem for Fedora 34 and higher. The EXT filesystem was the default for around 20 years prior to that.

2. The entire Linux hierarchical directory structure starting at the top (/) root directory.

In this section, we are using definition number 2 for "filesystem."

Filesystem Functions

Data storage is a necessity that brings with it some interesting and inescapable details. Filesystems are designed to provide space for nonvolatile storage of data. There are many other important functions that flow from that requirement.

A filesystem is all of the following:

1. **Data storage** – A structured place to store and retrieve data; this is the primary function of any filesystem. The hardware could be a hard drive (HDD), a solid state drive (SDD), or a USB thumb drive.

2. **Namespace** – A naming and organizational methodology that provides rules for naming files and structuring data. All filesystems need to provide a namespace, that is, a naming and organizational methodology. This defines how a file can be named, specifically the length of a filename and the subset of characters that can be used for filenames out of the total set of characters available. It also defines the logical structure of the data on a disk, such as the use of directories for organizing files instead of just lumping them all together in a single, huge data space.

3. **Security model** – A scheme for defining access rights.

4. **Application programming interface (API)** – System function calls to manipulate filesystem objects like directories and files.

5. **Implementation** – The software to implement the preceding.

We have already seen the first three of these functions. The last two are beyond the scope of this book as they are in the domain of developers.

The Linux Filesystem Hierarchical Standard

As a usually very organized Virgo, I like things stored in smaller, organized groups rather than in one big bucket. The use of directories helps me to store and then locate the files I want when I want them. Directories are also known as folders because they can be thought of as folders in which related files are kept in a sort of physical desktop analogy.

In Linux, and many other operating systems, directories can be structured in a treelike hierarchy. The Linux directory structure is well defined and documented in the Linux Filesystem Hierarchy Standard (FHS). This standard has been put in place to ensure that all distributions of Linux are consistent in their directory usage. Such consistency makes writing and maintaining programs easier for developers and SysAdmins because the programs, their configuration files, and their data, if any, should be located in the standard directories.

In Linux, there is no C: and D: drives as in Windows. Linux has one single unified directory tree which makes organizing things easy. This unified directory structure is defined in the Linux Filesystem Hierarchical Standard.

The Linux Filesystem Hierarchical Standard (FHS)

The latest Filesystem Hierarchical Standard (3.0)[1] is defined in a document maintained by the Linux Foundation.[2] The document is available in multiple formats from their website, as are historical versions of the FHS. Figure A-3 provides a list of the standard, well-known, and well-defined top-level Linux directories and their purposes.

---

[1] http://refspecs.linuxfoundation.org/fhs.shtml

[2] The Linux Foundation maintains documents defining many Linux standards. It also sponsors the work of Linus Torvalds.

These directories are listed in alphabetical order. I have highlighted the two directories that regular users need to be concerned with most of the time, /home and /tmp. Only the root user needs to deal with the rest of the directories and even then not very often for small businesses.

Directory	Description
/ (root filesystem)	The root filesystem is the top-level directory of the filesystem. All other filesystems are mounted on standard, well defined, mount points as subdirectories of the root filesystem. Unlike Windows, all directories, regardless of which physical storage drive on which they are located, are mounted into a single directory tree structure. There are no drive designations such as C: or D: because they are not required.
/bin	The /bin directory contains user executable files.
/boot	Contains the static bootloader and kernel executable and configuration files required to boot a Linux computer.
/dev	This directory contains the device files for every hardware device attached to the system. These are not device drivers, rather they are files that represent each device on the computer and facilitate access to those devices.
/etc	Contains a wide variety of system configuration files for the host computer.
/home	Home directory storage for user files. Linux was designed as a multiuser operating system so each user has a subdirectory in the /home directory. A user's home directory can contain many subdirectories into which files can be sorted into some sort of meaningful, related collections. Several subdirectories have already been created in your personal home directory but you can create any that you want.
/lib	Contains shared library files that are required to boot the system.
/media	A place to mount external removable media devices such as USB thumb drives that may be connected to the host.

Figure A-3. *The top level of the Linux Filesystem Hierarchical Standard*

Directory	Description
/mnt	A temporary mountpoint for regular filesystems (as in not removable media) that can be used while the administrator is repairing or working on a filesystem.
/opt	Optional files such as vendor supplied application programs should be located here.
/proc	Virtual filesystem used to expose access to internal kernel information and editable tuning parameters.
/root	This is not the root (/) filesystem. It is the home directory for the root user.
/sbin	System binary files. These are executables used for system administration.
/selinux	This filesystem is only used when SELinux is enabled.
/sys	This virtual filesystem contains information about the USB and PCI busses and the devices attached to each.
/tmp	Temporary directory. Used by the operating system and many programs to store temporary files. Users may also store files here temporarily. Note that files stored here may be deleted at any time without prior notice.
/usr	These are shareable, read only files including executable binaries and libraries, as well as the man[ual] files and other types of documentation.
/usr/local	These are typically shell programs or compiled programs and their supporting configuration files that are created locally and used by the SysAdmin or the regular users of the host.
/var	Variable data files are stored here. This can include things like log files, database files, web server data files, email inboxes, and much more.

Figure A-3. (*continued*)

Wikipedia also has a good description of the FHS.[3]

---

[3] Wikipedia, "Filesystem Hierarchy Standard," https://en.wikipedia.org/wiki/Filesystem_Hierarchy_Standard

APPENDIX 2

Introduction to the Command Line

Objectives

After reading this appendix, you will learn

- Command-line terminology

- To explore of the differences between the terms, terminal, console, shell, command line, session, and others

- To enter and execute commands using the Bash shell

- A few basic but important Linux commands

Tip This appendix provides introductory information about using the command line. You do not need to read this to be able to use Fedora for your small business. It is included here in case you are curious or find some need for it.

Introduction

As a small business owner, you perform a lot of tasks including that of the System Administrator, a.k.a. the SysAdmin. In this role, you must do a number of tasks that larger organizations may hire or contract people to perform. We do not intend to turn you into a full-fledged system administrator (SysAdmin) but merely to enhance your understanding of the command line enough so that it won't seem so daunting when you need to use it for performing updates, upgrades, and other software management.

327

© David Both, Cyndi Bulka 2022
D. Both and C. Bulka, *Linux for Small Business Owners*, https://doi.org/10.1007/978-1-4842-8264-9

Besides, the command line can be surprisingly powerful.

In this appendix, you will learn to use the primary tool of the SysAdmin, the command-line interface (CLI). We will start with the basics – how to access the command line; terminology; some basic commands that you might need as a regular, that is, a non-root user; and how to exit the command line.

CLI vs. GUI

We are all familiar with the graphical user interface (GUI) in which we use a mouse to point and click or even a touch screen to navigate and to perform tasks. For the most part, this type of human–machine interface is easy and intuitive, except when it is not. Some GUI interfaces are horrible, but that is the designer's fault.

We can easily use a tablet or computer GUI because most of us have grown up with computers, tablets, and game consoles.

Linux provides a GUI desktop which provides you as a user with a very familiar desktop-like interface. You can use all types of applications to perform your work in that graphical environment. This applies to applications like office suites, multimedia tools, and much more; it also applies to most of the tools you will need in order to manage and administer your Linux computer.

You may never need the command-line interface to use the applications you need to run your business. However, the command line offers an alternate means to perform system administration. Many administrative tasks can be performed more easily and faster at the command line.

My friend, Seth Kenlon, has this to say in a recent article[1] for Opensource.com:

> Similar to a restaurant menu, graphical interfaces for computers offer users a choice of actions. There are icons and windows and buttons, and you hunt for the one you're looking for, click on items, drag other items, and manipulate graphical representations until a task is complete. After a while, though, this can become cumbersome and, worse yet, inefficient. You know exactly what needs to be done, so wouldn't it be nice to just tell the computer exactly what you want to happen, rather than going through the physical and mental motions of hunting for components and repeating a mouse-based dance routine?

---

[1] Kenlon, Seth, "A guide to the Linux terminal for beginners," https://opensource.com/article/21/8/linux-terminal

I recommend you read this article which can be found at the link in Footnote 1. That article also contains links to other excellent articles in Kenlon's series for users just getting started using the command line.

Defining the Command Line

The command line is a tool that provides a text mode interface between the user and the operating system. The command line allows the user to type commands into the computer for processing and to see the results.

The Linux command-line interface is implemented with shells such as Bash. Other shells are available but are beyond the scope of this book. The function of any shell is to interpret commands typed by the user and pass the results to the operating system which executes the commands and returns the results to the shell.

Access to the command line is through a terminal interface of some type. This can be confusing when you are new to it so let's explore some of the components you will encounter when using the command line.

Command Prompt

The command prompt is a string of characters like this one that sits there in the terminal with a cursor, which may be flashing and waiting – prompting – you to enter a command:

```
[dboth@mycomputer ~]$
```

The structure of a typical Bash command prompt in a modern Linux installation consists of the [user_name @host_name present_working_directory]$. The present working directory (PWD) is also known as the "current" directory, all enclosed in square braces. The tilde (~) character is a shorthand notation for your home directory. The dollar sign ($) at the end of the prompt indicates that this is a regular user rather than the root user.

The root user command prompt ends with a pound sign (#) like this:

```
[root@mycomputer ~]#
```

This is intended as a visual cue to ensure that we know whether we are working as a regular user or as root.

Command Line

The command line is the line on the terminal that contains the command prompts and any command you enter. Graphical terminal emulators run in a window on the GUI desktop, and more than one terminal emulator can be open at a time.

Command Line Interface (CLI)

The command-line interface is any text mode user interface to the Linux operating system that allows the user to type commands and see the results as textual output.

Command

Commands are what you type on the command line in order to tell Linux what you want it to do for you. Commands have a general syntax that is easy to understand. The basic command syntax for most shells is

```
command [-o(ptions)] [arg1] [arg2] ... [argX]
```

Options may also be called switches. They are usually a single character and are binary in meaning, that is, to turn on a feature of the command, such as using the **-l** option in **ls -l** to show a long listing of the directory contents.

Arguments are usually text or numerical data that the command needs to have in order to function or to produce the correct results. For example, the name of a file, directory, user name, and so on would be an argument. Most of the few commands that you will discover in this book use one or more options and, sometimes, an argument.

To enter a command, type it on the command line and press the **Enter** key to execute it.

When you run a command that simply returns to the command prompt without printing any additional data to the terminal, don't worry – that is what is supposed to happen with most commands. If a Linux command works as it is supposed to, most of the time, it will not display any result at all. Only if there is an error will any message display. This is in line with that part of the Linux Philosophy[2] – and there is a significant discussion about that which I won't cover – that says, "Silence is golden." Yes, there really is a Linux Philosophy.

Command names are usually very short due to the "Lazy SysAdmin" part of the Linux Philosophy; less typing is better. The command names also usually have some literal relation to their function. Thus, the "**ls**" command means "list" the directory contents, "**cd**" means change directory, and so on.

Note that Linux is case sensitive. Commands will not work if entered in upper case. **ls** will work, but LS will not. File and directory names are also case sensitive.

Terminal

The original meaning of the word "terminal" in the context of computers is an old bit of hardware that provides a means of interacting with a mainframe or Unix computer host. The terminal provides the command-line interface to the user.

In this book, the term "terminal" refers to terminal emulator software that performs the same function and which runs in a window on the GUI desktop.

The terminal is not the computer; the terminals merely connect to mainframes and Unix systems. Terminals – the hardware type – are usually connected to their host computer through a long serial cable. Terminals such as the DEC VT100 shown in Figure B-1 are usually called "dumb terminals" to differentiate them from a PC or other small computers that may act as a terminal when connecting to a mainframe or Unix host. Dumb terminals have just enough logic in them to display data from the host and to transfer keystrokes back to the host. All of the processing and computing is performed on the computer to which the terminal is connected.

---

[2] Both, David, *The Linux Philosophy for Sysadmins*, Apress, 2018

Figure B-1. *An old DEC VT100 dumb terminal.Creative Commons Attribution 2.0 Generic license. Author: Jason Scott*

Terminals that are even older, such as mechanical teletype machines (TTY), predate the common use of CRT displays. They used rolls of newsprint-quality paper to provide a record of both the input and results of commands. The first college course I took on computer programming used these TTY devices which were connected by telephone line at 300 bits per second to a GE (yes, General Electric) time-sharing computer a couple hundred miles away.

Much of the terminology pertaining to the command line is rooted by historical usage in these dumb terminals. For example, the term TTY is still in common use, but I have not seen an actual TTY device in many years.

Terminals were designed with the singular purpose of allowing users to interact with the computer to which they were attached by typing commands and viewing the results on the roll of paper or the screen. The term "terminal" tends to imply a hardware device that is separate from the computer while being used to communicate and interact with it.

KVM

Stands for keyboard, video, and mouse, which are the primary tools with which we humans interact with the computer.

There are also some tools called "KVM switches" that allow connection of 2, 4, 8, 16, or even more computers to a single keyboard, display, and mouse.

Console

The console is the name for a terminal specifically intended for system administration rather than application programs.

Virtual Console

Modern personal computers and servers that run Linux do not usually have dumb terminals that can be used as a console. Linux typically provides the capability for multiple virtual consoles to allow for multiple logins from a single, standard PC keyboard and monitor. Fedora provides for one virtual console (virtual console 1, vc1) for the graphical interface and five virtual consoles for text mode logins.

Each virtual console is assigned to a function key corresponding to the console number. So vc1 would be assigned to function key F1 and so on. It is easy to switch to and from these sessions. Hold down the **Ctrl+Alt** keys, and press **F2** to switch to vc2. Then hold down the **Ctrl+Alt** keys and press **F1** to switch back to vc1 which is the graphical desktop interface. Figure B-2 shows the login on virtual console 2.

```
Fedora 34 (Xfce)
Kernel 5.14.9-200.fc34.x86_64 on an x86_64 (tty2)

mycomputer login:
```

Figure B-2. *Login prompt for virtual console 2*

Virtual consoles provide a means to access the command line if the desktop is unavailable or has failed in some way. That does not happen often, but it can. You may never need this capability, but it can be invaluable if you do. After logging in to a virtual console as the root user, the Bash shell works exactly the same way as it does in a GUI terminal session, so we won't go into any more detail here.

Terminal Emulator

A terminal emulator is a software program that emulates a hardware terminal. The objective is to provide a command-line interface on the GUI desktop.

There are many terminal emulators available for Linux. For this book, we use the Xfce4 terminal because it is the default for the Xfce desktop, it is very sparing of system resources, and it has all of the features we need. One of those features is the ability to open multiple tabs in the same window. Each tab contains a terminal session so that you can perform multiple command-line tasks. It is not necessary to wait for one task to complete before starting another.

To launch the Xfce4 terminal emulator, locate the icon on the bottom panel (panel 2), which looks like a little screen that contains the two characters ❯_ to indicate a command prompt. Click that icon to open an instance of the terminal emulator. The terminal emulator opens in a window on the desktop as shown in Figure B-3.

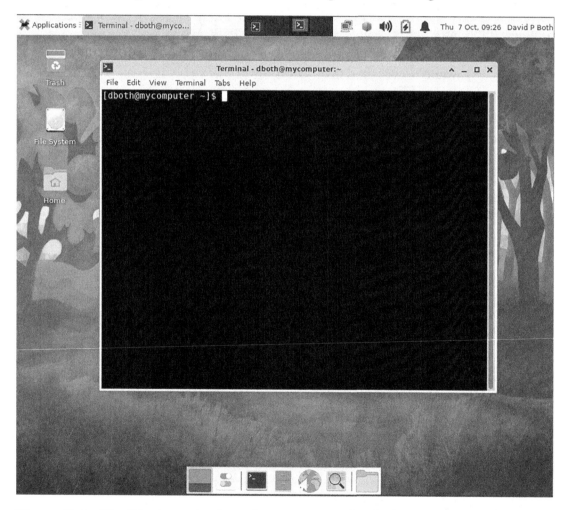

Figure B-3. *The Xfce4 terminal emulator open on the desktop*

To open a second tab, right-click anywhere in the black area of the terminal window to open a menu. Click the Open Tab menu item. A new tab appears to the right of the first.

Figure B-4 shows the same instance of Xfce4 terminal emulator with two tabs open. The PWD is displayed for each tab which can help you find the one you need when there are several open tabs. Figure B-4 also shows the context menu you can use to open a new tab. The active tab has a blue line underlining it. The color may vary depending upon the desktop color scheme being used.

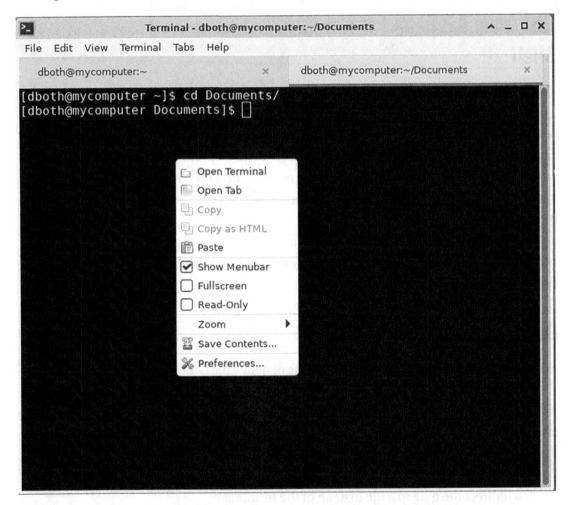

Figure B-4. *The Xfce4 terminal emulator with multiple tabs and the context menu open*

To exit from and close a tab, either click the "X" on the right side of the tab, or type the **exit** command in that session.

Session

Session is another of those terms that can apply to different things, and yet it retains essentially the same meaning. The most basic application of the term is a terminal session. That is a single terminal emulator connected to a single user login and shell. So in its most basic sense, a session is a single window or virtual console logged into a local or remote host with a command-line shell running in it. The Xfce4 terminal emulator supports multiple sessions by placing each session in a separate tab.

Shell

The shell is the command interpreter for the operating system.

The shell is the focal point of all of these other things. The terminal emulator, console, and session are only there to enable the shell to be displayed so that a user can interact with the computer. The shell creates and displays the command line and interprets the commands typed by the user or SysAdmin into a form usable by the operating system. When the results are returned to the shell program, it displays them on the terminal.

The default shell for Fedora is the Bash shell. Bash stands for Bourne Again Shell because the Bash shell is based upon the older Bourne shell which was written by Steven Bourne in 1977.

Data Streams

Everything in Linux revolves around streams of data – particularly text streams.

Data streams are the raw materials upon which the CLI tools perform their work. As its name implies, a data stream is a stream of data – text data – being passed from one file, device, or program to another using Standard Input/Output (STDIO). Pipes are used to connect streams of data from one utility program to another using STDIO. The function of these programs is to transform the data in some manner. Redirection can be used to redirect the data to a file instead of the terminal.

Data streams can be manipulated by inserting filter programs into the data stream using pipes. Each filter program is used by the SysAdmin to perform some operation on the data in the stream, thus changing its contents in some manner. Redirection can then be used at the end of the pipeline to direct the data stream to a file.

STDIO

The use of Standard Input/Output (STDIO) for program input and output is the foundation of the Linux way of doing things. STDIO was first developed for Unix and has found its way into most other operating systems since then, including DOS, Windows, and Linux.

> *This is the Unix philosophy: Write programs that do one thing and do it well. Write programs to work together. Write programs to handle text streams, because that is a universal interface.*
>
> —Doug McIlroy, Basics of the Unix Philosophy.[3,4]

STDIO was developed by Ken Thompson[5] as a part of the infrastructure required to implement pipes on early versions of Unix. Programs that implement STDIO use standardized file handles for input and output rather than files that are stored on a disk or other recording media.

There are three STDIO data streams, each of which is automatically opened as a file at the startup of a program. Each STDIO data stream is associated with a file handle which is just a set of metadata that describes the attributes of the file. These file handles are explicitly defined by convention and long practice as STDIN, STDOUT, and STDERR, respectively.

STDIN – is standard input which is usually input from the keyboard.

STDOUT – Is Standard Output which sends the data stream to the terminal by default. It is common to redirect STDOUT to a file or to pipe it to another program for further processing.

STDERR – The data stream for STDERR is also usually sent to the display.

If STDOUT is redirected to a file, STDERR continues to be displayed on the screen. This ensures that when the data stream itself is not displayed on the terminal, that STDERR is, thus ensuring that the user will see any errors resulting from execution of the program. STDERR can also be redirected to the same or passed on to the next filter program in a pipeline.

---

[3] Eric S. Raymond, *The Art of Unix Programming*, www.catb.org/esr/writings/taoup/html/ch01s06.html

[4] Linuxtopia, *Basics of the Unix Philosophy*, www.linuxtopia.org/online_books/programming_books/art_of_unix_programming/ch01s06.html

[5] Wikipedia, "Ken Thompson," https://en.wikipedia.org/wiki/Ken_Thompson

Getting Help – The Man(ual) Pages

Linux provides a powerful documentation tool you can use to get help on any command. The man(ual) pages have been around Unix since its beginnings in 1969, and Linux has inherited the concept of man pages as well.

Man pages place the documentation for Linux where regular users of the CLI and SysAdmins need them most – at the command line. Most of the commands covered in this appendix have many options, some of which can be quite esoteric. This appendix is neither meant to cover all of the Linux commands available (there are several hundred), nor is it intended to cover all of the options on any of these commands. This is meant only as a basic introduction to these very few commands and their uses.

You can explore them in more detail using the man pages. To see how the man command works, start with the man page for the **ls** command:

```
[dboth@mycomputer ~]$ man ls
NAME
       ls - list directory contents

SYNOPSIS
       ls [OPTION]... [FILE]...

DESCRIPTION
       List  information  about  the FILEs (the current directory
       by default).  Sort entries alphabetically if none of -cf-
       tuvSUX nor --sort is specified.

       Mandatory  arguments  to  long  options are mandatory for
       short options too.

       -a, --all
              do not ignore entries starting with .

       -A, --almost-all
              do not list implied . and ..

       --author
              with -l, print the author of each file
```

```
    -b, --escape
            print C-style escapes for nongraphic characters
<SNIP>
```

Use the **Page Up** and **Page Down** keys on your keyboard to page through man page documents, such as this one, that are too long to fit a single screen. To exit from a man page, simply press the "**q**" key. Either uppercase or lowercase works, and it is not necessary to press the Enter key.

Some Important Linux Commands

The most basic Linux commands are those that allow you to determine and change your current location in the directory structure; create, manage, and look at files; view various aspects of system status; and more. This section will introduce you to some basic commands that enable you to do all of these things. It also covers some commands that are frequently used during the process of problem determination.

Tip Unlike Windows, Linux commands and file names are case sensitive. So file-1 is not the same as File-1. Commands are almost always lowercase. There are some exceptions but none that will be covered in this book. If you have a problem with a command, be sure that you check carefully to ensure it was entered correctly including the case.

The PWD

The acronym PWD means present working directory, which you might know as the "current directory." The PWD is important because all command actions take place in the PWD unless another location is explicitly specified in the command.

The **pwd** command means "print working directory," that is, print the name of the present working directory on the terminal. Type the command and press **Enter**.

```
[dboth@mycomputer ~]$ pwd
/home/dboth
[dboth@mycomputer ~]$
```

This is the absolute path of the PWD for my home directory. Take a moment to briefly scan the man page for the **pwd** command. An absolute path is one that is specified completely starting at the root directory.

Using Directories and Paths

A path is a notational methodology for referring to directories in the Linux directory tree. This gives us a method for expressing the path to a directory or a file that is not located in the PWD. The term PWD refers to present working directory. Linux uses paths extensively for easy location of and access to executable files, making it unnecessary to type the entire path to the executable.

For example, it is easier to type **ls** than it is to type **/usr/bin/ls** to run the ls command. The shell uses the PATH variable where it finds a list of directories in which to search for the executable by the name "ls."

This simple command displays the content of the PATH environment variable for the user dboth. The **echo** command is used to print the contents of a file or variable to the terminal.

```
[dboth@mycomputer ~]$ echo $PATH
/home/dboth/.local/bin:/home/dboth/bin:/usr/local/bin:/usr/bin:/usr/local/
sbin:/usr/sbin
[dboth@mycomputer ~]$
```

Tip   Linux uses the forward slash (/) to separate directory names in path statements. This is different from Windows which uses the backslash (\).

The various paths – directories – that the shell will search are listed in the output from the preceding command. Each path is separated by a colon (:).

Let's list the contents of the PWD with the **ls** command. The -l option in the second version of the following command performs a long listing which provides more detail about the files and directories in the listing. Note that the "d" in the leftmost column of the long listing indicates that all of these items are directories. By default, directories are displayed in blue.

```
[dboth@mycomputer ~]$ ls
Desktop  Documents  Downloads  Music  Pictures  Public  Templates  Videos
[dboth@mycomputer ~]$ ls -l
total 0
drwxr-xr-x. 1 dboth dboth 0 May 25 14:12 Desktop
drwxr-xr-x. 1 dboth dboth 0 May 25 14:12 Documents
drwxr-xr-x. 1 dboth dboth 0 May 25 14:12 Downloads
drwxr-xr-x. 1 dboth dboth 0 May 25 14:12 Music
drwxr-xr-x. 1 dboth dboth 0 May 25 14:12 Pictures
drwxr-xr-x. 1 dboth dboth 0 May 25 14:12 Public
drwxr-xr-x. 1 dboth dboth 0 May 25 14:12 Templates
drwxr-xr-x. 1 dboth dboth 0 May 25 14:12 Videos
[dboth@mycomputer ~]$
```

This command does not print the so-called "hidden" files in your home directory, which makes it easier for you to scan the rest of the contents. Those hidden directories and files are configuration files that contain your personal configuration for many application programs. Each user on a Linux computer has their own set of configuration files in their home directory. Use **ls -la** to list all files including the hidden ones in a long format. You can see how options can be used together in this command making it unnecessary to use a syntax like **ls -l -a**.

There is nothing special about the so-called hidden files. The only thing different about them is that their names start with a period (.) such as .bashrc. It is just a recognized convention is that those files are treated as hidden.

Create Some Test Files

Let's create some files in your home directory that can be used to demonstrate some of the command-line tools you might need at some point.

Make sure your PWD is your home directory. The cd command with no options or arguments always returns you to your home directory for the PWD.

```
[dboth@mycomputer ~]$ pwd
/home/dboth
[dboth@mycomputer ~]$
```

This little Bash program creates 200 files with "Hello world filexxx" as the content for each, where xxx is the file number. You can edit the program and change "200" to any number of files that you need. For now, leave it at 200.

```
[dboth@mycomputer ~] for I in `seq -w 200` ; do echo "Hello world file$I" >
testfile$I.txt ; done
```

Use the ls command to display a list of the files that are located in the PWD, which should be your home directory. Depending on the width of your screen, and any other files or directories in your home directory, the output should look similar to the following:

```
[dboth@mycomputer ~]$ ls
Backgrounds      testfile046.txt testfile099.txt testfile152.txt
Desktop          testfile047.txt testfile100.txt testfile153.txt
Documents        testfile048.txt testfile101.txt testfile154.txt
Downloads        testfile049.txt testfile102.txt testfile155.txt
Music            testfile050.txt testfile103.txt testfile156.txt
Pictures         testfile051.txt testfile104.txt testfile157.txt
Public           testfile052.txt testfile105.txt testfile158.txt
Templates        testfile053.txt testfile106.txt testfile159.txt
testfile001.txt testfile054.txt testfile107.txt testfile160.txt
testfile002.txt testfile055.txt testfile108.txt testfile161.txt
testfile003.txt testfile056.txt testfile109.txt testfile162.txt
testfile004.txt testfile057.txt testfile110.txt testfile163.txt
testfile005.txt testfile058.txt testfile111.txt testfile164.txt
testfile006.txt testfile059.txt testfile112.txt testfile165.txt
testfile007.txt testfile060.txt testfile113.txt testfile166.txt
testfile008.txt testfile061.txt testfile114.txt testfile167.txt
testfile009.txt testfile062.txt testfile115.txt testfile168.txt
<SNIP>
```

Pipes

Pipes are interesting tools that allow us to do amazing things on the command line. Pipes – symbolized by the vertical bar (|) – are the syntactical glue that can connect command-line utilities together. Pipes allow the Standard Output from one command to be "piped," that is, streamed, from Standard Output of one command to the Standard Input of the next command.

A string of commands connected with pipes is called a pipeline. The programs that use STDIO are referred to officially as filters.

less Is More

One simple and common use of the pipe is to pipe the output from commands through the **less** tool which is a pager that is useful when the output from a command exceeds the number of lines of the terminal. That is, it allows the user to scroll through the data one page at a time.

Let's start by looking at what happens when too much data is displayed by a command and it scrolls off the top of the screen.

Now that we have a lot of files in the home directory, enter the **ls -1** command. It spews many lines of data to STDOUT – so many that we only see the bottom lines of data while the majority of the output scrolls off the top of the screen.

Enter the **ls -1 | less** command. You should see the top of the output from the command. At the bottom of the terminal, you should see a colon and the cursor as seen as follows:

To scroll down by a single new line, press the **Enter** key. Press the **Space bar** to see a whole new page of output from the command.

You can also use the **Up** and **Down** arrow keys to move one line at a time in the respective direction. The **Page Up** and **Page Down** keys can be used to move up or down a page at a time. Use these four keys to navigate the output stream for a few moments. You will see **(END)** at the bottom left of the screen when the end of the data stream has been reached.

You can also specify a line number and use the **G** key to "go-to" the specified line number. The following entry will go to line 100 which will display at the top line of the terminal.

100G

Capital G without a line number takes you to the end of the data stream.

G

Lowercase g takes you to the beginning of the data stream.

g

Press the **q** key to quit and return to the command line.

Redirection

Redirection is the capability to redirect the STDOUT data stream of a program to a file instead of to the default target of the display. The "greater than" (>) character, a.k.a. "gt," is the syntactical symbol for redirection.

Redirecting the STDOUT data stream of a command can be used to create a file containing the results from that command. There is no output to the terminal from the first command unless there is an error. The second command, **cat**, allows you to view the contents of the file you just created.

```
[dboth@mycomputer ~]$ echo "Hello World!" > file-01.txt
[dboth@mycomputer ~]$ cat file-01.txt
Hello World!
[dboth@mycomputer ~]$
```

When using the > symbol for redirection, the specified file is created if it does not already exist. If it already exists, the contents are overwritten by the data stream from the command. You can use double greater than symbols, >>, to append the new data stream to any existing content in the file as illustrated in this next example. Enter this command on one line to append the new data stream to the end of the existing file.

```
[dboth@mycomputer ~]$ echo "Using redirection to append data to a file"
>>  file-01.txt
[dboth@mycomputer ~]$ cat file-01.txt
Hello World!
Using redirection to append data to a file
[dboth@mycomputer ~]$
```

Time and Date

Time and date are important and the Linux **date** and **cal** commands provide some interesting capabilities.

Enter the date command to display the current date and time:

```
[dboth@mycomputer ~]$ date
Sun Sep 23 15:47:03 EDT 2018
[dboth@mycomputer ~]$
```

The **cal** command displays a calendar for the current month:

```
[dboth@mycomputer ~]$ cal
      August 2021
Su Mo Tu We Th Fr Sa
 1  2  3  4  5  6  7
 8  9 10 11 12 13 14
15 16 17 18 19 20 21
22 23 24 25 26 27 28
29 30 31
[dboth@mycomputer ~]$
```

The following command displays a calendar for the entire year of 1949:

```
[dboth@mycomputer ~]$ cal 1949
```

Both of these commands have many options for formatting the output. Be sure to at least glance at the man pages for these two commands:

Tab Completion Facility

Lazy SysAdmins like to minimize typing. Bash provides a facility for completing partially typed program and host names, file names, and directory names. Type the partial command or a file name as an argument to a command and press the **Tab** key. If the host, file, directory, or program exists and the remainder of the name is unique, Bash will complete entry of the name. Because the Tab key is used to initiate the completion, this feature is referred to as "Tab completion."

Tip   The Bash man page has a detailed and mostly unintelligible explanation of "programmable completion." The book *Beginning the Linux Command Line* has a short and more readable description[6] and Wikipedia[7] has more information, examples, and an animated GIF to aid in understanding this feature.

This is a very short introduction to command completion. Be sure that your home directory is the PWD. We will use completion to change into the ~/Documents directory. Type the following partial command into the terminal:

```
[dboth@mycomputer ~]$ cd D<Tab>
```

The **<Tab>** means to press the Tab key once. Nothing happens because there are three directories that start with "D." You can see that by pressing the Tab key twice in rapid succession which lists all of the directories that match what you have already typed.

```
[dboth@mycomputer ~]$ cd D<tab><Tab>
Desktop/   Documents/ Downloads/
[dboth@mycomputer ~]$ cd D
```

---

[6]Van Vugt, Sander, *Beginning the Linux Command Line* (Apress 2015), 22.

[7]Wikipedia, "Command Line Completion," https://en.wikipedia.org/wiki/ Command-line_completion

Now add the "o" to the command and press Tab twice more:

```
[dboth@mycomputer ~]$ cd Do<tab><Tab>
Documents/ Downloads/
[dboth@mycomputer ~]$ cd Do
```

You should see a list of both directories that start with "Do." Now add the "c" to the command and press the Tab key once.

```
[dboth@mycomputer ~]$ cd Doc<Tab>
[dboth@mycomputer ~]$ cd Documents/
```

So if you type cd Doc<Tab>, the rest of the directory name is completed in the command. Now press the **Enter** key to execute the command.

Let's take a quick look at tab completion for commands. In this case, the command is relatively short, but most are. Assume we want to determine the current uptime for the host.

```
[dboth@mycomputer ~]$ up<Tab><Tab>
update-alternatives       update-mime-database
update-ca-trust           update-pciids
update-crypto-policies    update-smart-drivedb
updatedb                  upload-system-info
update-desktop-database   upower
update-gtk-immodules      uptime
[dboth@mycomputer ~]$ up
```

We can see several commands that begin with "up," and we can also see that typing one more letter "t" will complete enough of the uptime command that the rest will be unique. Type "t" and then the Tab key to complete the command. Press the **Enter** key to execute the command.

```
[dboth@mycomputer ~]$ upt<Tab>ime
 07:55:05 up 1 day, 10:01,  7 users,  load average: 0.00, 0.00, 0.00
```

The completion facility only fully completes the command, directory, or file name when the remaining text string needed is unequivocally unique. Tab completion works for commands, some subcommands, file names, and directory names. I find that completion is most useful for completing directory and file names, which tend to be longer, a few of the longer commands, and some sub-commands.

Many Linux commands are so short already that using the completion facility can actually be less efficient than typing the command. The short Linux command name is quite in keeping with being a lazy SysAdmin. So it just depends on whether you find it more efficient or consistent for you to use completion on short commands. Once you learn which commands are worthwhile for tab completion and how much you need to type, you can use those that you find helpful.

Command Recall

Lazy SysAdmins don't like typing and all SysAdmins are lazy. We especially don't like repetitive typing, so we look for ways to save time and typing. Using the Bash shell history can help do that. The history command displays the last 1000 commands issued from the command line. You can use the Up/Down arrow keys to scroll through that history on the command line and then execute the same or modified commands with no or minimal retyping.

Command-line editing can make entering lots of similar commands easier. Previous commands can be located by using the **Up arrow** key to scroll back through the command history. Then some simple editing can be performed to make modifications to the original command. The **Left arrow** and **Right arrow** keys are used to move through the command being edited. The **Backspace** key is used to delete characters, and simply typing can complete the revised command.

Enter the **history** command to view the current command history. You can see many of the commands we have used in this appendix. In my case, there are commands that I used to test things for this appendix and a couple of the following ones:

```
[dboth@mycomputer ~]$ history
    1  ll
    2  su -
    3  exit
    4  ll
    5  echo "Hello World!" > file-01.txt
    6  cat file-01.txt
    7  echo "Using redirection to append data to a file" >>  file-01.txt
    8  cat file-01.txt
    9  history
[dboth@mycomputer ~]$
```

Use the Up arrow key to scroll through the history on the command line.

When you find a command you want to repeat, just hit the Enter key to issue that command again.

Use the history command to view the history again. Pick a command you want to execute again and enter an exclamation point (!) followed by the number of the command you want to run. Then press the **Enter** key.

Although using the CLI history as demonstrated in these examples seems a bit trivial, if you have to repeat some very long and complex commands, it can really save a lot of typing and perhaps mistyping which can be just as frustrating.

Summary

You can see from this appendix just a little of the vast power available to the SysAdmin when using the command line.

You briefly explored the use of tabs to enable multiple terminal sessions in the same window. However, the Xfce4 terminal emulator offers more functionality than we have covered in this appendix.

You have also explored using the man pages to get help, a few of the most important Linux commands for creating directories, moving around the directory structure. You explored how to recall commands from the Bash history.

Bibliography

Books

Binnie, Chris, *Practical Linux Topics*, Apress 2016, ISBN 978-1-4842-1772-6

Both, David, *The Linux Philosophy for SysAdmins*, Apress, 2018, ISBN 978-1-4842-3729-8

Gancarz, Mike, *Linux and the Unix Philosophy*, Digital Press – an imprint of Elsevier Science, 2003, ISBN 1-55558-273-7

Sobell, Mark G., *A Practical Guide to Linux Commands, Editors, and Shell Programming Third Edition,* Prentice Hall; ISBN 978-0-13-308504-4

van Vugt, Sander, *Beginning the Linux Command Line,* Apress, ISBN 978-1-4302-6829-1

Whitehurst, Jim, *The Open Organization*, Harvard Business Review Press (June 2, 2015), ISBN 978-1625275271

Web sites

BackBlaze, Web site, *What SMART Stats Tell Us About Hard Drives,* https://www.backblaze.com/blog/what-smart-stats-indicate-hard-drive-failures/

Both, David, *8 reasons to use the Xfce Linux desktop environment,* https://opensource.com/article/18/6/xfce-desktop

Both, David, *Using rsync to back up your Linux system,* https://opensource.com/article/17/1/rsync-backup-linux

Free Software Foundation, *Free Software Licensing Resources,* https://www.fsf.org/licensing/education

gnu.org, *Bash Reference Manual – Command Line Editing,* https://www.gnu.org/software/bash/manual/html_node/Command-Line-Editing.html

How-two Forge, *Linux Basics: How To Create and Install SSH Keys on the Shell,* https://www.howtoforge.com/linux-basics-how-to-install-ssh-keys-on-the-shell

Krumins, Peter, *Bash history,* http://www.catonmat.net/blog/the-definitive-guide-to-bash-command-line-history/

LibreOffice, *Home Page,* https://www.libreoffice.org/

LibreOffice, *Licenses,* https://www.libreoffice.org/about-us/licenses/

BIBLIOGRAPHY

Linux Foundation, *Filesystem Hierarchical Standard (3.0)*, `http://refspecs.linuxfoundation.org/fhs.shtml`

Linuxtopia, *Basics of the Unix Philosophy*, `http://www.linuxtopia.org/online_books/programming_books/art_of_unix_programming/ch01s06.html`

Opensource.com, `https://opensource.com/`

Opensource.com, *Appreciating the full power of open*, `https://opensource.com/open-organization/16/5/appreciating-full-power-open`

Opensource.com, *What is open source?*, `https://opensource.com/resources/what-open-source`

Opensource.com, *What is The Open Organization*, `https://opensource.com/open-organization/resources/what-open-organization`

Opensource.org, *Licenses*, `https://opensource.org/licenses`

Opensource.org, *The Open Source Definition (Annotated)*, `https://opensource.org/osd-annotated`

Wikipedia, *Linux console*, `https://en.wikipedia.org/wiki/Linux_console`

Wikipedia, *rsync*, `https://en.wikipedia.org/wiki/Rsync`

Glossary

Term	Definition
Account	An account on a computer is used to authenticate the user and as a means to determine what system resources, such as files and tools, that the user can have access to. This can also be called a user account or a login account. Linux user accounts require a user ID and a password for authentication. Once authenticated a user has access to their own files and home directory structure. Access to system files and other users' files is very limited or nonexistent.
BIOS	The Basic Input/Output System. BIOS is a small program embedded in the motherboard hardware that monitors and enables the computer to perform very low-level hardware Input and Output (I/O of data. It also allows the user to perform certain configuration actions. BIOS provides a means to view the hardware configuration of the computer. This is where you can easily determine whether a computer actually has the specified hardware installed. BIOS also runs a hardware test on all components of the computer immediately after power-on. Errors cause the computer to enter BIOS mode. See also UEFI.
Brute force attack	When crackers try to force their way into your computer without using any type of finesse. This type of attack usually consists of attempts to login using random user IDs and passwords. These attacks are automated and can perform thousands of attempted logins per second.

(continued)

© David Both, Cyndi Bulka 2022
D. Both and C. Bulka, *Linux for Small Business Owners*, https://doi.org/10.1007/978-1-4842-8264-9

Term	Definition
Bus	A multi-lane electronic channel on the motherboard for moving data between the major components of a computer such as between memory (RAM), storage devices, network adapters, and other devices.
Byte	A single computer character. Used when referring to storage or memory space. Typically used in multiples such as Kilobytes (KB). See the section, "Numeric Naming and Prefixes," in this Glossary for an explanation of these prefixes.
Command	Commands are what you type on the command line in order to tell Linux what you want it to do for you. Commands have a general syntax that is easy to understand. The basic command syntax for most shells is:
	`command [-o(ptions)] [arg1] [arg2] ... [argX]`
	Options may also be called switches. They are usually a single character and are binary in meaning; that is, to turn on a feature of the command, such as using the -l option in ls -l to show a long listing of the directory contents.
	Arguments are usually text or numerical data that the command needs to have in order to function or to produce the correct results. For example, the name of a file, directory, user name, and so on, would be an argument. Most of the few commands that you will discover in this book use one or more options and, sometimes, an argument.
Command line	The command line is the line on the terminal that contains the command prompt and any command you enter.
Command Line Interface (CLI)	The Command Line Interface is any text mode user interface to the Linux operating system that allows the user to type commands and see the results as textual output.

(continued)

Term	Definition
Command prompt	The command prompt is a string of characters like this one that sits there in the terminal with a cursor, which may be flashing, and waiting – prompting – you to enter a command.

`[dboth@mycomputer ~]$`

The structure of a typical Bash command prompt in a modern Linux installation consists of the [user_name @host_name present_working_directory]$. The present working directory (PWD), is also known as the "current" directory, all enclosed in square braces. The tilde (~) character is a shorthand notation for your home directory. The dollar sign ($) at the end of the prompt indicates that this is a regular user rather than the root user.

The root user command prompt ends with a pound sign (#) like this.

`[root@testvm1 ~]#`

This is intended as a visual cue to ensure that we know whether we are working as a regular user or as root. |
| Context menu | In a context menu, options for selection vary depending upon the context in which the menu was raised. For example a right click on the desktop brings up one set of menu options and a right click on LibreOffice Writer would open a menu with options needed for word processing. |
| Core | Each processor contains one or more computing cores. A core is the most basic hardware computing device of the computer. This term is sometimes used as a synonym for CPU. Many processors contain 2, 4, or even more compute cores. Some processors contain as many as 32 or 64 cores. The most common processors today have 4 cores. One of David's computers has 16 cores. |

(continued)

Term	Definition
CPU	Central Processing Unit. In some processors each computing core may be designed in such a manner as to be as powerful as 2 cores. Such a core is said to have 2 CPUs and uses Intel's Hyperthreading technology to achieve that. A processor with 4 cores may have 8 cores when used with Hyperthreading. David's 16 core processor therefore has 32 CPUs. For more detailed information on the CPU and how it works see my article, "The central processing unit (CPU): Its components and functionality[1]."
Cracker	A cracker is someone who does unethical or illegal hacking. The term derives from hacker and the fact that these people are trying to crack into your computer like "cracking into a safe." Crackers are responsible for infecting your computers with malware of all kinds, junk pop-ups, and ransomware. Crackers are the criminals of the Internet. See "Hacker."
Cruft	Cruft is the accumulation of things unpleasant or superfluous over time. When applied to system administration it generally refers to an accumulation of old files and directories that are no longer needed. One tasks Sysadmins typically perform is to find and remove the cruft.

(continued)

---

[1] Enable SysAdmin, Red Hat, *The central processing unit (CPU): Its components and functionality*, https://www.redhat.com/sysadmin/cpu-components-functionality

Term	Definition
Data stream	Everything in Linux revolves around streams of data – particularly text streams.
	Data streams are the raw materials upon which the CLI tools perform their work. As its name implies, a data stream is a stream of data – text data – being passed from one file, device, or program to another using Standard Input/Output (STDIO). Pipes are used to connect streams of data from one utility program to another using STDIO. The function of these programs is to transform the data in some manner. Redirection can be used to redirect the data to a file instead of the terminal.
	Data streams can be manipulated by inserting filter programs into the data stream using pipes. Each filter program is used by the SysAdmin to perform some operation on the data in the stream, thus changing its contents in some manner. Redirection can then be used at the end of the pipeline to direct the data stream to a file.
DDR SDRAM	DDR stands for Double Data Rate. That means data can be stored and retrieved from the memory DIMM twice as fast as older, single rate DIMMS. This is not about the memory clock speed. A DDR memory DIMM with a specific clock speed (different from CPU speed) can transfer data 2x the rate of an SDR DIMM of the same speed. Only work with computers that use DDR memory DIMMs.
	The types of DDR memory listed below, DDR3, DDR4, and DDR5, are not interchangeable. Each one has a notch in the connector that mechanically prevents it being inserted into a slot intended for a different type.
DDR2 SDRAM	Don't even consider a computer that uses DDR(1) or DDR2 for memory (RAM). DDR1 and DDR2 are no longer available at reputable computer stores.
DDR3 SDRAM	First available in 2007, this is the oldest memory type you should find in a reasonably useful used computer. Avoid it at all cost in new computers because it is becoming less available in computer stores. `https://en.wikipedia.org/wiki/DDR3_SDRAM`

(continued)

Term	Definition
DDR4 SDRAM	Released in 2017, this type of RAM is faster than DDR3. The physical DIMM packages can also contain much more RAM in the same size. Many new computers in lower price ranges still use this type of memory as do some higher end computers. `https://en.wikipedia.org/wiki/DDR4_SDRAM`
DDR5 SDRAM	Faster with more memory packed into the same size DIMMs than earlier ones. This version was released in 2020. DDR5 memory is typically used in high-end computers and is becoming more widely available as of this writing. Its initial use has been in fast GPUs. `https://en.wikipedia.org/wiki/DDR5_SDRAM`
Desktop(1)	A graphical user interface that uses the loose metaphor of a desk as a physical item of furniture with a flat top on which work can be performed with physical tools, file folders, and individual files.
	Likewise, the graphical desktop provides a visual space on which folders (directories) containing files can be opened and managed. Tools like LibreOffice can be used to create and edit documents and spreadsheets.
	See also Graphical User Interface.
Desktop(2)	Term generally applied to physical computers with a form factor that allow them to be placed on a desk. One typical configuration is to place the monitor on top of the desktop computer.
	See also Tower.
Dialog	A dialog is a window on a computer desktop that provides a method for users to enter data of various kinds. For example a dialog might request a user's ID and password.
Dictionary attack	A Dictionary attack is a brute force attempt to crack your computer but using a bit more finesse than a full-on brute force attack. In this case it uses well-known system level user IDs such as root, in combination with passwords based on words found in the dictionary
DIMM	Dual In-line Memory Module. The most common SDRAM memory physical packaging format.

(continued)

Term	Definition
Directory	Directories are logical structures that are part of a filesystem and are used to organize files. Each directory can have many subdirectories and each of those can contain many additional subdirectories. Your home directory contains all of your personal files and some additional subdirectories such as Downloads, Documents, Music, Pictures, and so on.
	The names of these directories can be used make clear the types of files they are used to contain. To state the obvious, the Documents directory can be used to store documents and the Music directory to store your music files.
	The term "directory tree" is used to refer to a directory structure with many subdirectories because it looks like an inverted tree with many branches when diagrammed.
	The directory structure you create in your home directory is strictly up to you and there are no "directory police" to force you to store downloaded files in your Download directory or music in the Music directory. However most tools such as web browsers that perform downloads will look for the Downloads directory even though they give you the option to store a downloaded file in some other location. The same with the Music and Video directories; media playback tools will look for your Music and Video directories.
	Two files with the same name cannot exist in the same directory. Two files with the same name can exist in your home directory tree but they must be in different directories.
Distribution	A prepackaged combination that includes the Linux operating system as well as many administrative tools and application programs such as accounting, word processing, multimedia, and more. We use the Fedora distribution in this book because it is modern, well supported, and is easily updated with fixes and upgraded to newer releases.
DVI	Digital Video Input. Like HDMI this is a protocol and hardware implementation for connecting a computer to a display screen.
Fedora	A popular Linux distribution that is supported by Red Hat and which contains advanced user features and thousands of application packages.

(continued)

Term	Definition
File	A file is a related collection of data such as a document, spreadsheet, financial account, a program, photograph, video, and much more.
	The metadata for a file includes its name, size, the dates it was created, last altered, last read, and the locations of its data on the storage device.
File attributes	Files in a Linux system have a number of attributes that are used to describe various aspects of the file such as its name, size, ownership, and security status. These attributes enable Linux to ensure that only authorized users are able to access the file to read or modify it.
File name	File names are used as a method to identify files and to access them via their entries in a directory.
	The BTRFS (B-Tree FileSystem) is the default for current releases of Fedora and is what you have installed with Linux. File names in the BTRFS can be made up of alphanumeric and most special characters. Although blanks and special characters except for slash (/) and null (which is not the same as a blank or space) are allowed, it is usually a good idea to not use blanks. Filenames can be up to about 125 characters in length including the extension.
	Upper- and lowercase filenames are different. Thus File1 is not the same as file1 is not the same as FILE1. This is unlike Windows in which the same file can be referred to with either upper- or lowercase characters.

(continued)

Term	Definition
File name extension	All Linux filesystems support file name extensions which are separated from the rest of the file name by a period and usually consist of 3 to 4 characters. These extensions are used to help applications and tools identify the type of files they are such as txt for text, doc and docx for MS Word documents, odt for LibreOffice open document text format, pdf for PDF documents, and so on.
	Many of the features of tools like the Thunar file manager and programs like the default Document Viewer and the Okular document viewer depend at least in part upon these extensions to determine how to handle files.
	For example, doc, docx, and odt files are all word-processing files. So Thunar uses those file name extensions to launch LibreOffice Writeer as the default application. Extensions xls and ods are spreadsheet files so Thunar would open LibreOffice Calc as the spreadsheet application.
Filesystem	1. A specific type of data storage format for disk and solid state storage devices. Types of filesystems include EXT4, BTRFS, XFS, and others. Each filesystem type has its own metadata structure on the storage device that defines where the data is stored and how the operating system can access it. BTRFS is the default filesystem for Fedora 34 and higher. The EXT filesystem was the default for around 20 years prior to that.
	2. The entire Linux hierarchical directory structure starting at the top (/) root directory.
Firewall	A firewall is a security tool that prevents external access to the host or network that it protects.
	Although a firewall may be a hardware device, in the context of this book, a firewall is a program that runs on a Fedora computer. The firewall blocks all attempts to initiate access the computer via the network connection while still allowing the computer to communicate to other hosts on the local network and the Internet.

(continued)

Term	Definition
FOSS	Free Open Source Software is software that everyone is free to use, copy, redistribute and modify. It is usually also free of charge, though anyone can sell free software so long as they don't impose any new restrictions on its redistribution or use.
Graphical Processing Unit (GPU)	A processing unit designed specifically for use with graphics. This is essentially heavy numerical calculations so GPUs can also be used in gaming and other applications that require intense numerric calculations.
Graphical User Interface (GUI)	The GUI is an interface that is used to provide an easier interaction with the computer. This reduces or eliminates the need for many users to use the command line interface (CLI) which is text-based. The GUI can simulate a physical desktop but not all GUI interfaces do.
Hacker	A hacker is anyone who builds, fixes, or modifies computer hardware or who writes, fixes, or modifies computer programs – software.
	For example I purchase all of the hardware components like motherboards, memory, storage devices, power supplies, and cases, for new computers from the local computer store or on-line. I build new computers out of those parts. I also fix old computers when they break and upgrade the hardware when they need it even if they are not broken.
	I also write programs to automate many administrative tasks for my computers, and modify configuration files so that various software packages work in ways more to my liking than the defaults. All of that constitutes hacking.
	See the antonym "Cracker."
Hard Disk Drive (HDD)	Magnetic media used for long term storage of data and programs. Magnetic media is nonvolatile; the data stored on a disk remains even when power is removed from the computer. Hard drives are connected to the motherboard through SATA connections. HDDs can store data for decades even when powered off.

(*continued*)

Term	Definition
HDMI	High Definition Multimedia Interface. HDMI is a digital standard for audio and video communication between hardware devices such as a computer and a display. It is designed to support High Definition (HD) video and audio on a single cable.
Host	Another term for a computer, particularly when it is connected to a network.
I/O	Input/Output. The transfer of data into or out of a computer or attached device such as a storage drive.
KVM	Stands for Keyboard, Video, and Mouse, which are the primary tools with which we humans interact with the computer. There are also some tools called "KVM switches" that allow connection of 2, 4, 8, 16, or even more computers to a single keyboard, display and mouse. These are usually only useful in a computer room.
Linux	Linux is a powerful operating system (OS) that runs on many types of computers including the Intel personal computers that most of us have in our homes and offices. The popular use of this term means all of the tools and application programs typically provided in a Linux distribution such as Fedora.

(continued)

Term	Definition
Live (ISO) image	Also called an ISO image, a live image is a file that contains an exact image of Linux that can be installed on a storage device such as a USB thumb drive. This creates a bootable device that can be used to test Linux on one or more computers. After a computer is booted using the live image USB device, Linux can be tested and even installed directly from the device. Installing an ISO image requires use of special software to create because it is not a simple copy operation. An ISO image can be stored on a CD, DVD, or USB thumb drive. However, due to the relatively low capacity and slow speeds of CD and DVD devices compared to modern USB thumb drives, ISO images can be much larger than CD or DVD devices can contain. USB devices are also faster and provide better testing environments. Many computers no longer come with DVD/CD drives but all come with USB connectors. After booting your Windows computer – or any computer for that matter – from the live USB device you will be able to test drive Linux on that computer. You can use the live USB to explore Fedora and to learn a little about the easy to use Xfce desktop. This will not touch or change your existing data in any way. Your data is safe unless you make some extraordinary effort to change it.
Local Host	The physical computer on which you are currently logged in and working at the keyboard and mouse. All other hosts are remote hosts.
M.2	A designator for a specific form factor of Solid State Drive (SSD). The M.2 connector is a very small connector that allows the SSD to connect directly into the PCIe system bus on the motherboard. This allows for much faster data transfer speeds so gives much better performance than SATA connections. M.2 SSDs look very similar to DIMMs but they cannot be installed in DIMM memory slots. Some M.2 SSDs use SATA connectors although those are limited to SATA transfer speeds.

(continued)

Term	Definition
Memory (RAM)	Random Access Memory (RAM) is used to store data and programs while they are being actively used by the computer. RAM can only store data while the computer is powered on. The term "memory" is used as a generic reference to any type of RAM memory.
Menu	A list of options from which a user can make one or more selections. The Xfce desktop has its own unique form and structure, not unlike other programs.
Metadata	Metadata is data that describes other data. The data that we see when we perform a long listing, ls -l, consists of the file name, user and group ownership, size, the date and time it was last modified, and its permissions. These are all metadata that are used to describe and identify the file. There is other metadata about files that is available but not displayed in a long listing. The filesystem itself has a complex set of metadata that includes information about its logical structure such as used and free space on the storage device, the locations of directories, and data that helps to define the location of the data belonging to each file.
Motherboard	A large circuit board that contains many hardware components of the computer and bus connections for installing parts such as memory and the processor as well as other plug-in components on a PCI bus.

(continued)

Term	Definition
Mount	This term can be a verb as in to mount a filesystem. It can also refer to the mount point on which a filesystem is mounted. This is different from Windows where each storage drive is assigned a letter such as C: and each drive is the root of its own directory tree.
	All storage devices must be mounted in order to allow access to the data on them. This is important to all users. When you insert a USB thumb drive or an external USB storage drive a new icon representing that device appears on the desktop. You can mount and unmount storage devices using that icon. Just be sure to unmount all external storage devices before unplugging them.
	This term's historical roots go back to the days of early mainframes. Reels of tape and removable hard disk packs that contained the magnetic recording disks were physically mounted on the appropriate drive and then logically mounted so that the operating system could access them.
Network	A means of connecting two or more computers together so that they can share data and other resources such as printers. Networks may be wired or wireless.
Network Interface Card (NIC)	An adapter that connects a host to the network to enable it to communicate with other hosts. The adapter is usually integrated on the computer motherboard or it may be an add-in card. Most modern desktop computers have one or two wired Gigabit NICs. Laptops usually have wireless NICs and some also have wired NICs.
Microprocessor	An explicit term for a complete processor on a single integrated circuit (IC) chip. This differs significantly from previous processors which were built from multiple IC chips or even tens of thousands of individual transistors.
Operating System (OS)	A supervisor program that manages all aspects of the computer's operation including the hardware, application programs, errors, and more.
PCI Express	Peripheral Component Interconnect (PCI) Express (PCIe) is a very high-speed computer bus for connecting hardware devices on the motherboard of a computer.

(*continued*)

Term	Definition
POST	Power On Self Test. A quick test of the computer hardware performed by BIOS immediately after power on. Errors usually cause the computer to enter BIOS or UEFI mode.
Processor	A physical package containing one or more compute cores. The processor package is plugged into a special socket on the motherboard.
RAM	Random Access memory. Memory in which any location can be accessed directly without the need to read preceding memory in order to get to it. Contrast with a tape drive in which the all of the tape content must be read from the beginning until the desired data is located.
	RAM is much faster than any type of magnetic tape, disk, or other type of magnetic storage medium. Because of this it is used for the main memory of all modern computers enabling fast access to any data needed by the CPU.
	The contents of RAM are lost when the computer is powered off.
Remote host	Any host that is not the local host and that must be communicated with via the network. In this sense remote can imply either another computer in the same room, or another computer in the next city or halfway around the world.
	Any host that is not "here."
Root directory	The root directory is the top-level directory of the Linux filesystem. All other filesystems are mounted on standard, well defined, mount points as subdirectories of the root filesystem.
	Unlike Windows all directories, regardless of which physical storage drive on which they are located, are mounted into a single directory tree structure. There are no drive designations such as C: or D: because they are not required.

(continued)

Term	Definition
Router	A device that transfers network data packets from one network to another. A router installed by an ISP transfers data packets from the internal network to the Internet. Most routers supplied by ISPs provide a wireless router as well as a 4-port switch for wired connections.
	A properly configured Linux computer with multiple network interface cards (NICs) can be used as a router.
SATA (bus)	The Serial Advanced Technology Attachment bus is used to connect HDD and SDD storage devices to the motherboard of a computer.
SDRAM	Synchronous Dynamic RAM. The modern form of RAM.
Session	Session is one of those terms that can apply to different things and yet it retains essentially the same meaning.
	The most basic application of the term is a to terminal session. That is a single terminal emulator connected to a single user login and shell. So in its most basic sense a session is a single window or virtual console logged into a local or remote host with a command line shell running in it. The Xfce4 terminal emulator supports multiple sessions by placing each session in a separate tab.
Shell	The shell is the command interpreter for for the operating system.
	The shell enables the user interaction with the computer. It displays the command line and interprets the commands typed by the user or Sysadmin into a form usable by the operating system. When the results are returned to the shell, it displays them on the terminal.
	The default shell for Fedora is the Bash shell. Bash stands for Bourne Again Shell because the Bash shell is based upon the older Bourne shell which was written by Steven Bourne in 1977.

(continued)

Term	Definition
Solid State Drive (SSD)	The solid state equivalent of hard drives (HDDs). They have similar characteristics in terms of long term data storage because it is persistent through reboots and when the computer is powered off. SSDs can read and write data much faster than the old HDDs.
	The main disadvantage to SDDs is that they can only store data for about a year while powered off. Thus they are not suitable for long-term backup or archival usage.
STDIO	The use of Standard Input/Output (STDIO) for program input and output is the foundation of the Linux way of doing things. STDIO was first developed for Unix and has found its way into most other operating systems since then, including DOS, Windows, and Linux.
	There are three STDIO data streams, each of which is automatically opened as a file at the startup of a program. Each STDIO data stream is associated with a file handle which is just a set of metadata that describes the attributes of the file. These file handles are explicitly defined by convention and long practice as STDIN, STDOUT, and STDERR, respectively.
	STDIO works at all levels of Linux but is exposed to the user at the command line.
STDIN	STDIN is the standard input which is usually input from the keyboard.
STDOUT	STDOUT – is standard output which sends the data stream to the terminal by default. It is common to redirect STDOUT to a file or to pipe it to another program for further processing.
STDERR	STDERR – The data stream for STDERR, that is error messages, is also usually sent to the display.
	If STDOUT is redirected to a file, STDERR continues to be displayed on the screen. This ensures that when the data stream itself is not displayed on the terminal, that STDERR is, thus ensuring that the user will see any errors resulting from execution of the program. STDERR can also be redirected to the same or passed on to the next filter program in a pipeline.

(continued)

Term	Definition
Storage	Storage is a general term that refers to any type of device designed to store large amounts of data for long periods of time. It can also be referred to as non-volatile storage because it retains the data stored on it even when power is not supplied to it.
	Today's storage devices are based on two technologies. The first and oldest is the hard disk drive (HDD) and the newest is the solid state drive (SSD). The primary function of both HDD and SSD devices is to store data in a non-volatile medium so that it is not lost when the power is turned off. Both technologies store the operating system, application programs, and your data so that they can be moved into main memory (RAM) for use.
Storage device	Any device that stores programs and data for long periods even when the computer is turned off. The two primary forms of internal storage for computers are hard disk drives (HDDs) and Solid State Drives (SDDs).
Spin	A spin is a term used to designate various types of live images that can be used to test and install specific configurations of Fedora. In addition to a basic installation of Fedora, each spin includes software designed for particular tasks or configurations.
	For example one spin installed Fedora with the KDE desktop and another installs Fedora with the Xfce desktop which is what we are using in this book. Other spins include one for software developers and one for The Xfce spin is the one most appropriate for inexperienced users who need to be productive while becoming familiar with Linux.
Storage device	Any type of device used for long-term storage of data such as a hard disk drive (HDD), a solid state drive (SSD), CD, DVD, or a USB thumb drive.
System Administrator (SysAdmin)	Person(s) in charge of managing and maintaining computer systems and networks. SysAdmin is a synonym.
	Activities performed by a system administrator include tasks such as monitoring security configuration, managing allocation of user names and passwords, monitoring disk space and other resource use, performing {backups}, and setting up new hardware and software.

(continued)

Term	Definition
Terminal	The original meaning of the word "terminal" in the context of computers is an old bit of hardware that provides a means of interacting with a mainframe or Unix computer host. In this book the term "terminal" refers to terminal emulation software that performs the same function and which runs in a window on the GUI desktop.

Figure G-1. *An old DEC VT100 dumb terminal. Creative Commons Attribution 2.0 Generic license. Author: Jason Scott*

The terminal is not the computer; terminals merely connect to mainframes and Unix systems. Terminals – the hardware type – are usually connected to their host computer through a long serial cable. Terminals such as the DEC VT100 shown in Figure G-1 are usually called "dumb terminals" to differentiate them from a PC or other small computer that may act as a terminal when connecting to a mainframe or Unix host. Dumb terminals have just enough logic in them to display data from the host and to transfer keystrokes back to the host. All of the processing and computing is performed on the computer to which the terminal is connected.
Terminals that are even older, such as mechanical teletype machines (TTY) predate the common use of CRT displays. They used rolls of newsprint-quality paper to provide a record of both the input and results of commands.

(continued)

Term	Definition
Terminal emulator	A terminal emulator is a software program that emulates a hardware terminal. The objective is to provide a command line interface on the GUI desktop. Graphical terminal emulators run in a window on the GUI desktop and more than one terminal emulator session can be open at a time.
Tower	Designates a computer case form factor that is designed to stand on the floor as it is rather tall. This form factor can be placed on a desktop but it fits better on the floor or a short stand next to the desk. Standard tower cases are the most flexible in terms of hardware repair and upgrade.
Twisty	A twisty is a triangle-shaped image that can appear in the Thunar file manager navigation panel next to a directory icon to indicate that there are subdirectories inside that directory. A click on the twisty displays the subdirectory tree. Another click closes it.
UEFI	The Unified Extended Firmware Interface (UEFI) is a modern and more secure replacement for the BIOS used in older personal computers.
USB	The Universal Serial Bus is a moderately high speed bus used to connect external devices such as external HDDs, SDDs, thumb drives, printers, keyboards, mice, and more to a computer.

(continued)

Term	Definition
Virtual consoles	Modern personal computers and servers that run Linux do not usually have external dumb terminals (hardware) that can be used as a console. Linux typically provides the capability for multiple virtual consoles to allow for multiple logins through a single, standard PC keyboard and monitor. Fedora provides for one virtual console (virtual console 1, vc1) for the graphical interface and five virtual consoles for command line logins.

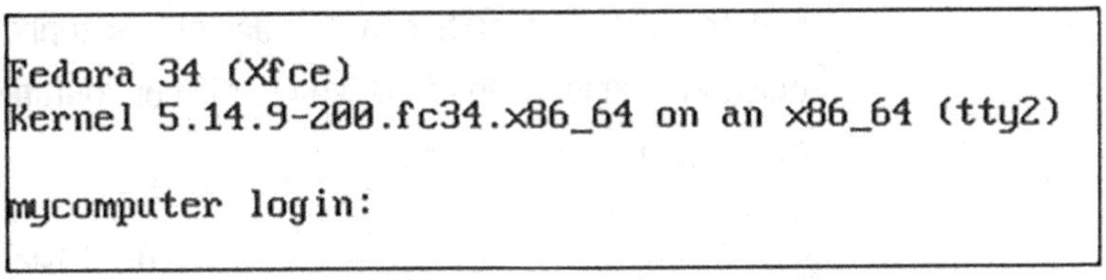

```
Fedora 34 (Xfce)
Kernel 5.14.9-200.fc34.x86_64 on an x86_64 (tty2)

mycomputer login:
```

Figure G-2. *Login prompt for virtual console 2*

	Virtual consoles provide a means to access the command line if the desktop is unavailable or has failed in some way. That does not happen often but it can. You may never need this capability but it can be invaluable if you do. After logging in to a virtual console the Bash shell works exactly the same way as it does in a GUI terminal session.
Virtual memory	Memory created by using the hard disk to simulate additional random access memory. Sometimes known as swap space, this type of memory is especially important in computers that have too little RAM for the tasks they need to perform.

(continued)

Term	Definition
Window	An area of the display that is bounded by a frame and which contains the visual interface to a running program. The window frame can be used to move the window or to adjust its size. The title bar contains information about the program running in the window, including its name.

The window in Figure G-3 shows the icon bar at the bottom of the window but the icon bar would usually be located at the top of the window underneath the menu bar. In the case of this application, the Konsole terminal emulator, the location of the icon bar is configurable to be either at the top or the bottom.

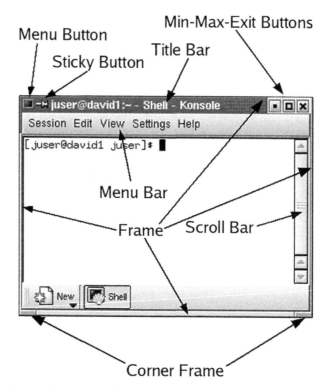

Figure G-3. *The parts of a typical window*

(*continued*)

Term	Definition
Workspace	A workspace is a desktop. Fedora allows for multiple workspaces to be used simultaneously and provides an easy way to switch between them using the workspace switcher. Similar to having multiple physical desks, multiple workspaces can be used to organize your work in any desirable manner. For one example, files and programs relating to different projects can be sorted onto different workspaces.
Workstation	A generic term for a Linux host used by an individual as their personal workstation. A workstation can be a desktop or tower form factor.

Numeric Naming and Prefixes

Numeric names and their corresponding orders of magnitude are often a point of misunderstanding. This is important when you purchase or upgrade a computer so that you know what these numbers mean when applied to various components such as memory and storage devices.

This table lists common numeric prefixes, their usual names, and provides their numeric representations in scientific and decimal formats.

Prefix	Name	Abbrev	Scientific	Decimal
	Unit		1	1
Kilo	Thousand	K	1×10^3	1,000
Mega	Million	M	1×10^6	1,000,000
Giga	Billion	G	1×10^9	1,000,000,000
Tera	Trillion	T	1×10^{12}	1,000,000,000,000
Peta		P	1×10^{15}	1,000,000,000,000,000

Typical examples are 8GB (Gigabytes) of RAM memory, a 1TB (Terabyte) storage device, and 100Mb/s (Megabit per second) Internet connection speed.

The case of the letter 'B' is also important for clarity. Lowercase 'b' indicates bits and uppercase 'B' refers to Bytes. The word Bytes is also typically capitalized for clarity.

Index

Symbols

Printed in the United States
by Baker & Taylor Publisher Services